Islamic Banking in Pakistan

Islamic banking and finance (IBF) has become a growing force over the past three decades, with Pakistan, one of the IBF pioneers, converting to an 'interest-free' banking system in 1985. However, since independence in 1947, there has been continual tension over Pakistan's essential character, between Islamic Minimalists, who favor a Modernist interpretation of Islam, and those who favor an Islamic Maximalist interpretation that sees Pakistan as a model Islamic state.

This book analyzes the push by Islamic revivalists to Islamize Pakistan and its financial system, from the early 1947 debates in the original Constituent Assembly to the final 2002 ruling on IBF of the *Shariat* Appellate Bench of the Pakistan Supreme Court. It examines the practice and theory behind contemporary Islamic, '*Shariah*-compliant,' banking. It offers extensive interviews with Pakistani Islamic bankers on the state of their industry and how they see it developing, and provides analysis on how the Islamic banks' customers differ from those of conventional banks.

Presenting a critical analysis of Pakistan's IBF experience and offering a new insight into Pakistan's banking industry that illustrates broader political and social trends in the country, this book will be of interest to specialists on Islam, South Asia and international economics.

Feisal Khan is Chair of the Economics Department at Hobart and William Smith Colleges in New York, USA. He has published in academic journals and edited volumes on economic development and corruption in Pakistan.

Routledge Contemporary South Asia Series

1 Pakistan
Social and cultural transformations in a Muslim nation
Mohammad A. Qadeer

2 Labor, Democratization and Development in India and Pakistan
Christopher Candland

3 China–India Relations
Contemporary dynamics
Amardeep Athwal

4 Madrasas in South Asia
Teaching terror?
Jamal Malik

5 Labor, Globalization and the State
Workers, women and migrants confront neoliberalism
Edited by Debdas Banerjee and Michael Goldfield

6 Indian Literature and Popular Cinema
Recasting classics
Edited by Heidi R.M. Pauwels

7 Islamist Militancy in Bangladesh
A complex web
Ali Riaz

8 Regionalism in South Asia
Negotiating cooperation, institutional structures
Kishore C. Dash

9 Federalism, Nationalism and Development
India and the Punjab economy
Pritam Singh

10 Human Development and Social Power
Perspectives from South Asia
Ananya Mukherjee Reed

11 The South Asian Diaspora
Transnational networks and changing identities
Edited by Rajesh Rai and Peter Reeves

12 Pakistan–Japan Relations
Continuity and change in economic relations and security interests
Ahmad Rashid Malik

13 Himalayan Frontiers of India
Historical, geo-political and strategic perspectives
K. Warikoo

14 India's Open-Economy Policy
Globalism, rivalry, continuity
Jalal Alamgir

15 The Separatist Conflict in Sri Lanka
Terrorism, ethnicity, political economy
Asoka Bandarage

16 India's Energy Security
Edited by Ligia Noronha and Anant Sudarshan

17 Globalization and the Middle Classes in India
The social and cultural impact of neoliberal reforms
Ruchira Ganguly-Scrase and Timothy J. Scrase

18 Water Policy Processes in India
Discourses of power and resistance
Vandana Asthana

19 Minority Governments in India
The puzzle of elusive majorities
Csaba Nikolenyi

20 The Maoist Insurgency in Nepal
Revolution in the twenty-first century
Edited by Mahendra Lawoti and Anup K. Pahari

21 Global Capital and Peripheral Labour
The history and political economy of plantation workers in India
K. Ravi Raman

22 Maoism in India
Reincarnation of ultra-left wing extremism in the twenty-first century
Bidyut Chakrabarty and Rajat Kujur

23 Economic and Human Development in Contemporary India
Cronyism and fragility
Debdas Banerjee

24 Culture and the Environment in the Himalaya
Arjun Guneratne

25 The Rise of Ethnic Politics in Nepal
Democracy in the margins
Susan I. Hangen

26 The Multiplex in India
A cultural economy of urban leisure
Adrian Athique and Douglas Hill

27 Tsunami Recovery in Sri Lanka
Ethnic and regional dimensions
Dennis B. McGilvray and Michele R. Gamburd

28 Development, Democracy and the State
Critiquing the Kerala model of development
K. Ravi Raman

29 Mohajir Militancy in Pakistan
Violence and transformation in the Karachi conflict
Nichola Khan

30 Nationbuilding, Gender and War Crimes in South Asia
Bina D'Costa

31 The State in India after Liberalization
Interdisciplinary perspectives
Edited by Akhil Gupta and K. Sivaramakrishnan

32 National Identities in Pakistan
The 1971 war in contemporary Pakistani fiction
Cara Cilano

33 Political Islam and Governance in Bangladesh
Edited by Ali Riaz and C. Christine Fair

34 Bengali Cinema
'An other nation'
Sharmistha Gooptu

35 NGOs in India
The challenges of women's empowerment and accountability
Patrick Kilby

36 The Labour Movement in the Global South
Trade unions in Sri Lanka
S. Janaka Biyanwila

37 Building Bangalore
Architecture and urban transformation in India's Silicon Valley
John C. Stallmeyer

38 Conflict and Peacebuilding in Sri Lanka
Caught in the peace trap?
Edited by Jonathan Goodhand, Jonathan Spencer and Benedict Korf

39 Microcredit and Women's Empowerment
A case study of Bangladesh
Amunui Faraizi, Jim McAllister and Taskinur Rahman

40 South Asia in the New World Order
The role of regional cooperation
Shahid Javed Burki

41 Explaining Pakistan's Foreign Policy
Escaping India
Aparna Pande

42 Development-induced Displacement, Rehabilitation and Resettlement in India
Current issues and challenges
Edited by Sakarama Somayaji and Smrithi Talwar

43 The Politics of Belonging in India
Becoming Adivasi
Edited by Daniel J. Rycroft and Sangeeta Dasgupta

44 Re-Orientalism and South Asian Identity Politics
The oriental Other within
Edited by Lisa Lau and Ana Cristina Mendes

45 Islamic Revival in Nepal
Religion and a new nation
Megan Adamson Sijapati

46 Education and Inequality in India
A classroom view
Manabi Majumdar and Jos Mooij

47 The Culturalization of Caste in India
Identity and inequality in a multicultural age
Balmurli Natrajan

48 Corporate Social Responsibility in India
Bidyut Chakrabarty

49 Pakistan's Stability Paradox
Domestic, regional and international dimensions
Edited by Ashutosh Misra and Michael E. Clarke

50 Transforming Urban Water Supplies in India
The role of reform and partnerships in globalization
Govind Gopakumar

51 South Asian Security
Twenty-first century discourse
Sagarika Dutt and Alok Bansal

52 Non-discrimination and Equality in India
Contesting boundaries of social justice
Vidhu Verma

53 Being Middle-class in India
A way of life
Henrike Donner

54 Kashmir's Right to Secede
A critical examination of contemporary theories of secession
Matthew J. Webb

55 Bollywood Travels
Culture, diaspora and border crossings in popular Hindi cinema
Rajinder Dudrah

56 Nation, Territory, and Globalization in Pakistan
Traversing the margins
Chad Haines

57 The Politics of Ethnicity in Pakistan
The Baloch, Sindhi and Mohajir ethnic movements
Farhan Hanif Siddiqi

58 Nationalism and Ethnic Conflict
Identities and mobilization after 1990
Edited by Mahendra Lawoti and Susan Hangen

59 Islam and Higher Education
Concepts, challenges and opportunities
Marodsilton Muborakshoeva

60 Religious Freedom in India
Sovereignty and (anti) conversion
Goldie Osuri

61 Everyday Ethnicity in Sri Lanka
Up-country Tamil identity politics
Daniel Bass

62 Ritual and Recovery in Post-Conflict Sri Lanka
Eloquent bodies
Jane Derges

63 Bollywood and Globalisation
The global power of popular Hindi cinema
Edited by David J. Schaefer and Kavita Karan

64 Regional Economic Integration in South Asia
Trapped in conflict?
Amita Batra

65 Architecture and Nationalism in Sri Lanka
The trouser under the cloth
Anoma Pieris

66 Civil Society and Democratization in India
Institutions, ideologies and interests
Sarbeswar Sahoo

67 Contemporary Pakistani Fiction in English
Idea, nation, state
Cara N. Cilano

68 Transitional Justice in South Asia
A study of Afghanistan and Nepal
Tazreena Sajjad

69 Displacement and Resettlement in India
The human cost of development
Hari Mohan Mathur

70 Water, Democracy and Neoliberalism in India
The power to reform
Vicky Walters

71 Capitalist Development in India's Informal Economy
Elisabetta Basile

72 Nation, Constitutionalism and Buddhism in Sri Lanka
Roshan de Silva Wijeyeratne

73 Counterinsurgency, Democracy, and the Politics of Identity in India
From warfare to welfare?
Mona Bhan

74 Enterprise Culture in Neoliberal India
Studies in youth, class, work and media
Edited by Nandini Gooptu

75 The Politics of Economic Restructuring in India
Economic governance and state spatial rescaling
Loraine Kennedy

76 The Other in South Asian Religion, Literature and Film
Perspectives on Otherism and Otherness
Edited by Diana Dimitrova

77 Being Bengali
At home and in the world
Edited by Mridula Nath Chakraborty

78 The Political Economy of Ethnic Conflict in Sri Lanka
Nikolaos Biziouras

79 Indian Arranged Marriages
A social psychological perspective
Tulika Jaiswal

80 Writing the City in British Asian Diasporas
Edited by Seán McLoughlin, William Gould, Ananya Jahanara Kabir and Emma Tomalin

81 Post-9/11 Espionage Fiction in the US and Pakistan
Spies and 'terrorists'
Cara Cilano

82 Left Radicalism in India
Bidyut Chakrabarty

83 "Nation-State" and Minority Rights in India
Comparative perspectives on Muslim and Sikh identities
Tanweer Fazal

84 Pakistan's Nuclear Policy
A minimum credible deterrence
Zafar Khan

85 Imagining Muslims in South Asia and the Diaspora
Secularism, religion, representations
Claire Chambers and Caroline Herbert

86 Indian Foreign Policy in Transition
Relations with South Asia
Arijit Mazumdar

87 Corporate Social Responsibility and Development in Pakistan
Nadeem Malik

88 Indian Capitalism in Development
Barbara Harriss-White and Judith Heyer

89 Bangladesh Cinema and National Identity
In search of the modern?
Zakir Hossain Raju

90 Suicide in Sri Lanka
The anthropology of an epidemic
Tom Widger

91 Epigraphy and Islamic Culture
Inscriptions of the Early Muslim Rulers of Bengal (1205–1494)
Mohammad Yusuf Siddiq

92 Reshaping City Governance
London, Mumbai, Kolkata, Hyderabad
Nirmala Rao

93 The Indian Partition in Literature and Films
History, politics, and aesthetics
Rini Bhattacharya Mehta and Debali Mookerjea-Leonard

94 Development, Poverty and Power in Pakistan
The impact of state and donor interventions on farmers
Syed Mohammad Ali

95 Ethnic Subnationalist Insurgencies in South Asia
Identities, interests and challenges to state authority
Edited by Jugdep S. Chima

96 International Migration and Development in South Asia
Edited by Md Mizanur Rahman and Tan Tai Yong

97 Twenty-First Century Bollywood
Ajay Gehlawat

98 Political Economy of Development in India
Indigeneity in ransition in the state of Kerala
Darley Kjosavik and Nadarajah Shanmugaratnam

99 State and Nation-Building in Pakistan
Beyond Islam and security
Edited by Roger D. Long, Gurharpal Singh, Yunas Samad, and Ian Talbot

100 Subaltern Movements in India
Gendered geographies of struggle against neoliberal development
Manisha Desai

101 Islamic Banking in Pakistan
Shariah-compliant finance and the quest to make Pakistan more Islamic
Feisal Khan

102 The Bengal Diaspora
Rethinking Muslim migration
Claire Alexander, Joya Chatterji, and Annu Jalais

103 Mobilizing Religion and Gender in India
The role of activism
Nandini Deo

104 Social Movements and the Indian Diaspora
Movindri Reddy

105 Identity Politics and Elections in Malaysia and Indonesia
Ethnic engineering in Borneo
Karolina Prasad

106 Religion and Modernity in the Himalaya
Edited by Megan Adamson Sijapati and Jessica Vantine Birkenholtz

Islamic Banking in Pakistan

Shariah-compliant banking and the quest to make Pakistan more Islamic

Feisal Khan

Routledge
Taylor & Francis Group
LONDON AND NEW YORK

First published 2015 by Routledge

2 Park Square, Milton Park, Abingdon, Oxfordshire OX14 4RN
52 Vanderbilt Avenue, New York, NY 10017

Routledge is an imprint of the Taylor & Francis Group, an informa business

First issued in paperback 2019

British Library Cataloguing in Publication Data
A catalogue record for this book is available from the British Library

Library of Congress Cataloging in Publication Data
Khan, Feisal, author.
Islamic banking in Pakistan: Shariah-compliant finance and the quest to make Pakistan more Islamic/Feisal Khan.
pages; cm. – (Routledge contemporary South Asia series; 101)
1. Banks and banking–Pakistan. 2. Banks and banking–Religious aspects–Islam. 3. Banking law (Islamic law)–Pakistan. 4. Interest (Islamic law)–Pakistan. I. Title. II. Series: Routledge contemporary South Asia series ; 101.
HG3290.5.A6K535 2016
332.1095491–dc23
2015018409

ISBN: 978-0-415-77975-3 (hbk)
ISBN: 978-0-367-23202-3 (pbk)

Typeset in Times New Roman
by Taylor & Francis Books

Contents

List of illustrations

Tables

Box

Preface: my first exposure to Islamic banking

In 1985 Pakistan became one of the first countries in the world to officially make the full transition from a conventional (interest based) banking system to an 'Islamic' (non-interest based) one. My first employment after graduating from Stanford University in 1988 was with ANZ Grindlays Bank in Karachi, Pakistan. Grindlays, alas, is no more, as it was subsumed within the Standard Chartered behemoth in 2000, but back then Grindlays still retained something of its old fashioned and ultra-conservative air, quite fitting for a bank that dated back to 1828 in the UK and had been in South Asia since 1854. As a consequence, it had the largest branch network, deposit base and management training program of all the foreign banks then operating in Pakistan. I was with Grindlays' Corporate Banking Division, beginning as a trainee, from 1988 to 1990. In that time I received very thorough instruction in all aspects of banking – retail, corporate, and merchant (i.e., investment) banking and foreign trade operations – in Pakistan, as well as excellent first-hand corporate banking experience handling some of the biggest domestic and multinational firms operating in Pakistan. As a trainee I was required to take – and miraculously passed on my first attempt – the Part I Exam of the Institute of Bankers Pakistan.[1]

As part of our preparation for the Part I exam we took evening classes at the Institute. I was immediately struck by the difference between the *theoretical* version of Islamic banking that we were taught in these classes and the very different *practical* version of it that we learnt in our training seminars and put into practice in our internships in each department of Grindlays. As far as I could tell, other than the use of some exotic (to me at the time) terms such as *murabaha, modaraba* and *ijara*, the rest of the practical training we received in the bank was very straightforward, conventional banking. The divide between the rhetoric of Islamic banking and the practice of it, as I soon realized, held true for all banks in Pakistan. I found out from my superiors that, for all practical purposes, nothing had really changed in Pakistani banking after the 1985 mandatory switchover to an ostensibly Islamic 'profit and loss sharing' banking system.

Some years later, during the course of my graduate work in the Economics department of the University of Southern California, I had the great good fortune to work with Professor Timur Kuran,[2] the King Faisal Chair in Islamic

Thought and Culture there, and one of the world's leading authorities on Islamic economics and finance. As both his research assistant and PhD student, I benefitted greatly from his encyclopedic knowledge of Islamic economic and financial institutions, law, norms and practices even though my dissertation had nothing to do with Islamic economics or finance. It is probably due to this early exposure that my current research interests are not in the traditional aspects of banking and finance usually handled by economists (such as return on equity or assets, or capital adequacy management, or even the causes of financial crises) but on the *political economy* side of the issue: *what* is Islamic economics, *how* is it now defined, and *why* did an Islamic banking system come about in Pakistan? I hope this book will answer, satisfactorily, these questions.

The genesis of the book lies with Dorothea Schaefter (Senior Editor – Central, South and Southeast Asia) at Routledge asking me at the South Asia Conference in Madison, Wisconsin, where I was presenting a paper on Islamic banking in Pakistan, if I had ever thought of writing a book on the subject. Unfortunately for her, I thought it was an excellent idea. I am extremely grateful for the faith in my ability to complete the task that Dorothea and her editorial team at Routledge, Rebecca Lawrence and Jillian Morrison, have shown since the project took far, far longer to complete than anyone had originally thought it would. I am also grateful to the Hobart and William Smith Colleges' Faculty Research Funds that gave me the opportunity to travel to Pakistan to do much of the research that went into the writing of this book.

Parts of the book have appeared in an early form as journal articles and I would like to thank the publishers of the original papers for giving me permission to use them here. These are parts of Chapter Six: The nuts and bolts of Islamic banking worldwide ('How "Islamic" is Islamic banking?' *Journal of Economic Behavior and Organization*, 76: 3, December 2010, pp. 805–820, © Elsevier Science) and Chapter Seven: 'Rebooting' Islamic banking in Pakistan to make it more Islamic ('Islamic banking by judiciary: the "backdoor" for Islamism in Pakistan?' *South Asia: Journal of South Asian Studies*, 31: 3, December 2008, pp. 535–555, © Taylor & Francis). I am grateful to the anonymous referees at these journals for their excellent comments on these papers, as well as to conference participants, friends and colleagues too numerous to list here with whom I have discussed various aspects of the book over the years.

However, I would especially like to thank my friend and colleague Dr. Vikash Yadav, who took time out of his busy schedule to read three very long chapters and give extensive and useful comments on them that helped clarify my own thoughts on the issues. I would also like to thank my sister Tehmina, who took a break from her own graduate research to read several chapters and give me her extremely helpful comments on them that made me realize what I thought I was saying was not what it came across as. And my daughters Melanie and Merrick, who put up with good grace far too many times with being told, 'Not this weekend, Abu has to work on his book.'

And above all else, I would like to thank my wife Jennifer Tessendorf for not only putting up with how long this book took to write but with me as well, and for encouraging me to finish it when I was ready to throw in the towel, and for reading several drafts of many chapters of the book. She always gave me detailed and very valuable comments on the chapters that narrowed and focused my often rambling prose, with several parenthetical clauses, that while extremely informative and fascinating in and of themselves, distracted the reader, perhaps by going off on alas irrelevant tangents, from the essential points being conveyed. The book is by far the better for her ruthless red pen. However, I did not always take her suggestions and I suspect that the book is the poorer for that.

I have usually used the standard Pakistani English transliteration of Arabic and Urdu terms, which is not used by all academics or linguists. For example, I write *murabaha* (a cost-plus sale) instead of *murabāḥa*, and *sukuk* (Islamic bond) instead of *ṣukūk*. Not only does the 'correct' transliteration disturb the flow of the sentence and distract the non-specialist (after all, it is Naples in English and not Napoli or Napule) but Arabized pronunciation and usage in Pakistan has become a *de facto* statement of where one's politico-religious sympathies lie. Just as I refuse to replace the time-honored South Asian *Khuda Hafiz* (May God keep you safe) with *Allah Hafiz* or use the 'correct' *Ramadan* instead of the traditional Pakistani pronunciation *Ramzan*, I refuse to replace *murabaha* with *murabāḥa*. The continual Arabization of Muslim culture has reached such ridiculous levels that I was informed, reasonably politely, that I was not pronouncing my own name correctly. My response to that was that, yes, my name was of Arab origin but I am not.

Finally, the opinions expressed in this book, except where they are explicitly identified as to the source, are my own and no-one else's. This book is my opinion and mine alone as to, among other things, whether or not Islamic banking is needed or even feasible, and what exactly is meant by *riba* and what was prohibited for Muslims. I think I am correct, but Allah knows best.

Notes

1 The old Part I and Part II exams, now replaced by a very different system of Junior Associate, Associate and Fellow, of the IBP were professional qualifications for Pakistani bankers, as the Certified Financial Analyst Levels I, II and III are in the USA for financial professionals.

2 Timur Kuran is now Professor of Political Science and Economics and the Gorter Family Professor of Islamic Studies at Duke University in the USA.

1 Islamic finance globally and why this book?

If Islamic banking was confined only to Pakistan or even just to South Asia, it would be an arcane field interesting only to either Islamic scholars or to South Asianists. But Islamic banking and finance (IBF) has far outstripped its relatively humble origins in international finance as an esoteric and obscure financial issue of as much (or as little) interest to the general public as St. Thomas Aquinas' 'Doctrine of the Just Price.' That is far from the case.

It is now common knowledge among those dealing with global finance and related issues that Islamic banking has become a growing force over the past three decades, with 716 Islamic banks in 61 countries worldwide (UK Trade & Investment 2013). By 2012 the world's Islamic financial assets were around $1.3 trillion, 90 per cent of this in Islamic banks, having grown 150 per cent since 2006 (Economist 2012) and an absolutely astounding thirteenfold from 2000 when they were a paltry $100 billion (Chin *et al.* 2008: 1). In 1999 Dow Jones created 'Islamic Indexes' to offer *Shariah*-compliant investment portfolios to cash-flush pious Muslims. Several major Western banks (e.g., Citibank, ABN Amro, Bank of America, HSBC, Standard Chartered, and the Union Bank of Switzerland) either have Islamic Banking subsidiaries or offer Islamic financial products to their customers. Clearly IBF has transformed itself into a major factor in global finance.

In the Muslim world the growth rate of Islamic financial assets far exceeds that of conventional ones. For example, in Bahrain, one of the Muslim world's two main money centers, between 1998 to 2005 Islamic bank assets grew at 111 per cent annually versus only a 6 per cent average annual growth rate for conventional bank assets (Bahrain Monetary Agency 2006). By 2013 the value of Islamic bank assets in Bahrain had reached $23.3 billion even though the average annual growth rate for 2005–13 had declined to a 'mere' 36.4 per cent.[1] Predictably, the increase in crude oil prices in the past several years has increased the growth rate of Islamic bank assets in the Middle East, and Islamic finance is often seen as an Arab phenomenon or, for the more knowledgeable, as an Arab and Malaysian phenomenon, as Malaysia is the other center of Islamic finance. Although still insignificant compared with conventional banking, e.g., in 2010 the US banking system alone held almost US$16.5 trillion in assets (Mishkin 2013: 43), the growth of Islamic banks demonstrates their importance to, and the growing financial clout of, the world's billion-plus Muslims.

What is less well known, even among those otherwise well informed about Islamic finance, is the importance of Pakistan to Islamic finance globally and the importance of Islamic finance to Pakistan. Given that South Asian, especially Pakistani, scholars such as Syed Abul Ala Maududi and Ashraf Qureishi laid the foundation of current IBF in the 1940s, it is not surprising that South Asians in general and Pakistanis in particular are 'over-represented' among the ranks of IBF theorists and practitioners. This is despite the fact that South Asia, and certainly Pakistan, has been quite isolated from the mainstream of global finance for most of the second half of the twentieth century. Pakistan was a leader in both the development of theoretical Islamic banking and how it was actually implemented, as Pakistanis and other South Asians are found in Islamic banks and financial firms throughout the Gulf at all levels, from tellers to the boardroom. There are also Pakistani and other South Asian analysts and scholars in major regional think tanks such as the Islamic Research and Training Institute of the Islamic Development Bank in Saudi Arabia[2] and in the central banks of many Gulf states. Thus there are Pakistanis involved at all levels of Islamic banking in the Gulf countries, and Pakistan continues to be important in the future development of Islamic finance even if it does not contribute much to it monetarily.

Why is IBF and its connection to Pakistan worth studying? Several reasons come to mind. Islamic banking and finance is a trillion-dollar component of global finance and one that is still growing rapidly. The original architects of contemporary IBF were/are disproportionately South Asian and especially Pakistani, although the Pakistani part of IBF is relatively small and so fairly insignificant in the global context – even though Pakistan is not an insignificant country for other reasons. More importantly, the fight over Islamic banking in Pakistan is a microcosm of the battle over what kind of a society Pakistan is going to be and over the nature of the Pakistani state itself. In some important aspects, this fight pre-dates the creation of Pakistan itself.

Thus the argument over Islamic banking in Pakistan is important because it illustrates the battle-lines between Islamic Minimalists who favor a Modernist interpretation of Islam and those who favor an Islamic Maximalist interpretation that sees Pakistan as a model Islamic state. For the latter, Pakistan's destiny is to be the 'New Medina' that will revive the (mythical) Golden Age of Islam. The contrast is between these Revivalists and the Modernists who, however devout they may have been personally, wanted a state that was effectively secular at the functional level, a state that would not make the religious inclinations and preferences of its people a matter of vital importance and concern to itself.

This decades-long battle between these two mutually antagonistic forces is why we see the level of sectarian chauvinism that is the norm for Pakistan now. And that is why I think this book matters. The book is not meant as a detailed 'how to' guide to Islamic banking in Pakistan or elsewhere, and neither is it meant to be a comprehensive history of Pakistan's Islamization. I hope to give the reader enough knowledge of the latter to understand the former because the two are irreducibly intertwined: Islamic banking would not exist without societal Islamization.

What is this book about?

My aim here is to examine how Pakistan came to be one of the first countries of the world to institute a fully 'Islamic' banking system. This was done by military diktat in 1985. That is the short answer.

The long answer is of course a much more complicated and convoluted one. To fully understand why the orders for a conversion were issued requires some knowledge of how and why Pakistan came into being and its complex relationship with Islam. The former requires some understanding of the basis and extent of Hindu–Muslim political antagonism in the British Indian Empire that led to the partitioning of British India into two separate Dominions, India and Pakistan, in August 1947. The latter requires an understanding of the overtly religious basis of both the Indian National Congress's and the Muslim League's mass following and the process by which the religion genie emerged onto the Indian nationalist scene. Without the salience of religion, both the Congress and the League lacked a mass following and the ability to mobilize at the grassroots. Before Mohandas Karamchand Gandhi, 1869–1948, began the transformation of the Congress Party after his return to India in 1915, it was little more than a glorified debating society for India's Anglicized native elite who sought 'Home Rule' from the British colonial rulers. Similarly, the Muslim League was little more than a lobbying association for some of India's Muslim grandees before the President of the Muslim League Mohammed Ali Jinnah, 1876–1984, and Pakistan's leader after independence in 1947, turned it into a real political party with mass appeal. In both cases the appeal of the respective parties to India's masses (to Hindus in the case of Congress and to Muslims in the case of the League) had an undeniable religious aspect to it. While the religious nature of the appeal may well have been stronger for the League than for Congress, it was vital to the success of both.

In the case of India, the Hindu genie could be more or less successfully stuffed back in the bottle by Jawaharlal Nehru, 1889–1964, India's first prime minister, because it had been discredited by the murder of Mahatma Gandhi by Hindu fanatics in 1948 and then further weakened by the death of Nehru's Deputy Prime Minister (the new regime's strongman) Sardar Vallabhai Patel, 1875–1950, relatively soon after independence. While certainly not as secular as Nehru, Patel was not a Hindu zealot like the extremists who killed Gandhi; he was, however, much closer to the extremely conservative (both religiously and politically) Hindu businessmen who funded both Congress and some of the Hindu chauvinist groups. Had these two events not taken place, it is highly likely that India's much vaunted secularism, a product of Nehru's personal beliefs and his virtually unopposed supremacy in Indian politics for a decade and a half after independence, would have been greatly weakened and challenged well before the *Bharatiya Janata* Party's *Hindutva* (i.e., Hinduness, an assertive brand of Hindu chauvinism) revival of the late 1980s. Pakistan was not as fortunate as India in being able to stave off the Islamists for as long as India could the *Hindutva* movement.

For Pakistan, the Islamic genie, once out, refused to go back in the bottle. Mohammed Ali Jinnah was personally secular and areligious but many of those who followed him had done so precisely because he was articulating a Muslim nationalism that was, for them at least, irrevocably linked to Islamic revivalism. *Pakistan ka matlab kya? La illaha il lallah!* ('What does Pakistan mean? There is no God but Allah!') was the extremely potent rallying cry in the Punjab during the 1946 elections that catapulted the League into power there. Some of those such as Syed Abul Ala Maududi, 1903–79, who had vigorously opposed Jinnah precisely because he had no use for religion in public or political life, went to Pakistan after independence to save the Muslim homeland from people like Jinnah who thought in modern (secular) terms that did not place Islam center stage. Maududi was, along with Imam Khomeini of Iran and Syed Qutb of Egypt, one of the three greatest theoreticians of political Islam in the twentieth century, and he and other Islamists opposed Jinnah's Muslim nationalism precisely because it would have an Islamic modernist, territorial basis and not a religious one.

This confusing and contradictory mix of circumstances – those who wanted a Muslim homeland were not in favor of an Islamic state, and those who most vociferously advocated for an overtly Islamic Pakistan were not originally in favor of a Muslim homeland – helps make this such a difficult and complicated case study. The importance of Islam here goes back directly to the only real tool the Muslim League had at its disposal to create a mass following for itself: mobilize the masses on an overtly religious basis to counter Gandhi's religion-tinged appeal to the Hindu masses.[3]

This was a real quandary for many of the Muslim League's leaders, who were mostly educated at the Oxbridge-patterned Aligarh Muslim University founded by the first major Indian Islamic modernist, Sir Syed Ahmad Khan, 1817–98. Theirs was a modernist interpretation of Islam that saw little conflict between modernity and religion even though most of them were at least certainly ceremonial deists when it came to the role of religion in public life.[4] Their call for Muslim nationalism had an ethnic basis. It was 'the Muslims are a separate nation and that is why they deserve their own state' and not 'the Muslims are a separate religion and that is why they deserve their own state.' Yet to succeed in their aim they had to utilize religion to mobilize the masses.

There were few *ulema* (Muslim religious scholars) of any standing who supported the Muslim League's call for a separate Muslim homeland. The most important among them was Maulana Shabbir Ahmad Usmani, 1886–1949, who was indispensable to Jinnah and the League both for countering Congress's conservative (mainly ultra-orthodox) Muslim allies who charged that the League's leaders were pro-British, irreligious and indeed well nigh non-Muslims for all practical purposes; and for mobilizing the Muslim masses in a way that the grandees who formed the Muslim League leadership never could. But Usmani did so not for Jinnah or the League, but for the opportunity to create a model Islamic state and society, an opportunity that would be denied to him in a secular, much less a Hindu-led, India. This was essentially the same reason why Maududi left India for Pakistan.

There is thus a continual tension in Pakistan from the first day over those who favor what the contemporary Iranian philosopher Abdul Karim Soroush has termed Maximalist Islam (where everything in a modern state has to be explicitly derived from well established Islamic principles – what is commonly but somewhat inaccurately termed *Shariah* [5]) and Minimalist Islam (where only broad conceptual outlines need be in conformity with Islam) (Fremont 2000). Most, but certainly not all, of the higher-level leadership of the Muslim League, the army and the civil service in the new state favored Islamic Minimalism (usually expressed as lip service to Islamic norms or other such perfunctory invocations of religion publicly): ceremonial deism.

This tension played out in several arenas in Pakistan, as seen in, for example, the early demand that the Pakistani education system include mandatory classes in *Islamiat* (the study of Islam)[6] or Maulana Usmani's demand that the government appoint a supra-parliamentary *Shaikh ul Islam* (Chief of the Muslim Clergy) who would have the right to oversee all public officials.[7] The particular manifestation that I am going to examine in depth here is how it affected the Pakistani financial system.

I shall examine in detail how it came about that Pakistan rather than, say, Saudi Arabia or a Persian Gulf country came to have one of the world's first Islamic banking systems. I shall also look in detail at both what Islamic finance is supposed to be, and what it actually is. That is, does Islamic finance as it is actually practiced differ from how its advocates envisaged it in theory? How, if at all, does Pakistani IBF differ from that practiced elsewhere in the world? And what is its likely future evolution?

Pakistan has received a great deal of notoriety and world attention for the past two decades, whether because of its nuclear weapons, or nuclear proliferation to other Muslim countries, or its ongoing brutal Islamist insurgency and terrorist campaign against the state, or its support of the ultra-Islamist Afghan Taliban, or Muslim terrorist attacks on India originating in Pakistan. Much of this attention has been openly scurrilous and in the extreme verging on outright scaremongering and sensationalism, and not just in the yellow press. For example, Bruce Riedel, the former US Central Intelligence Agency career officer, Special Assistant to the President of the United States and chair of the advisory group to President Barack Obama on South Asia, epitomizes the type of sensationalism used to sell books–he is the author of several books on Pakistan, Afghanistan and South Asia in general. Riedel personally briefed then US President-elect Barack Obama that 'Pakistan, the birthplace of global Islamic jihad and now its epicenter, had become a crucible of terror and was *the most dangerous country in the world*' (Riedel 2012: 2, emphasis added).

That being said, there are certainly more than ample grounds for much of the world to be concerned about what is happening in Pakistan and to try to make sense of it and why it has occurred. While Pakistan is not actually 'the most dangerous country in the world,' it certainly is a country that cannot be ignored by the rest of the world. The common denominator in most of what concerns security analysts in the outside world seems to be 'Islam' and how 'Islam' seems to be involved in everything that happens in Pakistan. Why is this so?

To work backwards then, using the particular issue that this book focuses on, for Pakistan, the demand for an Islamic financial system was irrevocably linked to the demand for an Islamic state. The underlying strength of this demand was because religion was the basis of the creation of Pakistan, and Muslim ethnic mobilization was not possible without their religious mobilization. And this meant that every Pakistani constitution had to be appropriately Islamic, culminating in the 1980 orders issued by Gen. Zia ul Haq, 1924–88, for Pakistan's banks to convert to an Islamic banking system.

Why an Islamic Pakistan with an Islamic banking system?

As the first modern state founded expressly because of the religion of its inhabitants, Islam has always been at the forefront of what makes Pakistan what it is and what it might become. But Islam and Pakistan have always had a curiously ambivalent relationship. As discussed above, many of the original leaders of the Muslim League, the army and the civil service inherited from the departing British colonial rulers were personally quite secular in their lives. They viewed Islam's role in Pakistan along lines similar to that of the role of Christianity in the United States in much of the twentieth century: nominally Christian and certainly ceremonially deist, but not a country where faith played a role in governing or legislating. Others though, notably Islamists such as Syed Abul Ala Maududi and the political party that he founded, the *Jamaat e Islami* (Party of Islam), saw Pakistan very differently. For Maududi and other Islamists like him, Pakistan's existence could only be justified if it were to serve Islam by being the world's first truly Islamic state. Although Maududi died in 1979, the *Jamaat* and its highly disciplined Islamist cadres are still a potent Islamist force in Pakistan, India and Bangladesh and are among the most vocal advocates of political Islam in South Asia.

Maududi and the other Islamist parties in Pakistan saw the Islamization of the financial sector in Pakistan not as an end in itself but merely as one aspect of the total Islamization of the nation, government, laws, culture and people. That is why no study of economic and financial Islam in Pakistan, and why Pakistan became a pioneer in Islamic finance, is possible without analyzing the role political Islam played in both the creation of Pakistan and its later history. For all Islamists and not just Maududi, Islam is not an *à la carte* menu that one can pick and choose from: it is all or it is nothing. Maududi wrote extensively not only on what made for an 'Islamic' state or an 'Islamic' form of government but also on what made an economic or financial system 'Islamic.'

But why does there have to be an 'Islamic' economic or financial system? The current conventional answer is that Islam prohibits charging or receiving interest, but this is far too simplistic a view and one, as I shall demonstrate, that was far from the uniform perception of all Muslims in the past.

In 1979 the military ruler of Pakistan, Gen. Zia ul Haq (ruled 1977–88), fully backed by the *Jamaat e Islami* and other Sunni Islamic political parties, announced that Pakistan would soon become the first country in the world to move to a wholly Islamic banking system. By 1985 all banks in Pakistan were ordered to offer only Islamic banking and financial services, although in practice there was no significant change in actual banking practices. However, the ultra-orthodox were not appeased by nominal changes to the system and sought legal redress which, given the explicit wording of the 1973 Constitution and Gen. Zia's changes to the Pakistani legal structure, they obtained.

Two court rulings (1991 by the Federal *Shariat* Court, an Islamic appellate court, and 1999 by the Supreme Court's *Shariat* Appellate Bench) declared that the financial Islamization decreed by Gen. Zia was inadequate and mandated a wholesale revision of the existing system to make it more Islamic. This would require shifting the emphasis from lending to direct equity participation as the sole permissible financing instrument. In 2002 the Supreme Court's *Shariat* Appellate Bench reversed its 1999 ruling and ordered the Federal *Shariat* Court restudy the issue before ruling on it afresh. Later in 2002 also, responding to the widespread criticism that the Pakistani banking system was not Islamic in any meaningful way, the country's central bank, the State Bank of Pakistan, decided to rename the hitherto Islamic banking system as 'conventional banking' and established a parallel – now truly Islamic and ostensibly fully *Shariah*-compliant – banking system while it studied how conventional banking could be overhauled.

Have things really changed since the 'reboot' of Islamic banking in Pakistan in 2002? What does current Islamic banking in Pakistan really look like? And how do its practitioners and customers feel about it? I shall also examine these and other issues and hope to be able to convey a full picture of Pakistani Islamic banking to the reader.

The organization of the book

The book is organized as follows:

Chapter One: Islamic finance globally and why this book?

Chapter Two: An Islamic Republic or merely a Republic of Muslims?

The importance of religion (both Hinduism and Islam) in Indian nationalism; the beginning of Muslim mass mobilization around religious symbols;

the resulting central role of Islam in the creation of Pakistan and the creation of an overtly Islamic Muslim political identity.

Chapter Three: The post-Jinnah Islamization of Pakistan

The Islamization of Pakistan, from the 1949 *Objectives Resolution* to General Zia's (1980s) amendments to the constitution creating the Federal *Shariat* Court and the *Shariat* Appellate Bench of the Supreme Court of Pakistan to attempts by democratically elected governments to expand the scope of Islamization.

Chapter Four: The debate over *riba*

The Koran's categorical prohibition of *riba* and different interpretations of what exactly is being prohibited; the arguments of Islamic Modernist/Islamic Minimalist scholars (such as Sir Syed Ahmad Khan, Fazlur Rahman, and others) and the perspective of Islamic Maximalists (such as Syed Abul Alal Maudoodi and Anwar Iqbal Qureishi); Islamic banking's role in strengthening and preserving a strong 'Muslim' identity and the prevention of the creation of 'partial Muslims.'

Chapter Five: The new orthodoxy of 'old' Islamic financial norms

The position of contemporary Islamic economists regarding the permissibility of charging interest on financial transactions; the time value of money in Islam; an alternate theory as to why Islam and other pre-modern societies prohibited the charging of interest on loans; the 1980 Council of Islamic Ideology report that formed the basis of the 1985 conversion from a conventional to an Islamic banking system and how it compares to historical financial practices in Muslim societies.

Chapter Six: The nuts and bolts of Islamic banking worldwide

The ideal form IBF is supposed to take and how current IBF is actually implemented in Pakistan and elsewhere; range and type of products offered; where and how they differ from conventional counterparts; how IBF institutions handle information asymmetry issues and the resulting problems of adverse selection and moral hazard; legal issues in offering IBF products in non-Islamic legal environments (USA, Western Europe); more 'liberal' Malaysian (Shaafi *madhab*) interpretation of Islamic banking rules versus more 'restrictive' Gulf/South-Asian (Hanafi/Hanbali *madhab*); how far IBF institutions have successfully offered alternatives to conventional financial products and whether IBF lives up to its claims.

Chapter Seven 'Rebooting' Islamic banking in Pakistan to make it more Islamic

The 1991 and 1999 Pakistani legal decisions invalidating the existing financial system on grounds it is unIslamic and hence unconstitutional; the possible impact on the economy of direct-equity participation as sole financing model; the 2002 Supreme Court *Shariat* Appellate Bench reversal of its 1999 ruling; the likelihood that the 2002 reversal will stay the law in the future; how Pakistani Islamic banking post-2002 differs from the version instituted by Gen. Zia in 1985.

Chapter Eight: Three decades of the Pakistani experiment

The main changes to Islamic banking in Pakistan post-2002; the size and scope of Pakistan's Islamic banking sector and how, if at all, it differs from the picture of Islamic banking presented in Chapter Six; the views of Pakistani Islamic and conventional bankers and others involved in the Pakistani financial sector; the behavior of the Pakistani retail and corporate clientele of both Islamic and conventional Pakistani banks; the differences between those that use Islamic versus those that use conventional banks.

Chapter Nine: *Quo vadis*, Islamic banking?

A reiteration of the main points of the book; the likely path Islamic banking in Pakistan will take in the future; an alternative vision of Islamic banking offered by some critics of its current form.

Notes

1 Calculated from 'Table 27: Aggregated balance sheet of the Islamic banks: retail banks and wholesale banks' of the Central Bank of Bahrain's (2014) *Statistical Bulletin.*

2 M. Umer Chapra, one of the world's most prominent Islamic economists and former advisor to the Saudi Arabian Monetary Agency (the Saudi central bank), is originally from Pakistan and was granted Saudi citizenship by the King, an honor so rare as to be almost unheard of.

3 Gandhi was also the leader of the *Khilafat* Movement 1919–24 to restore the Sunni Muslim Turkish Caliph. However, his unilateral decision to call off both his part of the Movement (and, incidentally, the Congress campaign to oust the British from India) led to great bitterness on the part of the Movement's Muslim leadership, who persisted for two years after his decision. The Movement fizzled out by 1924 when Mustafa Kemal Ataturk abolished the Caliphate and even Indian Muslims gave up the cause.

4 Ceremonial deism was the legal term coined in 1962 by Eugene Rostow, Dean of the Yale Law School, to describe the purely nominal and often perfunctory use of religion in public life in the United States, e.g., the invocation of God in the Pledge of Allegiance or on US currency. The United States Supreme Court affirmed the constitutionality of such usage in 1984. See Epstein 1996 for more details.

5 A necessary distinction should be made between *fiqh* (Islamic jurisprudence) and *Shariah* (literally 'path,' but here the Divine Path or Law that all Muslims must follow). While the two terms are often used interchangeably, what is usually termed *Shariah* is better called *fiqh. Fiqh* is simply the result of (fallible) human attempts to interpret *Shariah* and should not be viewed as immutable; only *Shariah* is immutable. There are currently four main Sunni (Hanafi, Shafi, Hanbali, and Maliki) and one main Shia (*fiqh e Jafaria* aka *Ithna Ashari* or Twelver Shia) schools of thought (*madhab*) regarding *fiqh*; in the past there were others that are now extinct. It is usual to characterize Hanafi as the most 'moderate/progressive' and Hanbali (of which Saudi Wahhabism is a direct outgrowth) as the most 'conservative' although no school is uniformly more 'progressive' or 'conservative' in all areas. The Sunni schools of thought are not exclusive and there is substantial overlap among them; similarly, the main Shia *madhab* has many commonalities with the Sunni ones. There are also fringe Sunni (e.g., the Ahmadia) and Shia (e.g., Ismaili) schools that differ greatly from the main five *madhabs* and some of these no longer call themselves Muslims (e.g., Druze or Baha'i); these groups are often persecuted by both mainstream Shias and Sunnis.

6 This was implemented at the primary school level in the early 1950s and massively expanded under General Zia ul Haq's military dictatorship (ruled 1977–88) until compulsory *Islamiat* classes and examinations were required through the first two years of the college curriculum.

7 See Chapter Two for more details on this.

2 An Islamic Republic or merely a Republic of Muslims?

The purpose of this chapter is to provide the necessary background to how and why Pakistan came about as an expression of Muslim nationalism that had an irrevocably Islamic revivalist tinge to it. This is why the Islamization of the Pakistani financial sector cannot be analyzed or understood without an understanding of the forces that drove Pakistan almost from its very inception towards Islamization. The development of a Muslim political consciousness in India during the period 1905–47 resulted in the Partition of the British Indian Empire into two successor states in August 1947: Hindu-majority India led by the Indian National Congress and Muslim-majority Pakistan led by the Muslim League.

This Muslim mass mobilization and the creation of a distinctly Muslim political identity in India under Muslim League auspices, even if not all Indian Muslims subscribed to it, meant that once Pakistan came into being it was destined to be 'Islamic.' Thus the real question that occupied center stage in Pakistani constitutional and politico-legal discussions almost from the first day of its existence onwards was 'How Islamic should Pakistan be?' and not 'Should Pakistan be Islamic?'

Muhammad Ali Jinnah, the leader of the Muslim League, was completely secular, indeed areligious, in his personal life and outlook, and his death in 1948 deprived the League of its most powerful advocate of a modern (i.e., *de facto* secular and only at most ceremonially deist) form of government for Pakistan. However, the secularists in the League were faced with a seemingly insurmountable problem: if Pakistan was not to be Islamic, then why have a Pakistan? Without Jinnah's towering personality and status in the new nation, they could neither effectively articulate nor press the case against the comprehensive Islamization of the new nation.

Pakistan was the result of a four-decade-long process that began with the British colonial government's partition in 1905 of the Indian province of Bengal into a Muslim-majority and a Hindu-majority region, and it culminated in the resounding electoral victory of the Muslim League in 1946. Between 1905 and 1946 the sense that Muslims were a separate 'nation' within India grew from being a belief held by only a few to becoming the deciding issue of the 1946 elections.

Jinnah saw Islam in the context of Indian Muslims not as a religious identity but as an ethnicity, a 'nation' in the preferred usage of the Muslim League.[1] This then became the crux of the League's quandary: its demand for Pakistan was really for ethnocratic power but to achieve this required that Muslims be mobilized along religious lines. By so doing, however, the League could not prevent Islamic revivalists from outflanking it and successfully conflating in the minds of much of the populace the League's demand for ethnocratic power with their demand for an Islamic state: a neo- or virtual theocracy in some key respects.

This was relatively easy for the Islamic revivalists to do because the creation of Pakistan was possible only due to the creation of an Indian Muslim religio-political identity, and this religio-political identity was possible only due to a religious awakening that, once awakened, could not be put back to sleep regardless of what the leadership of the Muslim League may have wanted. Thus the Pakistan that came into being on August 14, 1947 was destined to be Islamic. The only question was, how Islamic?

Accordingly, this chapter will, after a brief discussion of the pre-independence period, analyze how the 1946 All-India elections cemented the Muslim religious awakening in the areas that became Pakistan and how the Muslim League was unable to stave off the Islamic revivalist demands for an Islamic state. Despite the best efforts of many in the Muslim League leadership, the culmination of the first phase of this process was the approval of the 1956 Constitution that officially declared Pakistan to be an Islamic Republic. The politico-legal trajectory of the Pakistani state since then, despite some efforts in the 1962 Constitution to slightly water down its Islamic nature, has been firmly set on this path. The 1973 (i.e., current) Constitution reaffirmed the Islamic nature of the state, and the extensive amendments to it by Gen. Zia's military regime (1977–88) further strengthened it. The reaffirmation of Zia's Islamic amendments by subsequent Pakistani civilian governments confirmed that the state would remain 'Islamic.'

Pakistan, with or without the Islamic modifiers?

Pakistan[2] came into being on August 14, 1947 as a homeland for most, but certainly not all, of the British Indian Empire's Muslim inhabitants. Far from being enthusiastic supporters of the call for Pakistan, the vast majority of India's traditional *ulema* vociferously opposed its creation. To the extent that any country can be the single-handed creation of one man, Pakistan was that of Muhammad Ali Jinnah (1876–1948). Jinnah, an almost completely areligious and Anglicized UK-trained barrister – arguably one of the finest legal minds of his generation – was a rising young star of the nascent Indian nationalist movement and far from a Muslim separatist. Edwin Montagu, Secretary of State for India (the British Cabinet member responsible for India), after meeting him in 1916, wrote in his diary: 'Young, perfectly mannered, impressive looking, armed to the teeth with dialectics … Jinnah is a very clever man and it is, of course, an outrage that such a man should have no chance of running the affairs of his own country' (quoted in Embree 2011: 225). Jinnah, as it turned out, created his own country.

Muslims in undivided India were an overall minority but one that formed an absolute majority of the population in the western and eastern parts of India. The 1941 Census of India showed that its total population of 390 million was divided as follows: 256 million (65.6 per cent) Hindu; 94 million (24.1 per cent) Muslim; 26 million (6.7 per cent) Tribals;[3] roughly 6 million (1.5 per cent) each Sikh and Christian; and 1.4 million (0.4 per cent) Jain (Hoffman 1948: 96–98). The Muslim population was concentrated (56.4 million, 60 per cent of the total) in the provinces of Balochistan, Punjab, Northwest Frontier, Sind, Bengal, and Assam, most of whose areas eventually became Pakistan in 1947.[4]

Pakistan was the result of the demand of a large portion of the Muslims of the British Indian Empire for a Muslim majority state to be carved out of the Muslim-majority areas of the Indian Empire. The standard historical narrative contrasts the 'secular,' pan-Indian nationalism of the Indian National Congress (the political party which took power in independent India in 1947) with the Muslim nationalism/separatism of leaders such as the Islamic modernist Sir Syed Ahmad Khan (1817–98), Sir Muhammad Iqbal[5] (1877–1938; the ideological father of Pakistan), Muhammad Ali Jinnah (1876–1948), and the Muslim League. The basis of Muslim separatism in the Indian Empire was the 'two nation theory,' first espoused in a somewhat diffuse form by Sir Syed Ahmad Khan, a high-ranking native official in the colonial bureaucracy, who argued that Muslims and Hindus in India constituted two wholly separate and distinct communities: that there were two separate nationalities, as it were, in India. Some three decades after Sir Syed's death, at the December 1930 annual meeting of the Muslim League, its president Sir Muhammad Iqbal proposed a self-governing 'Muslim India' in the northwest of the British Indian Empire, i.e., Pakistan without Bangladesh (Jalal and Seal 1981: 439–440), to further separate Muslims from Hindus. Echoing this broad theme, in a speech to the inaugural session of the All India Muslim Students Federation in December 1937, Jinnah succinctly summarized the Indian Muslims' fears of Hindu domination in a nutshell when he said that 'We do not want to be reduced to the position of the Negroes of America' (quoted in Wolpert 1984: 156).

While the origin of Pakistan was undoubtedly grounded in a North Indian Muslim sense of being 'separate' from their Hindu neighbors, what became known eventually as the 'two nation theory,' there was no consensus among the leaders of that movement as to whether that separate Muslim homeland was to be an Islamic Republic or merely a republic with a Muslim majority. That is, was the new state to be an overtly confessional one that imposed a particular set of religious values on its populace and required both orthodoxy of thought and orthopraxy of observance? Or was it to be a nation of ceremonial deists? One that just happened to have a Muslim majority and so invoked Islam in public life in a purely *pro forma* fashion to, say, open the new session of Parliament or on other such public/ceremonial occasions.

The Islamization of the Pakistani financial system was and continues to be an integral and irrevocable aspect of the overall Islamization of the country advocated by the political parties affiliated with the great *madrassa* (school/seminary) at Deoband in India and the *Jamaat e Islami* (Party of Islam; founded by Maulana Syed Abul Ala Maududi[6] in 1941), and no understanding of how and why the Pakistani financial system was Islamized is possible without understanding how and why Pakistan was created and then how and why it became 'Islamic.' In short, a major – if not the most important – aspect of the impulse that created Pakistan was the same one that forced an overtly Islamic cast to its constitutional, legal and financial structures. The history of Pakistan is evidence that, once unleashed, these forces could not be denied.

This occurred despite the fact that the majority of the leadership of the Muslim League, the political party that created Pakistan, were Western-educated, Islamic progressive (to varying degrees) modernists who knew little of classical Islamic *fiqh* (i.e., Muslim jurisprudence; what is often erroneously termed *Shariah*).[7] They were certainly willingly to pay lip-service to the Islamic nature of the state by invoking the name of Allah on appropriate occasions and harkening back to the glory days of the great Muslim empires of the past. They were not willing to refashion, say, the criminal or financial codes to bring them into conformity with the rulings of any particular Islamic *fiqh*. Theirs was a ceremonial deism at a level not substantively different from that of the leadership of the United States' or the United Kingdom's in the 1920s or 1930s. This is in stark contrast with revolutionary Iran in 1979 where the Shia *ulema*, rigorously trained in *fiqh e Jaafaria*, assumed direct political control.

The Muslim League's Islam was reformist and modernist. It was the Islam of the Aligarh Movement started by Sir Syed Ahmad Khan (even if Sir Syed was not particularly progressive in his personal outlook) when in 1875 he founded the first institution of modern higher education (British style and deliberately offering an Oxbridge-patterned curriculum that stressed the English language and literature and the sciences) for Muslims in India.[8] A significant counter to Sir Syed, and Aligarh's bitter rival, was the great *Madrassa Dar ul Uloom* at Deoband founded only a few years earlier in 1866 but determinedly anti-Modernist and anti-Western in its outlook and resolute in its adherence to the *Dars e Nizami* curriculum established in India in the mid-eighteenth century. Deoband explicitly 'rejected any association with the British' (Akbar 2011: 96) and anyone such as Sir Syed Ahmad Khan.[9] The political parties affiliated with Deoband (the *Jamiat e Ulema e Hind* – JUH, the Party of the Islamic Scholars of India – and the ultra-reactionary *Majlis e Ahrar e Islam* – Association of Free Muslims) sided with the Indian National Congress against the Muslim League. At the risk of some oversimplification,[10] there was thus an internal struggle in the Indian Muslim community between Modernists and Traditionalists. Many of the Modernists favored a separate Muslim nationalism and thus opposed Congress's attempts to create a Hinduism-complected and Congress-led composite Indian nationalism. The Traditionalists, being bitterly opposed to anything that smacked of Westernizing Islam or Muslims (including Western-style Muslim nationalism and a Western education), naturally sided with Congress (Hindu-dominated and quasi-socialist though it might be) against what they viewed as heretical innovators who would inevitably destroy Islam. Heretical innovation (*bidah*) is a mortal sin in traditional Islamic jurisprudence and '"modernism" was the most dangerous heresy of the day, and they fought it vigorously' with every resource at their disposal (Binder 1961: 40).[11]

However, even within the Muslim League there were those who wanted a much more overtly Islamic Pakistan. This was certainly the desire of the small portion of India's Muslim *ulema* (traditional Islamic scholars) who supported the Muslim League. The most prominent among them was Maulana Shabbir Ahmad Usmani,[12] also of the great *madrassa* at Deoband. He enthusiastically supported the call for a separate Muslim homeland and was instrumental both in creating a mass base for the League among the generally illiterate Indian Muslim masses, and in countering attacks on the League's leadership by the Congress-allied traditional *ulema* opposed to their Islamic modernism and relative progressiveness. Usmani's desire was undoubtedly for a traditional Islamic state – one explicitly grounded in classical *fiqh* of the Hanafi school as interpreted by Deoband. Usmani's death in 1949 removed the main strength of the Islamization impetus within the League and shifted its focus to those outside it.

Usmani's role as the leading spokesman for Pakistan's Islamization was quickly taken up by the extremely influential Islamic revivalist, Koranic exegete, voluminous pamphleteer and prolific author Maulana Maududi. Despite Maududi's early opposition to the League's Pakistan because it would not be 'Islamic' enough for him, he decided to move there from India when he realized that the creation of Pakistan gave him the perfect opportunity to put his vision of the Islamic state into effect. Maududi's was a far more modernist, if not exactly progressive, vision of Islam and it was one that clearly transcended his Deobandi roots.

It is one of the great ironies of history that the Deoband-affiliated/influenced parties which had bitterly opposed Jinnah, the Muslim League and Pakistan had, by the end of the twentieth century, succeeded in shaping Pakistan in their image of what a Muslim state should be. At a basic level, and again at the risk of some oversimplification, the difference between the Muslim League leadership's interpretation of Islam and that of the Islamists such as Usmani or Maududi conforms to Abdul Karim Soroush's (Fremont 2000) differences between Maximalist Islam and Minimalist Islam discussed in Chapter One. Despite being routed at the polls in 1946, contemporary Pakistan is the triumph of the Islamic Maximalists and the overall defeat of the Islamic Minimalists.

Religion, communalism and mass mobilization in India before the 1946 general election

A detailed study of the Partition of the British Indian Empire into India and Pakistan is far beyond the scope of this work,[13] as is a discussion of how and why a strong Muslim national identity emerged in the decades leading up to the 1946 general election in India. The 1946 election resulted in the emergence of Congress and the Muslim League as the two largest and diametrically opposed political parties in the British Indian Empire, and the stage was set for the Partition of the Empire into India and Pakistan.

The 'blame' for the Partition of the British Indian Empire and the prevention of the emergence of a united India on the world scene is usually placed on an atavistic Muslim sense of separateness greatly aggravated by the political ambitions of Muslim leaders who saw in Pakistan a chance to be the big fish in a little pond. In short, 'it is still widely held that the Muslims prevented the creation of a modern unified India' (Ziring 1997: 4). Perry Anderson summarizes this succinctly:

> [it] has always been [the standard Indian view] that it was Jinnah's personal ambition that fired Muslim separatism, destroying the unity of the national liberation struggle and wrecking what would otherwise have been its natural culmination in a single ecumenical state coinciding with the borders of the Raj and bearing the proud name of India.[14]
>
> (Anderson 2012: 93)

The use of Islam and appeals to a separate Muslim identity that trumped all else was central to the Muslim League's electoral campaign. The League's resounding triumph in the 1946 Indian General Elections cemented its claim to be *the* voice of Indian Muslims and fully established Jinnah's status as the 'Sole Spokesman' for Indian Muslims, to use Jalal's (1994/1985) description of him. The use of Islam by Jinnah and the Muslim League is fully acknowledged, documented and analyzed by researchers and scholars of all nationalities, ethnicities, religions or ideological persuasions.[15] In short, in 1946 a vote for the Muslim League was a vote for Islam and not to vote for the League was to declare oneself a *kafir* (unbeliever) and so imperil one's soul (Gilmartin 1988: 218). The League's electoral campaign had vital assistance from the tiny minority of *ulema* who supported it – essentially the singlehanded effort of Maulana Shabbir Ahmad Usmani of the Deoband *madrassa*, the vast majority of whose scholars were formally allied with Congress. The League's campaign won it 76 per cent of the total Muslim vote cast in India in the 1946 elections; in the two largest Muslim-majority provinces of Bengal and Punjab it won 65 and 84 per cent, respectively (Singh 1991/1987: 139–140), with most of the rest of the vote going to other Muslim parties and not to Congress.

What is less well known (and even less acknowledged) is that the League's opponents, both Congress and its allied traditionalist Muslim parties, also played the Islam card, albeit completely unsuccessfully. Congress used its allies in the Deobandi *ulema* of the JUH in a propaganda counter-barrage. The President of the JUH, Husain Ahmed Madani, was a well known Deobandi scholar who went to the extent to issuing an official *fatwa* in October 1945 that joining the Muslim League was *haram* (religiously forbidden) for Muslims (Khairi 1995: 468).[16] However Congress's 'attempts to outdo the League in religious propaganda, without having a widespread popular base among Muslims, profited Congress little, and only contributed to the atmosphere of communal bitterness' (Singh 1991/1987: 138). This was not the first time that religion had been used in Indian politics. Religion was integral in the conversion of the Indian national movement from an elitist organization of a few Western-educated intellectuals to a mass movement capable of successfully challenging the British colonial rulers.

The injection of religion into the Indian nationalist movement, or at least of religious symbolism, in an effort to create the salience necessary to create a mass base for what had hitherto been a glorified debating society was the work of Mohandas Karamchand Gandhi (1869–1948). Gandhi's return to India in 1915 from South Africa was the force that changed the nationalist scene. While also a UK-trained barrister like Jinnah – the two were actually born roughly 30 miles apart from each other and were both Gujrati speakers – the two could not be more different in personality, dress, attitude to religion and the path to achieving Self-Rule for India.

It was Gandhi, who had cut his teeth in the much more hostile environment of South Africa and spent years learning how to build a grassroots movement that created Congress's mass base and transformed it from a glorified debating society into a national party capable of challenging British colonial rule. He 'rebuilt Congress from top to bottom, endowing it with a permanent executive at national level, vernacular units at provincial level, local bases at district level, and delegates proportional to population, not to speak of an ample treasury' from his highly successful fundraising efforts among the arch-conservative Hindu merchants (Anderson 2012: 17). While Gandhi served as Congress's President only once (in 1924), Congress belonged to him in a way that it never did to anyone else.

Increasing unrest (especially in the Punjab – both the breadbasket and the sword-arm of the Raj) at ever-increasing military recruitment demands, rising wartime shortages, and high inflation meant that the colonial administration had to resort to ever more draconian laws in World War I in India. This culminated in the infamous Rowlatt Act of 1919 (technically the 'Anarchical and Revolutionary Crimes Act') which extended the Raj's wartime powers of summary arrest and detention into peacetime in order to forestall any nationalist agitation. The Act set up a special court, a *de facto* Star Chamber, that could imprison suspects without trial and no right of appeal for up to two years and was not bound to follow normal rules of evidence or allow suspects legal representation. The Act also gave Provincial governments wide powers of search, arrest and detention. Jinnah resigned from the Central

Legislature – in which every single nominated or elected Indian member (though not the government servants serving *ex officio*) had voted against the Act – in protest, and Gandhi launched his *satyagraha* (insistence on truth) movement against the Act in 1920.[17]

Gandhi's *satyagraha* protest movement coincided with the *Khilafat* protest movements starting in India at the same time. The Treaty of Sèvres (which built upon the earlier Armistice and the 1919 Treaty of Versailles) that a victorious Britain and France imposed on a defeated Ottoman Turkey effectively dismantled its empire and transferred control of the Muslim holy cities of Mecca and Medina from the Ottoman Sultan (the Sunni Caliph) to the British Empire via its client Kingdom of the Hejaz. In 1919 the more traditional (i.e., the overwhelming majority) Indian Muslims led by the *ulema* started the All India *Khilafat* (Caliphate) Committee to protest against the dismantling of the last remaining Muslim empire and the imposition of *kafir* (infidel) rule over the holy cities. Earlier in 1916 the same *ulema* had condemned the Hashemite revolt against the Ottoman Turks[18] in no uncertain terms: the Sherif of Mecca, Hussein ibn Ali – the future British client King of the Hejaz – was declared a *kafir* by Maulana Bari (of the influential Farangi Mahal *madrassa* in Delhi) for daring to revolt against the Caliph (Akbar 2011: 128), obedience to whom had been ordained by God. Gandhi was offered the leadership of the *Khilafat* movement by the organizers, which transformed it from merely a Muslim protest to the national stage as Gandhi's leadership meant that the fate of the Turkish Muslim Caliph now assumed great importance for Hindus as well. For example, the All-India *Khilafat* Day, October 17, 1919, protest shut down virtually the entire country as a general strike was observed (Minault 1982: 76). Gandhi's decision to unilaterally call off both the *Khilafat* movement and *satyagraha* in 1922 following escalating mob violence and government use of force embittered many, especially the Muslims,[19] as it seemed that Gandhi had given the Raj a last-minute respite when it was clearly on the ropes.

The *Khilafat* movement among many Indian Muslims rapidly approached the status of a religious mania.[20] Tens of thousands of Muslim women donated their jewelry – which in the Indian context serves as their 'rainy day fund' and store of wealth/savings as well – to raise funds for the Turkish Army fighting Britain's Greek allies, and Muslim crowds at *Khilafat* rallies were larger than anything seen among Muslims to date. Tens of thousands of Muslims left India for Afghanistan as *ulema* associated with the JUH and Congress preached *hijrat ya jihad* ('emigration or holy war') arguing that it was impermissible for Muslims to live under infidel rule.[21] Fortunately, the religious mania stirred up by the *Khilafat* movement died down almost as quickly as it had started – the movement was officially ended in 1924 – since Mustafa Kemal Ataturk's abolition of the 400-year-old Turkish Caliphate made agitation on its behalf against the British irrelevant. However, the principle of mass mobilization and political action by Indian Muslims when Islam was in danger had been established.

For Gandhi, the goal was now 'Swaraj [self rule] within a year' (Anderson 2012: 26) and his initially non-violent mass movement was infused with Hindu symbolism (not least the name itself, at least for Muslims). Gandhi 'promised Dharmaraj (Rule of Dharma) which would evolve into Rama Rajya' (Akbar 2011: 152) in India with, presumably, Hindus in charge. As Rama is the seventh avatar of Vishnu, the supreme Hindu deity, and Dharma is the Hindu natural order of the universe, what Gandhi appeared to be promising was that the ouster of British Rule would return India to its natural Hindu order and this would then lead to Rama/Vishnu's kingdom on Earth. Just as a Christian political leader promising 'Christ's government' or a Muslim leader promising *Hukumat e Ilahi* ('Allah's government') in a country might worry, perhaps even terrify, many non-Christians and non-Muslims, respectively, many Muslims were deeply troubled by Gandhi's statements. This confirmed their view of him as merely the Hindu leader of a Hindu organization.[22]

It was not just Muslims who were concerned about Gandhi's injection of his religion, Hinduism, into politics. Jawaharlal Nehru, the first Prime Minister of India, 1947–64, and ostensibly Gandhi's most loyal disciple, himself wrote in his *Autobiography* that:

> Gandhiji was continually laying stress on the religious and spiritual side of the movement. His religion was not dogmatic, but it did mean a definitely religious outlook on life, and the whole movement was strongly influenced by this and *took on a revivalist character so far as the masses were concerned.* The great majority of Congress workers naturally tried to model themselves after their leader and *even repeated his language.* [But the rest of the Congress leadership] were not men of religion in the ordinary sense of the word, and they considered political problems on the political plane only. In their public utterances they did not bring in religion. But *whatever they said had far less influence* … I used to be troubled sometimes at the growth of this religious element in our politics, both on the Hindu and the Moslem side. … Even some of Gandhiji's phrases sometimes jarred upon me thus his frequent reference to Rama Raj as a golden age which was to return. But I was powerless to intervene, and I consoled myself with the thought that *Gandhi used the words because they were well known and understood by the masses. He had an amazing knack of reaching the heart of the people.* But I did not worry myself much over these matters. I was too full of my work and the progress of our movement to care for such trifles, as I thought at the time they were. … Often we discussed his fads and peculiarities among ourselves and said, half humorously, that when Swaraj came *these fads must not be encouraged.* Many of us, however, were too much under his influence in political and other matters *to remain wholly immune even in the sphere of religion.*
>
> (Nehru 1941: 71–72, emphasis added)

In this seemingly frank but still ultimately self-serving and highly political document, Nehru is essentially acknowledging that the only way for Congress to appeal to and connect with the masses was to explicitly appeal to Hinduism – Ram Raj – and that this continuous appeal to religion was affecting the non-sectarian and non-communal nature of Congress. However, Nehru consoled himself by thinking that religion could be shunted aside when he achieved power. In this he was able to succeed as Gandhi was murdered by Hindu extremists, rendering them relatively weak for the time being. Furthermore, Nehru's chief rival in Congress, the power behind the throne as India's Deputy Prime Minister and Interior Minister, was the much more overtly Hindu-revivalist and religiously conformist Sardar Vallabhai Patel who died in 1950.[23] Patel also acted as Congress's chief contact man for the all-important Hindu industrialists, extremely conservative men both politically and religiously, who had funded Congress in its decades of struggle against the British.

However, it has to be emphasized that Gandhi was not in any way a Hindu supremacist such as were found in the relatively mainstream *Akhil Bharat Hindu Mahasabha* (All India Hindu Assembly), of which many in Congress (including some at the highest levels) were also members,[24] much less the extreme right-wing and downright fascistic Hindu-supremacists of the *Rashtriya Swayamsevak Sangh* (the infamous RSS or National Patriotic Organization, some of whose members assassinated Gandhi in 1948 for being too conciliatory towards Muslims). Gandhi was not even a traditional Hindu.

Gandhi's relationship with his religion was an extremely complex and complicated one. Gandhi was by no means an orthodox Hindu, even if he staunchly defended many traditional Hindu practices such as the caste system until very late in his life. Neither was Gandhi in favor of centralising power in India under a Hindu-led Congress government.[25] What Gandhi was, however, was an extremely successful political entrepreneur, grassroots mobilizer, and organizer who knew that pushing a new agenda required the use of words, symbols, and concepts that have not just the necessary salience but a deep emotional impact on the intended audience. In this Gandhi succeeded admirably. Jinnah and the Muslim League merely used his demonstrated winning strategy.

However, as Nehru directly states in the passage quoted earlier, Gandhi's explicit use of Hindu symbols and terminology increasingly 'took on a revivalist character so far as the masses were concerned' and both the Congress leadership and the rank and file were influenced by Gandhi's use of overtly Hindu memes and repeated them. The problem was that while Gandhi may have used familiar Hindu symbols, his 'postmodern' – to use the Rudolphs' (2006) somewhat anachronistic description – understanding of what they meant was not what the average Congressman or even some in the Congress leadership thought he was advocating.

This issue came back to haunt Congress when, following its tremendous electoral victory in the 1937 elections,[26] Congress provincial administrations assumed power in eight of India's 11 provinces and some of them pushed

Hindu revivalist and chauvinist policies extremely aggressively. For example, the Congress government in the populous Central Provinces (CP – modern Madhya Pradesh and Chattisgarh states) did so to the point that not just the opposition Muslim League charged that it was pushing an extremely aggressive Hindu-chauvinist agenda, but non-CP Hindu Congress leaders urged Jawaharlal Nehru to intervene personally before the situation got completely out of control and relations with their Muslim populations were irrevocably damaged.[27] Nehru ordered an internal Congress investigation into the situation in 1938 which confirmed the bulk of the allegations and concluded that Congress had lost the Muslim masses[28] (Pandey 1978: 637). The report, brutally frank for an official document, ended with:

> It is evidently true that all our Congressite Hindu friends became openly communal. They completely forgot their creed [the official Congress position of secularism] and became partial to every [pro-Hindu] affair. In doing so they became so much unconscious that their masks dropped off and they looked quite naked to the public eyes.
>
> (quoted in Pandey 1978: 637)

Nehru (1941: 139) himself ruefully admitted in his autobiography 'That many a Congressman was a communalist [i.e., Hindu supremacist] under his national cloak. But the Congress leadership stood firm and, on the whole, refused to side with' the communalist element in the Congress rank and file. Given that Nehru wrote this in 1941 and the internal Congress inquiry on the actions of the Central Province's government was in 1938, his assessment of the situation was not exactly wrong but it was certainly putting the best possible light on events.[29]

A more nuanced analysis of the Partition of India would of course discuss many factors other than the growth of Muslim religio-nationalist consciousness. These could include, for example, the failed Cabinet Mission Plan[30] of 1946 or the role of the salariat[31] of the United Provinces, Bihar and eastern Punjab in Muslim nationalism. Any discussion of these issues, vital as they are to a better understanding of Partition, are outside the purview of this, perforce extremely brief, survey. The main aim here is to understand why there was this tremendous build-up of Muslim religious feelings in India and its subsequent seemingly irresistible impact on the socio-political policy debate in Pakistan, and how that led to the Islamization of the Pakistani financial sector.

The overwhelming Muslim vote for the Muslim League in 1946 was the culmination of decades of increasing Hindu–Muslim estrangement. It was not simply the result of a political party's decision to inject religion into politics in order to gain an electoral advantage, although such crass political motives did not help the situation any. Even a cursory glance at the history of British India in the first half of the twentieth century is enough to disprove the myth that Hindu–Muslim antagonism was simply manufactured out of whole cloth by a deliberate British colonial policy of *divide et impera* (divide and rule) or that Jinnah and other Muslim leaders created this Muslim sense of separateness where previously there had been a unified front against the British. The fissure existed independently of British colonial policy, which capitalized on it.[32] Jinnah, on the contrary, spent most of his career chasing what turned out to be the chimera of a Hindu–Muslim united front against the British Raj and he was a late and reluctant convert to both injecting religion into politics and a separate homeland for Muslims.[33] Pakistan was, at perhaps its most basic level, the culmination of a long-brewing Muslim political awakening that was inevitably, though in hindsight tragically, linked to religious revivalism.

The shape of Jinnah's short-lived Pakistan: Muslim but not Islamic

The state which emerged from the wreckage of Partition on August 14 as the Dominion of Pakistan had an inherent identity crisis: was it simply a nation of where its people just happened to be Muslims, a Republic of Pakistan as it were, or was it what Article 1(1) of its first (i.e., 1956, and shortest-lived) constitution proudly proclaimed it to be: 'The Islamic Republic of Pakistan?'

This is not a minor issue of semantics since this question lies at the very core of Pakistan's identity and what type of constitutional, legal, and economic system it would follow. Both Pakistani and foreign analysts (e.g., Khan 2001: 166, Oldenburg 2010: 67) have criticized Pakistan's Constituent Assembly (CA, which functioned as both the legislature of the new state as well as the drafting body for its constitution) for taking nine years to come up with a constitution when its sister Dominion, India, became the 'Republic of India' on January 26, 1950 following the promulgation of its new constitution.[34]

Jinnah lived long enough to see his Pakistan come into being on August 14, 1947 but he died on September 11, 1948. The 13 months that he was the undisputed, albeit dying, master of a new government trying to establish order among the bloody chaos of Partition – millions of refugees, the departure of virtually the entire Hindu and Sikh professional class and government bureaucrats, war with India over Kashmir, the shutting off of irrigation water to the Pakistani Punjab by India, and much more – were not enough to set Pakistan's socio-political orientation or to shape its fundamental institutions. That task was left to his Prime Minister and long-time chief aide, Liaquat Ali Khan.

There was a tiny minority of *ulema* (traditional Islamic scholars/jurisprudents) who supported the Muslim League's demand for Pakistan and 'the outstanding figure' (Binder 1961: 137) among them was Maulana Shabbir Ahmad Usmani of Deoband.[35] Usmani had been invaluable in countering the attacks on the Muslim League and Jinnah coming from the large majority of *ulema* and 'Nationalist (i.e., pro-Congress) Muslims' who had argued that Jinnah, who for almost all of his life had absolutely refused to pay even nominal lip-service to Islamic orthodoxy of thought or orthopraxy of behavior, was the most unlikely Muslim saviour imaginable and no true Muslim could ever follow such a *kafir* (infidel). Milder versions of these charges were levied against others in the League's leadership as well.

Representative of the anti-Jinnah propaganda put out by Congress's Nationalist Muslim allies is the couplet authored by Maulana Mazhar Ali Azhar, of the *Majlis e Ahrar e Islam* (Association of Free Muslims),[36] who took the title of *Quaid e Azam* (the Great Leader) given to Jinnah by the League and combined it with Jinnah's marriage to a non-Muslim to give the following doggerel: *Ik Kafira kay peechay Islam ko chora, Yeh Quaid-e-Azam hai kay Kafir-e-Azam* ('He abandoned Islam to chase an Unbeliever, Is he the Great Leader or the Great Infidel?').[37]

Jinnah's main argument was that in a country with a large majority community and a large minority community (which was itself a majority in some provinces) and a history of mutual, often violent antagonism, the two communities could not coexist without substantive constitutional safeguards for the rights of the minority. Thus the Muslims could not coexist in India, with its large Hindu majority, in the absence of major constitutional safeguards for the Muslims. It is clear that, other than general references to Islamic traditions and past Muslim glories in public speeches, all of Jinnah's substantive policy proposals, arguments, and counter-arguments were singularly devoid of any reference to Islam, *Shariah, Sunnah*, or *hadith*. For Jinnah, the Muslims of India were a separate ethnicity, a nation in his terms, rather than merely a religious minority and his demand for Pakistan was couched in national self-determination terms rather than religious self-determination. As he stated in a radio interview in 1947, 'nationality, rather than religion, is the basis for a separate homeland for the Muslims of India' (quoted in Mortimer 1982: 188).

The direct counter to this view of the connection between Pakistan and religion was the election slogan first coined by a Muslim lawyer for the 1946 elections (Wasti 2009: 4): '*Pakistan ka matlab kya? La illaha illallah!*' ('What does "Pakistan" mean? There is no god but Allah!'[38]). This is of course derived directly from the Muslim *shahada* (declaration of faith): *la Illaha illallah, Muhammad ur Rasool Allah* ('there is no god but Allah and Muhammad is His messenger') and this slogan was used extensively by the Pakistani military government of Gen. Zia ul Haq (ruled 1977–88) as part of its Islamization campaign.[39]

Jinnah's personal views on Pakistan as an Islamic state are provided by Amir Ahmad, Raja of Mahmudabad. Raja Amir Ahmad was one of the richest landowners in the United Provinces in the 1930s, the youngest member of the Muslim League Working Committee, leader of the Muslim League youth wing, and his family was as close to Jinnah as anyone could be.[40] Amir Ahmad essentially funded much of the Muslim League, including the all-important newspapers, in the late 1930s out of his personal fortune. At one point he had a temporary falling out with Jinnah over the role Islam would play in the new Pakistan:

> My advocacy of an Islamic state brought me into conflict with Jinnah. He thoroughly disapproved of my ideas and dissuaded me from expressing them publicly from the League platform lest the people might be led to believe that Jinnah shared my view and that he was asking me to convey such ideas to the public. As I was convinced that I was right and did not want to compromise Jinnah's position, I decided to cut myself away and for nearly two years kept my distance from him, apart from seeing him during the working committee meetings and on other formal occasions. It was not easy to take this decision as my associations with Jinnah had been very close in the past. Now that I look back I realise how wrong I had been.
>
> (Mahmudabad 1997/1993: 425)

This was not an isolated incident. At the Delhi session of the Muslim League in 1943 Jinnah pre-empted a member's intention to move a resolution that 'the Constitution of Pakistan would be based on the concept of *Hakumat-i-Ilahiya* (godly government)' by stating unequivocally in his Presidential opening address that 'The Constitution of Pakistan can only be framed by the *millat* [nation] and the people' (quoted in Khairi 1995: 463). Similarly, at the Muslim Legislators Convention in Delhi, Jinnah stated flatly 'What are we aiming at? It is not theocracy, not for a theocratic state' (quoted in Khairi 1995: 463) and successfully blocked every attempt to introduce resolutions committing the Muslim League 'to the establishment of an Islamic state' (Khairi 1995: 463). However, Khairi (1995: 464) overstates his case when he states unequivocally that while 'Jinnah would refer to [the future] Pakistan as a "Muslim state", he never called it an "Islamic state".' Jinnah was after all a politician seeking votes and, like Gandhi before him, played the winning strategy: religion.

Jinnah's public speeches were often filled with general references to Islam and some of these public and semi-public utterances are less ambiguous than others. A sample of these are given below:

> Let us lay the foundations of our democracy on the basis of truly Islamic ideals and principles. Our Almighty has taught us [to] be guided by discussion and consultations.
>
> In the end, I would appeal to all … to forget past disputes and differences and join hands with the Government of Pakistan in setting up a truly democratic Islamic State.
>
> [There is misinformation spread by the Congress-allied *Khudai Khidmatgar* – God's Servants – party that the Pakistan Constituent Assembly] will disregard the fundamental principles of the Shari'ah and Qur'anic laws. This, again, is absolutely untrue.
>
> (Hoodbhoy 2007)

And most damningly in this context, in the run-up to the 1946 elections, Jinnah wrote to the Pir of Manki Sharif, a major religious leader in the

Frontier (now renamed Khyber-Pakhtunkhwa province) offering to enforce the *Shariah* in exchange for his support against the Congress-allied *Khudai Khidmatgar* party (Hoodbhoy 2007: 3301). Hoodbhoy stresses that Jinnah was known for a remarkable bluntness of speech uncommon among politicians and, again uncommon among politicians, was known to be willing to take unpopular stands. Thus for Jinnah to give evasive answers when asked about the nature of Pakistan is extremely uncharacteristic. Jinnah arguably knew virtually nothing of classical Islamic jurisprudence (*Shariah* or *fiqh*) and there are no references to be found in Jinnah's speeches to an Islamic state in the sense that the term would be understood by the *ulema*.

Jinnah's main policy statement as to the form Pakistan was to take in the future was the speech he made to the Constituent Assembly on August 11, 1947. This speech, while too long to quote in full here, is truly remarkable for the sentiments expressed in it as, in effect, Jinnah was giving clear guidelines to the drafters of Pakistan's first (of several unfortunately) constitution as to what he expected the constitution to contain. Jinnah clearly states:

> You are free; you are free to go to your temples, you are free to go to your mosques or to any other place of worship in this State of Pakistan. You may belong to any religion or caste or creed, that has nothing to do with the business of the State. As you know, history shows that in England, conditions, some time ago, were much worse than those prevailing in India today. The Roman Catholics and the Protestants persecuted each other. Even now there are some States in existence where there are discriminations made and bars imposed against a particular class. Thank God we are not starting in those days. We are starting in the days where there is no discrimination, no distinction between one community and another, no discrimination between one caste or creed and another. We are starting with this fundamental principle that we are all citizens and equal citizens of one State. … Today, you might say with justice that Roman Catholics and Protestants [as political distinctions and basis for civic discrimination] do not exist; what exists now is that every man is a citizen, an equal citizen of Great Britain and they are all members of the Nation.
>
> Now I think we should keep that in front of us as our ideal and you will find that in course of time Hindus would cease to be Hindus and Muslims would cease to be Muslims, not in the religious sense, because that is the personal faith of each individual, but in the political sense as citizens of the State.[41]

In this presidential address, arguably among the most important speeches ever delivered by Jinnah, there is no reference to Islam, the Koran, *Shariah*, or *Sunnah* (the life and sayings of the Prophet Muhammad that set binding precedents for devout Muslims), and only four references to Muslims or the Muslim community, and all in a descriptive and not a religious context. There is nothing to indicate that the status of religious minorities in Pakistan was to be set by classical Islamic concepts of *dhimmi* (religious minorities with somewhat limited civic rights allowed to live in an Islamic state) or indeed even that Islam *per se* was to play any role in the formulation of the Pakistani constitution. On the contrary, the 'ideal form' of the state to be emulated was not the Prophet Muhammad's *Alleh us Salam* (AS) 'Charter of Medina'[42] but Great Britain's 'unwritten' Constitution. Jinnah's understanding was clearly that the state was to transcend religion even if its people could not.

Nevertheless it seems that not even Jinnah could stem the Islamist tide forever. In a speech in early 1948 a noticeably sick – he died on September 11 – Jinnah denied that the future constitution would be 'in conflict with the Shariat Law' and criticized both those agitating for *Shariah* and those against it (Binder 1961: 100). However, even then Jinnah did not endorse *Shariah* as the basis for Pakistan's constitution; he merely denied that the new constitution would be 'in conflict with' it.

The stage is set for the Islamic Republic

Nehru's Congress Party could, after Gandhi's death, effectively discard Hinduism in ruling India – exactly as Nehru in 1941 had said he would do – the Muslim League after Jinnah's death could not discard Islam in ruling Pakistan. Jinnah died on September 11, 1948. His death removed from the Pakistani political stage the one man who could perhaps have kept the Islamist forces at bay.

Even before Jinnah's death, Maulana Shabbir Ahmad Usmani, the only Islamic scholar of any standing who had backed Jinnah, had demanded that the Pakistani government form a supra-governmental Ministry of Religious Affairs and his colleagues had drawn up an elaborate proposal for the Ministry which 'would not only control and supervise religious institutions, mosques and endowments and qadi [religious] courts, but it would act as general censor of all government activities, and exercise general supervision over the behavior of all government servants' (Binder 1961: 33), i.e., a quasi-Roman supervisor of public morality that would be above parliament. This ministry would be patterned on the Ottoman Turkish control of religious institutions and create an offical *Shaikh ul Islam* (Binder 1961: 193–194) as the head of the Islamic clergy in Pakistan (i.e., a Pakistani version of the Archbishop of Canterbury).[43] This was clearly the first step towards creating an Islamic state that would be recognizable to the Deoband *ulema* steeped in classical Islamic *fiqh*.

Jinnah apparently ignored this demand and no such ministry was ever established or even seriously considered. None of Jinnah's successors, not even his powerful Prime Minister, Liaquat Ali Khan, enjoyed either Jinnah's popularity among the masses nor his control over the Muslim League. After Jinnah's death the Muslim League's internal fissures and conflicts became apparent very quickly as the League was not able to maintain its united front for long against the demand of the Islamist forces, led by Syed Abul Ala

Maududi after Maulana Shabbir Ahmad Usmani's death in 1949, that the new constitution had to be an overtly Islamist one that enforced both Islamic (Sunni) orthodoxy of though and orthopraxy of behavior.

Notes

1 The immediate and quite longstanding, although not entirely accurate, comparison of Pakistan is with Israel in the sense that both states were created in the name of a religious identity that was defined as a nationality and so used as their founding *raison d'être.* The latest such comparison is Faisal Devji's (2013) *Muslim Zion: Pakistan as a Political Idea.* However, Devji somewhat overstates these similarities since there was no significant Jewish population in Palestine before the Twentieth century while the areas that became Pakistan had had a substantial Muslim majority population for several hundred years. However, it is certainly true that both Israel and Pakistan have become more overtly ideologically religious in the past few decades, an ideological religiosity quite at odds with the intents and personal proclivities of their respective founders.

2 In December 1971, following the decisive Indian intervention on the side of the Bengali separatists in the Pakistani civil war, what was then East Pakistan became the sovereign nation of Bangladesh.

3 Hoffman (1948: 96n1) gives the 'Tribals,' a catch-all term for what are believed to be India's earliest, aboriginal inhabitants, communal breakdown as follows: 16 million Hindu, 8 million animist, 1 million Christian and the remainder Muslim and Buddhist. The Tribals are now officially designated in India as 'Scheduled Tribes' (or Other Backward Classes) to distinguish them from 'Caste Hindus' and are given preferential educational and employment access via constitutionally mandated affirmative action policies.

4 Although Assam went to India, its Muslim majority districts were assigned to Pakistan. Both Bengal and Punjab were partitioned along communal lines, the latter saw great communal violence and mutual ethnic cleansing that resulted in hundreds of thousands of deaths and a massive transfer of populations. Approximately 15 million people, split almost equally among Muslims and Hindus/Sikhs, moved from Pakistan to India (in the case of Hindus and Sikhs) or *vice versa* (in the case of Muslims).

5 Arguably the leading Islamic modernist philosopher and poet in India; he was posthumously declared the national poet and *de facto* ideologue of Pakistan.

6 Maududi's key role in developing Islamic economics and finance is examined in more detail in Chapter Four.

7 For example, Liaquat Ali Khan, the first Prime Minister of Pakistan (1947–51) and Jinnah's right-hand man, had both a degree in political science and a first law degree from Aligarh Muslim University; he did his postgraduate law degree at Exeter College Oxford before being called to the bar at the Inns of Court in London. Sir Khawaja Nazimuddin, Liaquat's successor as prime minister (1951–53) and before that Governor General – head of state – after Jinnah from 1948 to 1951 was educated at a British Grammar School before attending first Aligarh Muslim University and then Trinity Hall, Cambridge. Nazimuddin's successor as Governor General, Ghulam Muhammad (1951–55), was also educated at Aligarh Muslim University after which he joined the British Indian civil service. Iskandar Mirza, the fourth Governor General and then first President of Pakistan (1955–58), attended Bombay University before joining the British Royal Military Academy, Sandhurst, as its first Indian cadet. Nazimuddin's successor as prime minister was Muhammad Ali Bogra (1953–55), a graduate of Calcutta University. While

some, e.g., Nazimuddin, were personally quite devout, their formal training, if any, in Islamic *fiqh* (jurisprudence) was minimal.

8 Aligarh was founded as the *Madrassatul Uloom Musalmanan e Hind* (Institution of Learning for the Muslims of India) and then became the Mohammedan Anglo-Oriental College and then finally Aligarh Muslim University in 1920. Despite the original, very ostensibly Islamic name given to the institution, presumably to allay the fears of more conservative Muslims, Aligarh was a radical departure for Muslims in India. The complete break with the past can be gauged by the fact that this apparent *madrassa*'s first headmaster was British, H.G.I. Siddons, the second was Hindu, Bajinath Prasad, and the first Bachelor of Arts graduate, the well known early historian Ishwari Prasad, was also a Hindu (see the Aligarh website, www.amu.ac.in accessed September 9, 2012, for more details). One of Aligarh's main tasks was to prepare Muslim students for advanced study in Britain and success in the competitive examination for the Indian Civil Service. Sir Syed himself was a senior judge in the Raj's legal system and his son Syed Mahmood was the first Muslim High Court judge in British India.

9 At one point in his career Sir Syed Ahmad Khan referred to himself as a Wahhabi but this was in the context of considering himself as being a radical Muslim reformer – which he certainly was – and contrasting it with the traditionalism then espoused by Deoband; it was not by way of identifying himself with the extremely conservative form of puritanical Islam found in Saudi Arabia which had actually begun as an earlier attempt to bring major reform to classical Islamic *fiqh*.

10 Neither Maulana Abul Kalam Azad, one of the few high-ranking Muslims in Congress in the interwar period, nor Abdul Ghaffar Khan, founder of the *Khudai Khidmatgar* (Servants of God) association, easily fit into this schema. Azad was an arch-Traditionalist early on in his life but seemed to have changed his views as he grew older and drew close to Jawaharlal Nehru's brand of socialism and to Nehru personally. Ghaffar Khan was also a graduate of Aligarh Muslim University but seemed to have imbibed Gandhian non-violence and asceticism and stayed close to Gandhi personally until the creation of Pakistan, which he opposed strenuously, and then espoused Pashtun nationalism.

11 See Metcalf (2004) for details on Deoband and the Aligarh Movement, and Malik (2006) for Sir Syed's views on Islamic Modernization and cooperation with the Indian National Congress.

12 'Maulana' is a religious title best rendered as 'learned/scholar' or the old English usage of 'master' to denote a respected scholar; it is derived from the Arabic for 'Master' (as in lord-and-master). For a masterful analysis of the key role played by Usmani, a neglected figure in the history of the Pakistan Movement, in rallying the 'average Muslim' to Jinnah see Dhulipala 2008. The League had significant support from assorted *sajda nashins*, *makhdooms*, *pirs*, etc. (essentially large landowners who derived their power and prestige from being the descendants of *sufi* saints, of whose shrines they were hereditary guardians) who exercised a great deal of influence among rural voters, but these rural notables are very different from *ulema* and carried virtually no weight in the urban areas. The tiny minority of JUH/Deobandi *ulema* who later supported Jinnah's call for Pakistan formed the *Jamiat e Ulema e Islam* (JUI – the Party of the Scholars of Islam) in 1940 under Usmani's leadership. Some of its later Pakistani adherents became quite reactionary and, after the JUI split into two, one faction became closely allied to Saudi Wahhabism and provided the *madrassas* that trained the Afghan Taliban in the 1990s.

13 The literature on the circumstances around the Partition of India is too large to detail here but those interested in greater depth on the circumstances that led to Partition, and especially Jinnah's role, should refer to Ayesha Jalal's (1994/1985) *The Sole Spokesman: Jinnah, the Muslim League and the Demand for Pakistan* (originally a highly revisionist analysis but now generally accepted as the standard

work on Jinnah's role in Partition). Stanley Wolpert's (1984) *Jinnah of Pakistan* is still the definitive biography of Jinnah. Ian Talbot's (1999) *Pakistan: A Modern History*, and Barbara and Thomas Metcalf's (2006) *A Concise History of Modern India* are standard historical works on these two countries by highly respected South Asian historians (the Metcalfs are particularly good on South Asian Islam). Philip Oldenburg's (2010) *India, Pakistan and Democracy: Solving the Puzzle of Divergent Paths* is a comparative (though favorable towards India) analysis of the very different post-Partition trajectories followed by these two countries.

14 There has, however, been a spate of recent Indian work on Partition (e.g., Nanda 2010; Singh 2010; Jawed 2009) which critically re-evaluates Jinnah's and Congress's role in the process, and reaches conclusions more favorable to Jinnah and more critical of the part played by Nehru and Congress in pushing Jinnah and the Muslim towards separation than is found in the Indian nationalist narrative.

15 See earlier references and e.g., Ahmed 1997, Gilmartin 1988, Ziring 1997, Jalal 2000, and others too numerous to list, for more details on the 1946 elections and the Muslim League's electoral strategy.

16 Initially, at least for Muslims, the JUH also planned a separatist agenda post-independence, at least in their private life. For example, the JUH envisaged a separate legal system for Muslims as a part of the *de facto* apartheid necessary to achieve the 'mental partition of India' for Muslims to live a truly Islamic life (Metcalf 2004: 140).

17 See Khan (2001: 20) for details on the Rowlatt Act.

18 Known to most in the West only from David Lean's highly romanticized 1962 film epic *Lawrence of Arabia*.

19 In the Punjab, relations between the two groups deteriorated massively and gave an ominous portend of the 1947 Partition violence and mass slaughter. The worst communal mass riots in decades swept across large towns and small villages alike, leaving dozens killed, hundreds injured, and massive property damage in their wake (Mittal 1977: 199–200). A 1923 Congress fact-finding mission to the Punjab concluded that relations between the Hindus and Muslims 'were so greatly strained that each community had practically arrayed itself in an armed camp against each other' (quoted in Hasan 1980: 63–64). The situation was worsened across north India by the publication by Hindu chauvinists of a scurrilous pamphlet on the private life of the Prophet Muhammad – the *Rangila Rasul* ('Pleasure Loving Prophet'). There was a long history in India of each side publishing such pamphlets about key religious figures on the other side.

20 See Akbar (2011), Qureshi (1999) and Minault (1982) for more on the importance of the *Khilafat* movement among Indian Muslims.

21 By August 3, 1919 British records show that about 13,000 *muhajirin* (immigrants) had entered Afghanistan from India; a week later the number was over 20,000 and still climbing (Qureshi 1999: 206). By August 1920 the number was well over 40,000 (Qureshi 1999: 214). But these were only the official figures registered by the British at one crossing point. Unofficial estimates range from 60,000 to 120,000 (Qureshi 1999: 231) and some even higher.

22 The Indian National Congress, even before Gandhi gained control of it and pushed more overtly Hindu memes, had always been a Hindu dominated organization (Anderson 2012). For example, B. G. Tilak (1856–1920), an early Congress leader, Indian nationalist and Hindu revivalist, opposed allowing Muslims to join the Congress Party and his 'fanaticism appealed to the more narrow minded and militant among his coreligionists and he enlisted a huge following' (Ziring 1997: 3). At the founding convention of the Indian National Congress in 1885 there were only two Muslims out of 72 delegates, while the second convention in 1886 had only 33 Muslims out of 431 delegates (Akbar 2011: 92). In order to counter criticism that it was really the *Hindu* National Congress, a token Muslim (Badruddin Tyabji) was

elected as its third (rotating, usually annual) President (Akbar 2011: 92). Muslims were never more than a minute fraction of Congress despite its occasional half-hearted outreach efforts to bring Muslims into its fold: in the 1930s, five decades after its founding, 97 per cent of Congress's membership was Hindu (Anderson 2012: 56).

23 Patel, variously dubbed the Bismarck of India or the Iron Man of India, was the man who actually ran Congress, maintained party discipline and enforced policy: in short, he was the Iron Fist to Nehru's Velvet Glove. Unlike Nehru, who was born with a silver spoon in his mouth, the self-made Patel – while also a London-trained barrister – was not an Anglophile perfectly at ease having High Tea with the Viceroy reminiscing about his schooldays at Harrow or debating the merits of spin versus fast bowling. Gandhi allegedly persuaded him to step aside to allow Nehru to become Congress Party President in 1946 as this would allow Nehru to negotiate with the British over Indian Independence and, incidentally, make Nehru the first Prime Minister of India; Patel was appointed Deputy Prime Minister and Home (i.e., Interior) Minister – where he was in direct control of the intelligence agencies, police force, and the rest of the extensive internal security apparatus inherited from the Raj. Patel's early death also allowed Nehru to push his Fabian Socialist agenda without effective opposition in the party. See Kumar (2007) or Balraj (2008) for more on Patel.

24 It was not until 1938 that Congress's leadership forbade joint membership in the Hindu *Mahasabha* (Akbar 2011: 198). Presumably this was caused in part by Congress's failure to attract more than a tiny percentage of the Muslim vote in the 1937 elections and the failure of Nehru's outreach campaign to attract more Muslims to Congress. Meetings of the *Mahasabha* were regularly attended by many high-ranking Congress members, presumably in their private capacity, such as Rajendra Prasad (President of independent India, 1950–62) and Madan Mohan Malaviya (four times President of Congress – 1909, 1918, 1932, and 1933 – and from 1924–46 the Chairman of the Board of the *Hindustan Times* newspaper group, India's largest) and 'when communal feelings were running high in the country the presence of such men at the Hindu Mahasabha meeting could only serve to [further] estrange many Muslims from the Congress' (Hasan 1980: 66n36).

25 The literature on Gandhi is far too vast to list here. A good beginning to the study of the political Gandhi, especially in the context of the Partition of the British Indian Empire, is the collection of essays by Lloyd and Susanne Rudolph (2006).

26 This was the first election held under the Government of India Act of 1935 that had greatly expanded the electoral franchise and for the first time devolved some real self-governance to the Indians. The Act was far short of the full self-governing Dominion status, i.e., the same status as Canada or Australia then, sought by men such as Jinnah and the earlier Congress leadership, and much less than the near-independence sought by Gandhi, Nehru, and Patel. See Shakoor (2005) for details on the 1937 elections.

27 At its peak in 1938, after Nehru's 'Mass Contact Movement,' Congress numbered barely 100,000 Muslims in a total party strength of 3.1 million; by 1944, in contrast, the Muslim League had grown to 2 million members (Sharma 2008: 72).

28 See Sarkar (2006) for more on one of the most contentious issues ordered by the Central Province's Congress government: the compulsory singing of *Vande Mataram* ('I Bow Before the Goddess') in CP schools by Muslim school children standing 'with folded hands [i.e., in a prayer-like fashion] and offer reverence to Gandhi's portrait' (Shakoor 2005: 83). Nehru considered *Vande Mataram*, a hymn to the Hindu goddess Durga as the personification of Mother India, and the 1882 novel *Anandamath* by Bankim Chandra Chattopadhaya (1838–94, the creator of the Bengali novel and a leading light of the Bengali literary renaissance) that made it famous, were 'likely to irritate the Muslims' (quoted in Sarkar 2006: 3963). *Anandamath* was about the defeat of an 'evil' Muslim ruler by devout Hindus, the

subsequent ethnic cleansing of Muslims and the restoration of a resurgent Hindu Bengal in which Muslims had been killed, expelled, or reconverted to Hinduism. Even Gandhi himself, after the communal slaughter of 1947, conceded that his earlier (1915) view of *Vande Mataram* as 'ardently patriotic' was erroneous and the hymn was best left unsung since it was purely 'political … a chant to insult or offend the Muslims' (quoted in Sarkar 2006: 3963). This was because during the 1905 Bengali Hindu agitation against the partition of Bengal, which Bengali Muslims favored, Hindu mobs used *Vande Mataram* as their battle hymn and war cry (Sarkar 2006: 3693; Kumar 1999), a direct counterpart to the traditional Muslim *Allah o Akbar* (God is Great). Starting in 1894 the full hymn was sung, after being set to music by the Bengali Hindu Nobel Laureate Rabindranath Tagore, who strongly opposed the 1905 Partition, before all Congress meetings. It remained Congress's official anthem until 1937 when the vehement objections of Congress's few Muslim members resulted in only the first two stanzas of the song (which extoll the beauty of the Bengal landscape and have no overtly religious or violent content) being approved for use at official Congress functions (Sarkar 2006: 3963). In the post-Independence Indian Constituent Assembly, *Vande Mataram* came close to being chosen as the Indian National Anthem and only lost out to Tagore's *Jana Gana Mana* ('Thou Art the Ruler of the Minds of All People') after ferocious behind-the-scenes arm-twisting by Jawaharlal Nehru; the advocates of *Vande Mataram* had to be content with the official consolation prize of its first two stanzas being designated as India's 'National Song.' The full hymn is still used by the Hindu-supremacist RSS as their party and marching song. Thus ordering Muslim schoolchildren to sing *Vande Mataram* was guaranteed to antagonize all Muslims, even those who were not sympathetic to the Muslim League, across India, and drive a further wedge between Congress and the vast majority of Indian Muslims.

29 Almost four decades earlier, Jawaharlal Nehru's father Motilal had used exactly the same words to describe the actions of many Congress members in the violent agitation against the 1905 division by the British of the province of Bengal into two (a Hindu-majority one and a Muslim-majority one). Although united Bengal had a small Muslim majority, it was completely dominated economically and politically by its relatively small Caste (i.e., high-caste) Hindu minority. The Caste Hindu agitation against the division rapidly took on an extremely communalist, very anti-Muslim as well as anti-British hue. The anti-Muslim nature of agitation distressed Motilal Nehru (twice President of Congress, 1919–20 and 1928–29) enough to write to his son Jawaharlal, the future Prime Minister of India, that 'Many a Congressman was a communalist under his nationalist cloak' (quoted in Hasan 1980: 58). For the *bhadralok* (literally 'well mannered folk' as the Caste Hindu elite of Bengal called itself), Bengali Muslims, who favored partition as it would let them escape *bhadralok* domination, were 'little better than a mongrel breed of circumcised low-caste Hindus' (Jalal and Seal 1981: 427).

30 In 1946 Jinnah had accepted the Cabinet Mission Plan of the British government, ultimately rejected by Congress, which essentially created an Indian confederation with 'self-rule' for the Muslim majority parts of India but not a separate Pakistan (Jalal 1994/1985); Jinnah argued that this gave Muslims their 'homeland' and so partition was not necessary. Congress rejected the Plan as it did not give it the powerful central government that they would dominate in a unitary Indian state (see Anderson 2012 for more on this).

31 The salariat was the class of (mainly) lower-level Muslim government functionaries in the United Provinces, Bihar, and eastern Punjab who feared their relatively privileged position (their representation in the British colonial administration was far disproportionate to their number in the population, especially in Muslim minority provinces) would be endangered by more competition from better Western-educated (i.e., fluent in English) Hindus under a Hindu-dominated

post-colonial government. These fears were well founded as the number of Muslims in the ranks of the British colonial administration in the United Provinces had already been reduced from 64 per cent in 1857 to 35 per cent by 1913 and declining (Alavi 1989).

32 In his memoir the acclaimed (in the Anglophone West if not in his native India) *bhadralok homme de lettres* Nirad Chaudhuri (2001/1951: 244) recalls the Hindus of East Bengal living in relative harmony with their Muslim neighbors until they realized that the Muslims favored the 1905 Partition of Bengal by the British and extremely powerful, if hitherto dormant, hatreds came out in the open. Chaudhuri (2001/1951: 243) recounts 'the arrogant contempt for the Muslims and deep seated hostility towards them' exhibited by the Calcutta (i.e., West Bengali) Hindu *Bhadralok* and contrasts it with the more 'live and let live' attitude prevalent in East Bengal (the Muslim majority portion of the province). This attitude did not outlast the Partition of Bengal.

33 Jinnah joined Congress in 1906 and refused to even attend the formation meeting of the Muslim League. When he, one of the most prominent Muslims in Congress and a rising star in its ranks, finally joined the Muslim League in 1913, he made it absolutely clear that 'the Muslim interest would in no way and at no time imply even the shadow of disloyalty to the larger national cause' and described himself as a 'staunch Congressman' with 'no love for sectarian cries' (quoted in Jalal 1994/1985: 7). In 1914 Gopal Krishna Gokhale (1866–1915; President of Congress in 1905 and Jinnah's mentor) called him 'the best Ambassador of Hindu–Muslim unity' (Akbar 2011: 113) because of Jinnah's ceaseless efforts to work out a *modus vivendi* between Congress and the Muslim League. Jinnah resigned from Congress in 1920 over his objections to the *Khilafat* Movement's injection of religion into politics – he was booed off the dais when he attempted to voice his objections at the meeting (Jalal 1994/1985: 9).

34 Although presented to the Indian Constituent Assembly on November 26, 1949, it didn't take effect until January 26 of the following year; however, since 'some 250 out of its 395 articles were taken word for word from the Government of India Act' of 1935, the burden on the Assembly was not as great as it may otherwise appear (Anderson 2012: 107). In the case of Pakistan also Khan (2001: 166) concludes that '… the 1956 Constitution was based on the pattern of the Government of India Act of 1935' and that this feat required 'nine years of effort.' The Indian Constituent Assembly took almost exactly the amount of time – two years – that Jinnah had estimated it would take the Pakistani Constituent Assembly to deliver its Constitution (Khan 2001: 88).

35 See Dhulipala (2008) for more details on this now almost forgotten leader of the Pakistan movement.

36 An extremely radical Deobandi offshoot from the *Khilafat* Movement.

37 While the reference to Jinnah as the *Kafir e Azam* is well known to most educated Pakistanis, the source of the couplet (translation mine) is page 11 of the Munir Commission Report (more formally 'The Report of the Court of Inquiry Constituted under the Punjab Act II of 1954 to Enquire into the Punjab Disturbances of 1953'). This was a two-member judicial commission (Mr. Justice M. Munir and Mr. Justice R. Kayani) instituted to examine the circumstances leading to the vicious anti-Ahmadi (a minority sect of Muslims viewed by more Orthodox Sunni Muslims as heretics) riots that led to perhaps 2,000 being killed in 1953. Another source (Khairi 1995: 468) gives *waastey* for *peechay*, i.e., 'for the sake of' instead of 'chasing after;' the meaning is essentially unchanged (translation mine).

38 Translation mine.

39 There is some evidence that Jinnah directly disowned this slogan after the League's tremendous electoral win in 1946, where it was undoubtedly used very effectively by at least the Punjab Muslim League. At the only meeting of the

All Pakistan Muslim League presided over by Jinnah, in Karachi in December 1947: 'During the meeting a man who called himself Bihari put to the Quaid [Jinnah] that "we have been telling the people *Pakistan ka matlab kya, La Illaha Illallah.*" "Sit down, sit down," the Quaid shouted back. "Neither I nor my working committee, nor the Council of the All Muslim League has ever passed such a resolution wherein I was committed to the people of Pakistan. Pakistan *ka matlab*, you might have done so to catch a few votes" (Khairi 1995: 466). The incident was recounted in an Urdu book *Daghon ki Barat* by Malik Ghulam Nabi, a former high-ranking member of the Muslim League who was present at the meeting, and reviewed by Ahmad Bashir, 'Islam, Shariat and the Holy Ghost,' in Peshawar's *Frontier Post*, June 6, 1988. When Khairi (1995: 466) attempted to interview Maulana Jamal Mian Farangimahli, an Indian citizen, who was one of the last survivors of those known to be at the meeting, Farangimahli refused to meet him.

40 Mahmudabad *père* provided the wedding ring for Rattenbhai at Jinnah's wedding and the Jinnahs spent part of their honeymoon at the Mahmudabad estate in the hill resort of Nainital. Jinnah was the executor of Mahmudabad *père*'s estate and Amir Ahmad called Jinnah 'Uncle' – presumably in private only (Mahmudabad 1997/1993: 420). An intensely private man, after Jinnah's death Amir Ahmad essentially retired from public life, moved abroad and refused all Pakistani government posts, even honorary ones.

41 The full text of the address is available at www.pakistani.org/pakistan/legislation/constituent_address_11aug1947.html (accessed April 5, 2011).

42 The charter by which the Prophet Muhammad AS agreed to rule Medina after the *hijra* (the migration from Mecca to Medina) in 622 CE, Year 1 of the Muslim calendar. The Charter of Medina is held by devout Muslims to be the ideal form of government and worthy of emulation by all Islamic states, just as the life of the Prophet is the *uswa hasana*, the *beau ideal*, of a human being and is to be emulated by all devout Muslims.

43 Sunni Islam, as is well known, has no 'church' in the Western sense of a hierarchically organized clergy *à la* Roman Catholicism or the Church of England. The Ottoman Sultans attempted to create such an organized 'mosque' but were ultimately unsuccessful. The Safavid Shahs of Persia, however, did manage to create such a structure for Twelver Shi'ism, especially the Persian form.

3 The post-Jinnah Islamization of Pakistan

The purpose of this chapter is to explain why the Islamization of the Pakistani financial sector cannot be analyzed or understood without an understanding of the forces that drove Pakistan almost from its very inception towards Islamization. Once Pakistan was achieved, Jinnah may have been done with Islam but the Islamists were not done with Jinnah's Pakistan. Accordingly, this chapter will show how the 'Dominion of Pakistan' became 'The Islamic Republic of Pakistan' and, over time, transformed itself from Jinnah's ideal of a state where religion had 'nothing to do with the business of the State,' to a minimally Islamic state, to one where everything, including the financial system, has to be in accordance with the *Shariah*. Thus while Jinnah did not envisage an Islamic State, an Islamic State is what his Pakistan became.

Post-Jinnah Pakistan: failed attempts at Islamic ceremonial deism

As it turned out, despite his undoubted importance in rallying the Muslim masses to Jinnah and Pakistan, Maulana Shabbir Ahmad Usmani's was not the most important voice agitating for a confessional cast to the new state. Maulana Syed Abul Ala Maududi (1903–79) was an influential and extremely prolific journalist and author; a somewhat auto-didactic Islamic scholar who had moved far beyond his early Deobandi training. In 1941 Maududi established a new socio-political movement, the *Jamaat e Islami* (JI, the Party of Islam) in India as a Leninist cadre party dedicated to the revival and revitalization of Indian Islam. Nasr (1996: 3) describes Maududi,[1] quite accurately, as 'the most influential of contemporary Islamic revivalist thinkers,' a man whose writings influenced Sayyed Qutb and the Egyptian Muslim Brothers as well as Imam Khomeini.

Maududi had an extremely ambivalent attitude towards Jinnah and consequently Pakistan. While in favor of Muslim separatism as a way to avoid Hindu rule (i.e., a Congress-dominated government), Maududi had opposed Jinnah precisely on the grounds that Jinnah's 'Muslim state' would not be an 'Islamic state' and would be too Westernized.[2] In fact Maududi went so far as to call such a state 'Napakistan' (meaning 'religiously polluted')[3] and one that would, for example, permit non-Islamic practices such as conventional banking and allow too many rights to minorities and various Muslim sects that Maududi deemed heretical (Nasr 1994: 108). Maududi was so disturbed by Jinnah's complete lack of interest in an Islamic structure for Pakistan that he had issued his own *fatwa* forbidding Muslims to vote for a 'secular' Muslim League. However, following the Muslim League victory in the 1946 elections, Maududi trimmed his sails to the prevailing wind and appealed to the Muslim masses of India to opt for Pakistan (Nasr 1994: 114–115). Maududi moved the JI to Pakistan to save the fledgling state from Jinnah's '*napak*' vision and the Muslim League, and immediately began public agitation for a state structured along his definition of what made for an Islamic one.

While this was not simply 'the *Shariah* implemented' – Maududi was an original thinker and quite critical of traditional *ulema* and their inability to come to terms with modernity – his concept of the Islamic constitution would still be *Shariah*-based, even if it was a more rational (his) interpretation of the *Shariah* than would sit well with his old Deobandi teachers. This however would not be secularism with an Islamic façade (i.e., Islamic Minimalism) but it, Maududi thundered, would 'mean nothing less than the demolition of the entire structure built by your [the Muslim League's] British masters and the erection of a new [wholly Islamic] one in its place' (quoted in Nasr 1996: 97). Unsurprisingly this view did not endear Maududi to many of the new state's bureaucrats and military officers.

Maududi, in January and February of 1948, delivered two lectures at the Lahore College of Law where he outlined his vision of an Islamic State and escalated the level of Islamic rhetoric used against Prime Minister Liaquat Ali Khan's government (Gaborieau 2002: 242). In August 1948 Maududi and the JI again attacked government policies and reiterated their stand that oaths of office sworn by officials of the new Dominion of Pakistan were not just illegal but actually *kufr* (an act that renders a Muslim an unbeliever) since they had sworn loyalty to the British Crown and a Muslim could only swear allegiance to Allah; therefore government service, including in the Pakistani Army, was forbidden for all Muslims (Nasr 1994: 123). Unsurprisingly, the Pakistani Government reacted harshly. All JI publications were shut down on sedition charges, government servants were forbidden from belonging to the JI (those who refused to relinquish their membership had their employment terminated) and it was, along with the Communist Party, declared to be a seditious organization and banned, and Maududi was jailed (Nasr 1994: 122).

But the Muslim League was now caught in a trap of its own making. It had used Islam to win votes, it had cloaked itself with the garb of Islam's savior, and many of its own rank and file (and some high-ranking officials as well) were overtly Islamist – just as many in the Congress were overtly Hindu revivalists. Jinnah's personality had been enough to keep the Islamists in check and his personal standing with the Muslim masses was such that no-one could even remotely criticize him;[4] his successor Liaquat did not enjoy such total control over the League or the Muslim masses.

As the authors of the determinedly Islamic Modernist 'Munir Commission Report' into the origins of the murderous riots against the heterodox Ahmadiya Muslim sect (see later in this chapter for more details) ruefully conceded, the relentless propaganda and agitation by the Islamists was extremely successful: the 'common man' believed Pakistan to be an 'Islamic State' and that 'This belief has been encouraged by the ceaseless clamour for Islam and Islamic State that is being heard from all quarters since the establishment of Pakistan' (Munir 1954: 231). Bowing to this pressure, Liaquat Ali Khan agreed to what he thought would be token concessions that would garb the essentially secular order of the state in an Islamic veil (Callard 1957: 216). These concessions would, Liaquat hoped, satisfy the Muslim *ulema* and the common people as to the Islamic nature of the state without any actual change being necessary to its secular institutions. The aim was to be, in effect, one part Islamic (the trappings) but nine parts secular (the essence). Thus ceremonial deism would be reaffirmed.

Accordingly, in February 1949, Liaquat Ali Khan introduced the 'Objectives Resolution' to the Pakistan Constituent Assembly. This was a completely unexpected move by Liaquat and immediately quieted the Islamic opposition to the Government. The Resolution was greeted enthusiastically by all but one of the Muslim members of the CA but not by its Hindu members (Callard 1957: 89–95).

The Constituent Assembly, formed on the basis of the 1946 Elections, had 69 members, of whom 18 were to be non-Muslims (mainly Bengali Hindus but including at least one Christian from Punjab) (Binder 1961: 122–123). However the emigration, at irregular intervals, of the Hindu and Sikh members for India meant that the full number of non-Muslims were never present in the Assembly and rarely, for that matter, were even a large number of Muslim members there. When one of the many amendments offered by the Bengali Hindu members was finally put to the vote, it lost 21:10 with the vote being strictly on religious lines (Khan 2001: 104–105).

The Objectives Resolution seemed to satisfy the demand for an Islamic state. This is made clear by the Islamic content in the Resolution:[5]

> In the name of Allah, the Benificent, the Merciful;
>
> Whereas sovereignty over the entire universe belongs to God Almighty alone and the authority which He has delegated to the State of Pakistan through its people for being exercised within the limit prescribed by Him is a sacred trust; …
>
> Wherein the principles of democracy, freedom, equality, tolerance and social justice, as enunciated by Islam, shall be fully observed;
>
> Wherein the Muslims shall be enabled to order their lives in the individual and collective spheres in accord with the teachings and requirements of Islam as set out in the Holy Quran and the Sunna;
>
> Wherein adequate provision shall be made for the minorities freely to profess and practise their religions and develop their cultures;

'In the name of Allah, the Benificent, the Merciful' is of course simply the English translation of *Bismillah ur Rehman ur Raheem*, the salutation that begins every *sura* (chapter) of the Koran but one. In spite of this, the Objectives Resolution was not intended by Prime Minister Liaquat Ali Khan to be the first step in the Islamization of the state, but near to the last. It was, however, a double-edged sword as the Resolution can be readily interpreted as the first step.

The Objectives Resolution is by itself an expression of Minimalist rather than Maximalist Islam. This is because it is actually quite vague as to what exactly is to be done to make the state Islamic: there is no explicit reference to *Shariah* or to the role of the *ulema* or to what exactly is meant by 'Islam' since not only is there a Sunni–Shia split in Islam, Sunni Islam is further subdivided into four main *madhab* (schools of thought, although Pakistan is predominantly Hanafi Sunni). There is no mention of how heterodox Muslim minorities are to be dealt with and it is unclear if non-Muslims are to be treated as *dhimmis*, i.e., *de jure* second-class citizens, as required under classical interpretations of *Shariah*.

At the same time a Basic Principles Committee, comprising 25 Constitutent Assembly (CA) members and 10 *ex-officio* ones appointed by the Government, was established and charged with writing a draft constitution to present to the CA (Callard 1957: 90–91). In a major concession to the Islamists, the CA also established the *Idara e Talimaat e Islam* (Organization for the Teaching of Islam) to advise the Basic Principles Committee on whatever religious issues might arise (Callard 1957: 90–91). Since the *Idara*'s recommendations were almost uniformly and laughably medieval in flavor,[6] unsurprising since it was dominated by traditional *ulema* almost unwholly unversed in modern political thought, their formal recommendations were essentially ignored by the Basic Principles Committee which was still dominated by Islamic Modernists. However, ignored or not, the essential point had been conceded.

This Committee accordingly presented its draft constitution to the CA in September 1950; the draft was immediately attacked as much as the Objectives Resolution had been praised since it lacked a 'clearly defined Islamic character' and, much like the Indian Constitution, was a near clone of the Government of India Act 1935 (Callard 1957: 92). Maududi and the *Jamaat e Islami* were prominent in the protests. Prime Minister Liaquat Ali Khan 'bowed before the storm of criticism' and immediately withdrew the draft and asked for general suggestions on the form of the Constitution (Callard 1957: 92; see also Binder 1961: 115). There were serious objections from the CA's Bengali Muslim members on the issue of federalism, official language policy, and the subordination of Bengal to the Center but Liaquat declared that the reason for the withdrawal of the draft Constitution was that it was not Islamic enough (McGrath 1996: 76).

To counter charges levied by the more secular-minded in the Muslim League and the government that there was no consensus among the *ulema* as to what exactly constituted an 'Islamic' government, the *Jamaat e Islami* organized a conference of *ulema* in January 1951 that in a mere three days produced a document titled 'The Principles of the Islamic State;' this was duly forwarded to the CA for its deliberations (Maududi and Ahmad 1960: 29). As a further concession to the *ulema* and the strengthening demand for a more Islamic Pakistan, the Liaquat Administration set up a commission to bring British-era laws into conformity with aims of the Objectives Resolution (i.e., to conform with Islam),[7] ordered the federal and provincial education departments to start mandatory Islamic education in schools, and that the mandate of the *Idara e Talimaat e Islam* be enhanced so that it could 'make the Muslim population of the country truly Muslim' (McGrath 1996: 77). Most importantly for the Islamists, the Chairman of the *Idara* Maulana Syed Sulaiman Nadvi,[8] a widely respected, non-Deobandi but highly traditionalist Islamic scholar, was inducted as a full member of the Basic Principles Committee and *Idara* members were regularly invited to address the Committee on Islamic issues (Callard 1957: 94).

The reason for Liaquat's attempts to appease the *ulema* are quite simple. The Muslim League was facing a strong challenge from resurgent Bengali political parties, the League was itself splitting into various factions and Liaquat did not want to fight a two-front war with both the *ulema* (over religion) and the Bengalis (over federalism).[9] The Muslim League's factionalization reached a near crisis point after Liaquat Ali Khan's assassination in October 1951[10] but a reworked draft constitution was finally presented to the CA in December[11] 1952. It was again strongly criticized from all sides. The Islamists, refusing to be placated with minor gestures, held that it did not make Islam central to the Constitution and that the Islamic provisions were clear afterthoughts; the Bengalis objected that it did not give Bengal (the majority province) enough, and Punjab (the second-largest province but massively overrepresented in the Federal government bureaucracy and the military) objected that it gave Bengal too much.

The contents of the draft constitution had apparently been leaked to the Islamic parties and they had mobilized their street power. The day before it was presented to the CA, in a massive show of strength 'thousands of men with banners and placards paraded before the [Constituent] Assembly building' clearly intended to intimidate the Assembly members and so forced the Speaker to impose Section 144 of the colonial penal code that allowed 'the police to suppress political demonstrations and speeches' (McGrath 1996: 88). The political situation in Pakistan was becoming increasingly unstable as the Muslim League hastily cobbled together cabinets from its various factions and a series of weak, almost revolving-door Prime Ministers were unable to stabilize the situation.

Attempted Islamization by *coup de main*

In November 1949 the *Majlis e Ahrar* (Association of Free Muslims), earlier staunch allies of Congress against the Muslim League but now in Pakistan along with the JI, had started agitation in Punjab to officially declare the *Jamaat e Ahmadiyya* (colloquially referred to as Ahmadis) as non-Muslims[12] and demanded that they be removed from all government offices since non-Muslims could not hold official posts in an Islamic state. The Ahmadis were a small fraction of the population of Punjab Province but were then relatively over-represented in the government bureaucracy and especially the military as the sect favored modern education and eschewed *jihad* or other agitation against the British colonial administration. The Ahmadis had been widely persecuted by orthodox Muslims – Ahmadis had been executed for apostasy in Afghanistan – and, *divide et impera*, were patronized by the British colonial rulers.

The most prominent Ahmadi in government, Foreign Minister Sir Zafrulla Khan, became the focal point of the agitation. In the course of this agitation, several Ahmadis (or suspected Ahmadis) were killed and the Ahrar leaders, instead of being prosecuted, were merely officially admonished to refrain from such acts in the future. The unwillingness of the Punjab government to act decisively against the *Ahrar* led to a continual increase in the acts of violence against Ahmadis and an escalation of the rhetoric employed against them.

The agitation reached a climax with mobs 10,000 strong rampaging through city streets, hunting down Ahmadis, and looting Ahmadi-owned businesses. Ahmadi estimates of the numbers killed, in what were essentially pogroms as the provincial government was complicit at many levels, is upwards of 2,000. The mass appeal of the anti-Ahmadi movement and the official sanction of the ruling party can be gauged by the fact that a crowd of 50,000 attended the funeral prayers of a man killed in (a rare incident of) police firing on an anti-Ahmadi mob; Punjab Muslim League provincial assembly members and other prominent Muslim League politicians were regularly seen leading anti-Ahmadi processions and addressing crowds of agitators.[13]

The Muslim League Chief Minister (i.e., highest elected official) of Punjab, Mumtaz Daultana, had regularly made speeches highly critical of the religious beliefs of Ahmadis and on March 6, 1953 he in effect surrendered his administration and Punjab to the mob. Daultana addressed a large anti-Ahmadi crowd and assured them that his government would put their demands before the Central (i.e., Federal) government and do his best to ensure they were met. Daultana's administration had been secretly funding the four newspapers at the forefront of the anti-Ahmadi agitation and he succeeded in paralyzing the Central government (Binder 1961: 253). Daultana's motives in this were most likely not religious *per se*[14] but aimed at bringing down the Central government and either winning much greater autonomy for the Punjab or becoming Prime Minister himself (see Binder 1961: 252–254).

Daultana personally dictated the following passage for addition to a cyclostyled sheet to be distributed in all the mosques in Punjab announcing the capitulation of the provincial government to the demands of the anti-Ahmadi agitators:

> *Suba'i hukumat ka ek Wazir taiyare ke zari'e in mutalibat aur hamari ta'yid ke sath aj hi Karachi bheja ja raha hai aur hamari purzor sifarash hai keh Chaudhri Zafrullah ko wazarat se musta'fi hone par fauran majbur kiya ja'e.*
>
> (Munir 1954: 166)
>
> [A minister of the provincial government is being sent to Karachi today by aeroplane to present these demands and our support [of them] and it is our strongest recommendation that Chaudhuri Zafrulla be forced to resign from his ministerial duties immediately.][15]

The provincial Governor then directed the chief of police to send out loudspeaker-equipped vans to broadcast the proclamation in all the towns and villages of Punjab. At 1:30 pm that afternoon, in an emergency cabinet meeting, the Central government ordered Martial Law be imposed in Lahore, Punjab's capital, and the Army turned out to restore law and order. By May 1953, with the provincial government and official backing for the rioters removed, the province was back to normal. Officially (the unofficial count is higher) the Army reported 11 killed and 49 wounded in Lahore alone, with an indeterminate number in other towns where force had to be used to restore calm (Munir 1954: 1).[16]

Two prominent advocates of an Islamic constitution for Pakistan, also active in anti-Ahmadi agitation – Maulana Maududi of the *Jamaat e Islami* and Maulana Abdus Sattar Niazi[17] of the *Jamiat e Ulama e Pakistan* – were arrested for incitement to riot and murder, tried by a special military court, and sentenced to death. Both of these sentences were commuted by the Governor General to 20 years imprisonment and both were quietly released after serving less than two years.

Given the weakness, factional infighting, and incompetence of the politicians, unelected bureaucrats who had learnt how to administer their charges under the British Raj gained ascendancy over the politicians. The most important among them were two heads of state, Chaudhury Ghulam Muhammad (October 19, 1951 to August 7, 1955) and Iskandar Mirza[18] (August 7, 1955 to October 27, 1958), who transformed the theoretically ceremonial office into the real power center by playing off different Muslim League factions against each other and appointing and dismissing Prime Ministers at will.[19] This transformed Pakistan from a parliamentary to a *de facto* presidential form of government.

Ghulam Muhammad dissolved the CA on October 24, 1954 when it attempted to curb his powers and so established the general principle that the Governor General, the executive, was above Parliament; the new CA was more circumspect in the exercise of its powers.[20] Iskandar Mirza went further and, in October 1958, declared Martial Law and dismissed the CA before parliamentary elections under the new 1956 Constitution could be held.

Three weeks later Mirza was himself deposed by his Army chief General Ayub Khan, Mirza's own nominee as the new Prime Minister; Ayub had earlier served in the cabinet as Defense Minister.[21]

The 1956 and later Constitutions: an Islamic Republic after all?

The new Constitutent Assembly, reconstituted after Governor General Ghulam Muhammad's 1954 dissolution, did pass the draft constitution in January 1956 despite the strong objections of the Bengali members.[22] The 1956 Constitution, short-lived though it was, had seemingly vindicated those in the Pakistan Movement who saw Pakistan as an Islamic State. The Constitution enshrined several Islamic articles, as follows.

- The name of the country was to be the Islamic Republic of Pakistan – Article 1(1).
- The Objectives Resolution was to be the preamble of the Constitution.
- The government was required 'to strengthen the bonds of unity among Muslim countries,' i.e., begin an attempt to recreate the Muslim *Ummah* – Article 24.
- Muslims would be 'enabled' to live their lives in accordance with the 'Holy Quran and Sunnah,' studying the Koran was to be compulsory for all Muslim students, and the Government would support mosques and other Islamic institutions – Article 25 (various sections).
- Alcohol was to be banned for Muslims 'otherwise than for medicinal' purposes – Article 28(f).
- The State was to 'eliminate *riba* [usury/interest] as early as possible' although the term *riba* was not actually defined in the constitution – Article 29(f).
- The President of the Islamic Republic had to be a Muslim – Article 32(2).
- The President was required to establish an 'organization for Islamic research and instruction' whose task it was to 'assist in the reconstruction of Muslim society on a truly Islamic basis' and that special tax on Muslims was to be imposed to fund it – Article 197(1–2).
- No laws could be passed that were not in accordance with the Koran and Sunnah, 'the injunctions of Islam;' the President was to establish a commission to bring 'existing law into conformity with the Injunctions of Islam,' and to 'compile in suitable form, for the guidance of the National and Provincial Assemblies such Injunctions of Islam as can be given legislative effect' – Article 198(1 and 3).

While the 1956 Constitution had indeed moved away from ceremonial deism, it was far from a capitulation to the orthodox *ulema* and other Islamists. It did not mention the *Shariah* or enshrine any explicit role for the *ulema* other than to serve on the various advisory and consultative bodies created under Article 197. It also did not declare non-Muslims as *dhimmis* but instead reiterated their full citizenship rights in the Islamic Republic; in addition to the rights allowed religious minorities in the Objectives Resolution, the Constitution stated that:

- full freedom of religion was established for all faiths, and discrimination on the ground of 'race, religion, caste or place of birth' was prohibited, as were special tax exemptions not available to all faiths – Article 13(1–3); also Articles 8–12 contain general provisions of the rights of all citizens;
- no specific tax could be levied on persons of one religion to propagate or maintain 'any religion other than his own' – Article 21.[23]

So while not Jinnah's Islamic minimalism or the United States' ceremonial deism, it certainly was not the Islamic maximalism demanded by the ultra-orthodox or Maududi.

However, the 1956 Constitution was not able to effect Pakistan's effective Islamization as the October 1958 declaration of Martial Law by President Iskandar Mirza, while not quite the last gasp of secularism in Pakistan, was the last successful attempt to hold off the Islamist forces there. Although President Iskandar Mirza was on record as having stated bluntly that 'religion and politics could and must be kept separate' (Gaborieau 2002: 238), Martial Law was not imposed to prevent the country's Islamization.[24] General Ayub Khan, who deposed Iskandar Mirza three weeks after the imposition of Martial Law, promulgated his own constitution in 1962 that removed the modifier 'Islamic' from the name of the country although the general Islamic nature of the 1956 Constitution was maintained in a more watered-down form. While the Preamble to the new constitution retained the Objectives Resolution of 1949, the watering down of the Islamist provisions meant that while the 1962 Constitution also mandated the elimination of *riba* as soon as possible, *riba* was now defined as usury rather than any and all interest.

However, the strength of the Islamist reaction to the Aligarh-tinged Islamic Modernism espoused by Ayub Khan[25] forced the military regime to immediately backpedal. The First Amendment to Ayub Khan's 1962 Constitution restored the 'Islamic' modifier to the official name of the country so that it was once again the 'Islamic Republic of Pakistan' (Khan 2001: 278). The strength of the Islamists should not have been surprising to Ayub Khan given the scale of the anti-Ahmadi riots of the 1950s or the *Ruet i Hilal* controversy of 1961.[26]

However, in other, perhaps more substantive areas Ayub Khan's Muslim modernism prevailed. The mildly progressive 1961 Muslim Family Law Ordinance[27] was promulgated by the military government despite the vehement objections of the orthodox *ulema* and the *Jamaat e Islami* who denounced it as wholly un-Islamic and started considerable political agitation to repeal it. While issued by the military government, the Ordinance was actually the result of a 1956 commission report that had been promptly shelved by the civilian government when its sole *ulema* member issued a scathing dissent (Feldman 2001: 164).

The 1962 Constitution also established the Central Institute of Islamic Research (CIIR) and the Council of Islamic Ideology (CII) but Ayub Khan appointed the Islamic Modernist Fazlur Rahman as the head of the CIIR.[28] Rahman's progressive interpretation of Islam eventually caused him to flee into self-imposed exile in the USA in 1968 when Ayub Khan's weakening grip on power led to the orthodox *ulema* denouncing him as a heretic and an apostate, and demanding his death.[29]

Ayub Khan's resignation as president in 1969, following weeks of protests by college students and labor unions, ushered in a somewhat more conservative military regime (1969–71) that scrapped Ayub Khan's constitution, but it was the civilian Pakistan People's Party 'Islamic socialist' regime which followed it in late December 1971 that completed Pakistan's *de jure* Islamization. Coming to power after the disastrous 1971 Civil War that saw the creation of Bangladesh and the collapse of the ruling military junta, the democratically elected Pakistan People's Party government crafted Pakistan's current Constitution in 1973. The 1973 Constitution and its various amendments firmly re-established Pakistan as an explicitly Islamic state: 'Islam shall be the State religion of Pakistan' Article 2 declared, while Article 227(1) reiterated that 'All existing laws shall be brought in conformity with the Injunctions of Islam as laid down in the Holy Quran and Sunnah, in this Part referred to as the Injunctions of Islam, and no law shall be enacted which is repugnant to such Injunctions.' Article 38(f) also enjoined the government, as had been the case in both the 1956 and 1962 constitutions, to 'eliminate *riba* as early as possible.' The main difference now was that *riba* was no longer defined in the Constitution itself as 'usury.'

And finally, in a complete reversal of the 1950s, after further political agitation and rioting by the *Jamaat e Islami* and other Islamic parties, the People's Party government amended the Constitution in 1974 to formally declare the Ahmadia sect as non-Muslims (Khan 2001: 515–516). This time there was no military intervention to prevent Jinnah's Pakistan from minutely scrutinizing the religious beliefs of its citizens.

Pakistan's *de jure* Islamization was complete when, in the face of mounting political opposition to the People's Party's victory in the 1977 general elections (widely considered to have been marred by at least some rigging and other electoral malfeasance),[30] the People's Party began to fracture under pressure (seven People's Party Members of Parliament, the Finance Minister and other high-ranking party officials resigned in protest) and a panicky Bhutto ordered the arrest of opposition political leaders (Khan 2001: 564). The leadership of the street opposition to Bhutto's Pakistan People's Party now devolved to mosque prayer leaders and 'other spokesmen of the Islamic establishment, who added the demand to Islamize society' in addition to the existing call by the opposing Pakistan National Alliance for new elections (Khan 2001: 564). Completely alarmed at the scale of the public demonstrations and by the refusal of some security forces to open fire on opposition mobs, Bhutto capitulated to the Islamic demands on April 17, 1977 and 'banned drinking and gambling, shut down night-clubs and race-courses, and reconstituted the Islamic Advisory Council with the mandate to propose measures for Islamizing the country's laws within six months' (Khan 2001: 564).

However, on July 5, 1977 the Army under General Zia ul Haq (ruled 1977–88) staged a coup and deposed Bhutto. While ostensibly promising to hold fresh elections in 90 days, General Zia continually postponed the polls until a stage-managed referendum in 1985 'validated' his actions and 'legitimized' his Presidency.[31] It was General Zia's government that made the first concerted effort to actually 'Islamize' all of Pakistan's society and economy although, given the explicit Islamic constitutional provisions found in the 1973 Constitution, one can make the argument that Zia was merely implementing the clear intent of the framers of the Constitution.

In 1980 Gen. Zia ordered the amendment of the country's judicial structure in order to incorporate a five member Federal *Shariat* Court (FSC) to vet all laws for conformity with the *Shariah* and the creation of a separate *Shariat* Appellate Bench of the Supreme Court to hear appeals from FSC rulings; traditional *ulema* (albeit in a minority) were a permanent part of the membership of both these courts (Khan 2001: 640–641, 662).

Zia argued that his continued rule was necessary to implement *Nizam e Mustafa*[32] in Pakistan and that he could not step down as President as long as this task remained unfinished, i.e., a *de facto* President for Life. While his policies were undoubtedly motivated as much by political expediency as by his personal orthopraxic piety and orthodox Hanafi (of the Deoband variety) Sunni beliefs, Zia's call for the creation of an Islamic state in Pakistan did strike a strong chord among average Pakistanis. In 1980, along with a host of other Islamic measures imposed by military diktat,[33] the Zia government implemented the 1980 Council of Islamic Ideology (CII) Report[34] on the elimination of interest from the economy (Kennedy 2004: 102) and ordered all commercial banks in Pakistan to open 'profit and loss sharing (PLS) accounts' (Khan 2001: 663). This measure allowed Muslims, in theory at least, to use their savings in an Islamically permissible manner by sharing in a bank's profits rather than receiving a fixed rate of interest on their deposits. At the same time Pakistani banks were ordered by the government to phase out traditional (i.e., Western, interest-based) banking by 1985 and become fully Islamic in their operations (Khan 2001: 665). The CII had recommended in 1969 and again in 1971 that *riba* be abolished and the banking system overhauled but thus far these reports had been studiously ignored by successive governments, both military and civilian.

Nevertheless, for all his ostensible commitment to Islamization, General Zia explicitly exempted financial matters from the FSC's purview until 1990 (Kennedy 2004: 106).[35] Given Pakistan's delicate fiscal situation (chronic budget deficits and dependence on foreign aid and worker remittances), allowing the FSC's Islamic Maximalist *ulema* to upset the fiscal apple cart was a risk that even Zia was not willing to take. This exemption delayed the crunch for several years.

However, once the financial exemption had expired the Federal *Shariat* Court and the *Shariat* Appellate Bench of the Supreme Court moved quickly against the existing system, ruling that 'real' Islamic banking should be introduced. This was because the form of Islamic banking that came to be adopted in Pakistan in 1985 was not greatly different from Western banking.

L'état, c'est Islamique!

By the mid-1980s Pakistan had been Islamized according to the interpretation of Islam favoured by the Deobandi *madrassas* in Pakistan,[36] i.e., a Maximalist, traditional interpretation of Islam now held undoubted sway. While the *Jamaat e Islami* had initially supported Gen. Zia's Islamization very enthusiastically, it distanced itself somewhat from his administration when it became clear that he was using them to prolong his personal rule rather than preparing to hand power over to them.

The *de facto* marginalization of the *ulema* in the 1950s and 1960s was indeed ancient history and, far from being content with token gestures, the orthodox *ulema* now held a practical veto over all acts of state. Even Gen. Zia's death in a mysterious plane crash in 1988 and the election of Benazir Bhutto and a reinvigorated Pakistan People's Party twice to power could not shake the Islamic Maximalism imposed by Zia. On the contrary, far from seeking to repeal Zia's Islamization measures, some elected governments have sought to massively expand them. The most egregious example of this was in 1998 when Prime Minister Nawaz Sharif, of the 'Pakistan Muslim League – Nawaz' (PML-N), proposed the 15th Amendment to the 1973 Constitution. This amendment would have altered Article 2 of the Constitution so that a new Article 2B would now read:[37]

2b Supremacy of the Quran and Sunnah

> (1) The Holy Quran and Sunnah of the Holy Prophet (peace be upon him) shall be the supreme law of Pakistan. **Explanation**:– In the application of this clause to the personal law of any Muslim sect, the expression 'Quran and Sunnah' shall mean the Quran and Sunnah as interpreted by that sect.
>
> (2) The Federal Government shall be under an obligation to take steps to enforce the Shariah, to establish *salat* [the five daily prayers], to administer *zakat* [Muslim poor tax], to promote *amr bil ma'roof* and *nahi anil munkar* (to prescribe what is right and to forbid what is wrong), to eradicate corruption at all levels and to provide substantial socio-economic justice, in accordance with the principles of Islam, as laid down in the Holy Quran and Sunnah.
>
> (3) Nothing contained in this Article shall affect the personal law, religious freedom, traditions or customs of non-Muslims and their status as citizens.

(4) The provisions of this Article shall have effect notwithstanding anything contained in the Constitution, any law or judgment of any Court.

This amendment, which would have put Pakistan at par with Taliban-ruled Afghanistan in the degree of its 'Islamicness,' was passed overwhelmingly by the National Assembly but narrowly defeated in the Senate. Before it could be re-presented in the next Senate session (where the ruling party would have undoubtedly gained a majority), General Pervez Musharraf's 1999 coup removed Prime Minister Nawaz Sharif from power. However General Musharraf, his much avowed desire for a 'moderate Islam' notwithstanding,[38] did not dismantle any of the Islamic structures created by General Zia.

Thus the existence of the Federal *Shariat* Court and the *Shariat* Appellate Bench of the Supreme Court in effect established a milder form of Maulana Usmani's 1949 demand for a censor of public morals who would determine if the actions taken by the state and its people passed Islamic muster. The overtly Islamic nature of the Republic of Pakistan would continue unabated. The Islamization of the Pakistani financial system was not to be as seemingly straightforward as envisaged by Gen. Zia when he ordered that all banks would curtail 'conventional' banking by 1985 and it was the Islamic parties that proved the most zealous in insisting that *riba* be eliminated at all costs.

But what exactly is *riba* and why are orthodox Muslims so intent on eliminating it?

Notes

1 The subject of numerous biographies and studies, perhaps the best study of Maududi's work and ideology is still Vali Nasr's 1996 *Mawdudi and the Making of Islamic Revivalism*; there is no standardization of the spelling of the name and Maudoodi and Maududi are probably still the most common South Asian variants. Interestingly, both Sir Syed and Maududi agreed on the proper place of women in society: in *purdah* (sequestered at home). This is more understandable in Sir Syed than in Maududi since the former was born 86 years before the latter. However, in her youth at least, Maududi's wife, a distant cousin whose family wealth allowed Maududi the luxury of not having to work for a living (Nasr 1996: 33–34), openly flouted *purdah* by riding a bicycle to her English-medium school (Akbar 2011: 235). Akbar (2011: 235) recounts an old accusation that the real source of her family's wealth was moneylending as he describes her as 'the daughter of the biggest Muslim moneylender in Delhi.' Contrary to his public position on the proper role for a Muslim woman, it was joked about that Maududi was a henpecked husband at home. Nasr (1996: 33–34) indirectly alludes to this by describing her as 'strong willed, liberal and independent minded' and that the 'standards that prevailed in his household were very different from the standards he required of others.' In 1964 Maududi reversed his public stand on women to support Jinnah's sister, Fatima, as a presidential candidate against Pakistan's reformist military ruler Ayub Khan; this cost him extensive support among the traditionalists (Nasr 1996: 44–45).

2 Maududi's father spent some time at Aligarh as the family was distantly related to Sir Syed but was immediately removed from there when Maududi's grandfather's suspicions about the institution were confirmed: he was horrified to learn that his son was dressing in Western clothes and playing cricket (Nasr 1996: 10).

This was the end of the Maududi family's flirtation with Westernization and the Aligarh mistake was not repeated with Maududi.

3 See Nasr (1994: 103–110) for details. The name Pakistan is an acronym derived from Punjab, Afghania (the old North West Frontier Province of British India), Kashmir, and Sind, with 'tan' added on as the Persian suffix denoting 'land.' Pakistan also serendipitously means religiously pure in Urdu. It is common knowledge among many educated Pakistanis that Maududi had referred to the Muslim League's demand for a Muslim homeland as 'Napakistan' (*napak* means religiously impure/polluted in Urdu). This was apparently done in the JI's magazine *Tarjumanul Quran* in 1942 but I have not been able to find a more detailed reference to it. Maududi's son Farooq Haider Maududi, in a television interview, confirmed that his father did refer to Jinnah's concept of Pakistan as 'Napakistan' (a YouTube upload of the interview, in Urdu, is available at www.youtube.com/watch?v=8KQG_7nWQA4 accessed May 8, 2012).

4 My late father described to me how, as a young boy of 14, he went to hear Jinnah address a public gathering in Lahore in late 1947. Jinnah began his address in highly stilted Urdu and then almost immediately switched to English – a language that hardly a handful of the crowd of several thousand understood. During the entire address, the crowd stood silent, as if hypnotized, and broke into riotous applause when the speech ended, even though virtually no-one in the crowd had understood more than a few words of it at most.

5 Other sections of the Resolution deal with the democratic nature of the state, an independent judiciary, territorial integrity and so on, and are not reproduced here. The entire text is available online at www.pakistani.org/pakistan/constitution/annex_objres.html#1 or see also Islamic Research Institute (2009) for the text and more details on some of the debate, pro and con. When in 1985 Gen. Zia, then military ruler of Pakistan, incorporated the Resolution, hitherto only in the Preamble of all three Pakistani constitutions, into Article 2(2) of the 1973 Constitution, the word 'freely' was omitted from the clause that reads 'Wherein adequate provision shall be made for the minorities freely to profess and practise their religions and develop their cultures;' 'freely' was restored to the Resolution by the 18th Amendment of 2010.

6 For example, the *Idara*'s formal recommendation on the ideal form of Islamic governance was that of a neo-Caliph appointed for life by the *ulema* and who would be advised by them on how to govern according to *Sharia* (Gaborieau 2002: 242).

7 The 'Laws Commission' established under Justice A. S. Mohammad delivered its report in 1954 but it was promptly forgotten given the tumultuous political climate then in Pakistan (Callard 1957: 229).

8 A moderate Islamist, Nadvi's religious training was from *Darul-uloom Nadwatul Ulema* and not from Deoband; he received an honorary doctorate from Aligarh in 1940. *Nadwatul Ulema* was originally founded as a 'middle ground' between the Islamic modernism of Aligarh and the extreme traditionalism of Deoband but, over time, has moved much closer to the latter, so much so that now it is considered as a Deoband-allied institution.

9 See Callard (1957), Binder (1961) and McGrath (1996) for excellent detailed accounts of the political situation in Pakistan then.

10 The mystery surrounding the assassination of Prime Minister Liaquat Ali Khan has never been satisfactorily resolved. The assassin Said Akbar was an Afghan residing in Pakistan and a part-time police informant, and was himself shot by the police seconds after killing Liaquat. Akbar has been variously held to be (i) mentally unstable, (ii) a religious fanatic, (iii) an Afghan nationalist demanding the return of 'lost' territory, or (iv) acting on behalf of Liaquat's Punjabi opponents in the Muslim League. See Zaidi (2010) for a detailed account. In 2007 another Pakistani Prime Minister, Benazir Bhutto, making what seemed

likely to be her second political comeback, was assassinated leaving the same venue, since renamed Liaquat Bagh after Liaquat Ali Khan.

11 McGrath gives the date as November (McGrath 1996: 88) but he was much further removed in time from the actual events than Callard.

12 The Ahmadi sect, formally *Jamaat e Ahmadiyya* (Party of Ahmad), was founded by Mirza Ghulam Ahmad (1835–1908) as a reform movement within Islam. The major point of controversy, and why Ahmadis are considered heretics by orthodox Sunni Muslims, arose with his proclamation that he was not just a reformer but a prophet – albeit a minor one – of God. In Islamic tradition, Muhammad AS was the last Prophet of God and for anyone to lay claim to prophethood after him is blasphemy in the extreme. The Ahmadi sect occupies roughly the same place *vis à vis* Islam that the Church of Latter Day Saints, better known as Mormons, occupies with respect to mainstream Christianity.

13 See Munir (1954) for details on the specifics of the anti-Ahmadi movement and the role of the Muslim League therein.

14 Daultana, from one of Punjab's great landed families, was educated at Punjab University and then Oxford, where he was the President of the India Society.

15 Translation mine.

16 There are reliable reports that Major General Azam Khan (a non-Ahmadi) commanding military troops in Lahore had on his own initiative ordered the Army to draw up plans to contain the agitation and unilaterally impose Martial Law. Apparently Azam was ordered to act by the Central government just as he was about to issue the orders himself. In any case, given the speed of the Army's reaction, it is clear that contingency plans were already in place and had been activated.

17 Unlike Maududi, Niazi had been prominent as a Muslim League student leader and later president of the provincial League in Punjab.

18 Although often styled as 'Major General' Iskandar Mirza, Mirza was not actually a senior Army officer. Despite being the first Indian to be commissioned from the (British) Royal Military Academy Sandhurst in 1920, Mirza transferred from the Army to the Indian Political Service in 1926 and served mainly in the North West Frontier. From 1926 on his service was in the colonial civil bureaucracy and not the military; the rank of 'major general' was an honorary one conferred on him by Prime Minister Liaquat Ali Khan in 1950.

19 The following list of Pakistani Prime Ministers and their term of office should suffice to show the increasing political instability in Pakistan: Liaquat Ali Khan (August 14, 1947 to October 16, 1951), Khawaja Nazimuddin (October 17, 1951 to April 17, 1953), Muhammad Ali Bogra (April 17, 1953 to August 12, 1955), Chaudhry Muhammad Ali (August 12, 1955 to September 12, 1956), Hussain Shaheed Suhrawardy (September 12, 1956 to October 17, 1957), Ibrahim Ismail Chundrigar (October 17, 1957 to December 16, 1957) and finally Feroz Khan Noon (December 16, 1957 to October 7, 1958).

20 See Khan 2001: 130–143, for more details. The crux of the matter was that the Governor General's powers to unilaterally dismiss the cabinet were curtailed by the CA amending the Government of India Act 1935. The Speaker of the CA appealed the dismissal and it was upheld by the High Court but dismissed by the Supreme Court on an absolute technicality. The Supreme Court ruled that all Acts of Parliament (here the CA) had to receive the Governor General's assent before they could become law; since the Governor General did not assent to the curtailment of his powers, he could still dissolve the CA at will and so the High Court judgment negating his dissolution was set aside. This ruling is widely held in Pakistan to be the beginning of the end of democracy in the country.

21 See Feldman (2001: 24–25) for details.

22 The Bengali members wanted a more Federal form of government that devolved greater powers to the provinces, and bitterly resented the equal representation clause, 150 parliamentary seats to each wing, that equated their 54 per cent of the population with West Pakistan's 46 per cent.

23 The full text of the 1956 Constitution is available on various websites, e.g., www.pakistani.org/pakistan/constitution.

24 Why exactly Iskandar Mirza imposed Martial Law is still quite controversial but certainly factors that must have played a role in his decision were the weakening position of the ruling Muslim League *vis à vis* the Bengali opposition, beginning with the League's rout in the East Bengal provincial elections of 1954 (Callard 1957: 57–59), the ever-growing internal fissures within the League itself that threatened its collapse and the certain knowledge that a non-League parliamentary majority would have undoubtedly removed him from office.

25 Ayub Khan was a student at Aligarh Muslim University but left before graduating when he was one of the few Indians selected for a King's Commission in the British Indian Army and sent to the Royal Military Academy, Sandhurst. In his autobiography Ayub speaks glowingly of Sir Syed Ahmad Khan and disparagingly of the traditional *ulema* (Khan 1967: 201–204).

26 The *Ruet i Hilal* (Sighting of the Moon) issue has to do with when *Ramzan* (i.e., *Ramadan*, the month of fasting) ends. Since Islam uses a modified lunar calendar, traditionally the month ends when the new moon is sighted. Ayub Khan's reformist military government decreed that the task of determining when the new moon actually occurred, being a fact of astronomical unambiguity, would fall to the Pakistan Meteorological Department. In March 1961 the Karachi *Ruet e Hilal* Committee, whose members apparently could not see the new moon with the naked eye that evening, determined that the Meteorological Department was wrong and that *Ramzan* had not ended, and so it happened that large portions of the country were still fasting while others were celebrating *Eid ul Fitr* (or the Lesser Eid; the second most important Muslim religious festival in Pakistan). To put this in context, imagine supporters of the current US administration celebrating Christmas on Tuesday while opponents celebrate it on Wednesday, and fights and riots break out as to who is correct. Ayub Khan's attempt to argue that the phases of the moon could be determined with scientific accuracy carried no weight with the *ulema* and the illiterate masses and, with the military in full retreat, 'the services of the meteorological Department were dispensed with, in this connexion' (Feldman 2001: 266). While now an obscure footnote in Pakistani history, the *Ruet i Hilal* controversy demonstrated the power of the Islamists to force even a modernizing military government to reconsider its agenda. It was a defeat for Islamic rationality and modernism and a victory for Islamic Maximalist traditionalism. The current situation has improved to the extent that a 'Central *Ruet e Hilal* Committee' now coordinates reports of moon sightings across the country but, almost invariably, in the Federally Administered Tribal Areas some people still celebrate Eid on different days.

27 The Ordinance departed from traditional Islamic family law in such areas as a husband requiring his first wife's written assent before marrying a second wife, written notice in the case of a husband divorcing his spouse, the wife's right to divorce her husband, the formal registration of all marriages, raising the legal age of female marriage to 16 years, and so on. See Feldman (2001: 162–166) for more details on the circumstances surrounding the Ordinance and its issuance.

28 These were constitutional bodies mandated by the 1956 Constitution as well.

29 After leaving Pakistan Rahman began a long and very distinguished academic career in the US that culminated with him as the Harold H. Swift Distinguished Service Professor of Islamic Thought at the University of Chicago. Apostasy in Islam renders the person *wajib ul qatl*, permissible to kill, according to traditional

Islamic *fiqh*, a position endorsed by the Deobandi *ulema* and virtually all other Islamic Maximalists.

30 The extent of the rigging has been hotly debated but there is no doubt that the ruling People's Party made extensive use of government resources and coercive power to at least 'shade' the results in its favor. There is also evidence to suggest that Bhutto was at first astounded and then openly dismayed when the sheer size of the People's Party 'victory' became clear: 155 out of 200 open seats (Khan 2001: 555). However, most analysts concede that the People's Party would have in all likelihood won on the order of 110+ open seats (Khan 2001: 560) but that it would have faced a much stronger opposition than it was hitherto used to, Bhutto having alienated a large section of the populace. Bhutto did himself no favors when his little-known opponent in Bhutto's home constituency, Larkana, mysteriously disappeared before he could file his nomination papers and so let Bhutto be returned 'unopposed;' the man later charged that he had been held incommunicado by the police and prevented from filing his papers (Khan 2001: 561). The provincial People's Party leaders all took their lead from Bhutto and followed suit, and were also returned 'unopposed' (Khan 2001: 561).

31 Zia's official position until 1985 was President, Chief of Army Staff, and Chief Martial Law Administrator (CMLA). Given how many times elections were postponed and rescheduled, the joke became that CMLA actually stood for 'Cancel My Last Announcement.'

32 *Nizam e Mustafa* (the System of the Prophet; Mustafa, the chosen one, is an epithet of the Prophet Muhammad AS) is a common way of describing the implementation of an orthodox interpretation of the Islamic state.

33 For example, revising the laws of evidence, mandatory breaks in the workday for prayers, compulsory instruction in *Islamiyat* through the first two years of college for all Muslims, compulsory deduction of *zakat* (Islamic poor tax), and so on. See the collection of essays in Hathaway and Lee (2004) for more on the economic aspects of Islamization in Pakistan; and Weiss (1985) on the impact of often discriminatory legislation on Pakistani women.

34 Usually referred to as the *Tanzil ur Rahman Report* after its author, then chairman of the Council of Islamic Ideology and later Chief Justice of the Federal Shariat Court during 1990–92.

35 The initial exclusion was for three years, later extended three times by the Pakistani government; see successive amendments to Clause 203(b) of the 1973 Pakistani Constitution for details. Rumor has it that Prime Minister Benazir Bhutto's administration, remarkably inept even by Pakistani standards, simply forgot to extend the exemption for another three years. It is also possible that, faced with a hostile President (a Zia-era holdover) and an unsympathetic Senate, the Benazir government had been unofficially informed that no further extensions would be granted.

36 The Pakistani Deobandi *madrassas* are now considerably more conservative and closely aligned to Saudi Wahhabist thought than the mother *madrassa* in India.

37 Available at www.pakistani.org/pakistan/constitution/amendments/15amendment_new.html (accessed March 3, 2003).

38 Unlike Zia, Musharraf was notoriously non-orthopraxic in his personal life. Reputedly fond of Scotch whisky, shortly after his coup Musharraf scandalized the orthodox by posing for a photo-op carrying his pet Pekinese dogs, Dot and Buddy. While not technically *haraam* (religiously forbidden the same way pigs are for Muslims – and Jews for that matter), dogs are considered *makruh* (religiously detestable) by devout Muslims who will go out of their way to avoid them since touching a dog violates *wudu* (pronounced *wuzu* in South Asia; the ritual washing procedure that must be followed before a Muslim can say his prayers); following the furor, his pets were rarely seen in public again.

4 The debate over *riba*

The purpose of this chapter is to give a detailed discussion of why Islamic Maximalists and Traditionalists argue that the Koran prohibits charging or receiving interest in any form and why Minimalists and Modernists argue that this is not the case. After a brief discussion as to what 'interest and usury' actually refers to, it provides an overview of the history of interest/usury bans in non-Islamic societies and its treatment in the Koran, and covers in detail the arguments of the most important advocate of Islamic financial Maximalism, Syed Abul Ala Maududi, and those of major financial Minimalists such as Sir Syed Ahmad Khan, Fazlur Rahman, Muhammad Asad, and Mahmud Shaltut. It also lays out the role Islamic finance plays in the overall structure of a truly Islamic society and the creation of a strong 'Muslim' identity in South Asia.

The aim here is to show why no complete analysis of Islamic banking and finance in Pakistan is possible without an understanding of how it fits into the bigger picture of Islamizing Pakistan. This chapter also examines the position of many contemporary Islamic economists regarding the permissibility of charging interest on financial transactions. It examines the 1980 Council of Islamic Ideology report that formed the basis of the 1985 conversion from a conventional to an Islamic banking system, how that report compares to historical Islamic financial practices, and the ideal form that an Islamic financial system is supposed to take.

Interest, conventional and Islamic banking

All conventional banking systems are interest based. This means that a client obtaining a loan from a bank to, say, purchase an automobile is charged an interest rate on that loan, meaning that the amount repaid by the client to the bank is greater than the nominal sum lent. In effect then, in a conventional banking system, the client has the temporary use of funds, made available by the bank for a stated purpose, which then have to be repaid with some compensation due to the bank for the use of its funds; quite often, the bank has a charge or lien over the asset purchased with the funds (or on some other asset put up by the client as collateral) until the loan is repaid. Similarly, a client who keeps her funds on deposit at the bank – which are then used, lent out, by the bank to earn its income – is also due compensation from the bank for using her money for its own purposes. Naturally the spread (the difference) between the rate paid to depositors and that paid by borrowers is used to cover the bank's payroll, overhead and other costs. The residual spread (net of costs) provides the bank's profits.

From the basic fact that borrowing money incurs a monetary cost for the borrower follows the standard (textbook) definition of interest as 'the cost of borrowing or the price paid for the rental of funds (usually expressed as a percentage of the rental … per year)' (Mishkin 2013: 3).[1] Whether the money is borrowed 'cheaply' or 'expensively' is a function of the interest rate charged by the lender to the borrower. As there is no absolute definition of what constitutes cheap money and at what point it becomes expensive, cheap and expensive are relative terms. Contemporary Western society does, however, now differentiate between 'interest' and 'usury.' The Oxford English Dictionary defines usury as 'The fact or practice of lending money at interest; esp. in later use, the practice of charging, taking, or contracting to receive, excessive or illegal rates of interest for money on loan' (OED online). The use of the term 'excessive or illegal rates of interest' in the definition carries with it the clear connotation of exploitation and injustice. It is in this context that the *sine qua non* of contemporary Islamic banking and finance has become that it is an 'interest free' financial system that, by virtue of it being interest free, is non-exploitative and inflicts injustice on neither the borrower nor the lender. This is because, unlike Western society now, the current Islamic orthodoxy does not differentiate between usury and interest. For today's devoutly orthodox Muslim, as for many devoutly orthodox Christians in times past, interest and usury are one and the same – even if this did not always hold true for Muslims.[2]

In addition to the ban on *riba* in financial transactions, the Koran and the *hadith*[3] lay down general guidelines for what are and are not permissible forms of economic activity for Muslims. Over the centuries, the *ulema* of the various schools of Islamic thought (*fiqh*) have concluded that, along with *riba* which is banned outright in the Koran, all practicing Muslims must also avoid financial transactions that involve excessive *gharar* (uncertainty; i.e., where the outcome is extremely uncertain), *maysir* (outright gambling), and *haram* (religiously forbidden) products. Engaging in trade is encouraged but, ideally, profits must be the result of assuming a proportionate share of the risk involved in the transaction by taking an equity stake in it; profits must not be earned 'risk-free' by making a collateralized loan.[4]

Non-Islamic interest bans and the condemnation of usury

It is common knowledge that Islam was not the first, and certainly far from the only, religious tradition to condemn charging interest on financial transactions. Neither was Pakistan the first society (or state) to attempt to remove interest from financial transactions. There is a long history of religious, moral, and ethical objections to interest-based financial transactions, and not just to what would be considered usurious today. Aristotle, for example, famously argued that money was barren and thus cannot beget more money (Visser and McIntosh 1998: 181), so paying interest for the use of someone else's money was a truly unnatural act. Plato banned lending at interest in his *Republic* (Glaeser and Scheinkman 1998: 21). In addition to the more well known condemnations of charging interest in the Old Testament/Torah of Christianity and Judaism (e.g., in *Leviticus* 25:35–37 or *Exodus* 22:25), Visser and McIntosh (1998) give a detailed account of ancient Hindu (*ca.* 600–400 BCE) texts that prohibit higher castes from engaging in it; Buddhist texts (also *ca.* 600–400 BCE) that condemn 'hypocrites' who practice it; and the Roman *Lex Genucia* reforms of 340 BC that banned interest outright.[5] Even such leading figures of the Protestant Reformation as John Calvin and Martin Luther, who are commonly held to have had a favorable outlook towards trade and profit, were bothered enough by the practice of lending money at interest to have:

> [E]xpressed some reservations about the practice of usury despite their belief that it could not be universally condemned. Calvin, for instance, enumerated seven crucial instances in which interest remained 'sinful', but these have been generally ignored and his stance taken as a wholesale sanctioning of interest.
>
> (Visser and McIntosh 1998: 179)

However reluctant the West, starting with the Protestant parts of it, was at coming to terms with lending at interest, many other parts of the world had already moved on past a uniform ban. The West was simply, slowly, playing catch-up with the more complex and sophisticated economies of the pre-modern world. In those parts, the absolute nature of the condemnation of usury had already changed into a more nuanced understanding of what was at work. That is, a distinction was being drawn between 'usury' and 'interest.' For example, in India by the second century CE only charging above some stipulated interest rate was illegal; the later Roman Republic (*ca.* 40 BCE) set a maximum rate of 12 per cent on loans (Visser and McIntosh 1998: 178), but for Senators (i.e., members of the Roman elite) the maximum rate chargeable by them was only 6 per cent (Glaeser and Scheinkman 1998: 23). The Romans further differentiated between *mutuum* (personal consumption) loans and *stipulato* (commercial) loans and the former were required to be made interest-free (Glaeser and Scheinkman 1998: 23). Earlier in India, in the fourth century BCE, some laws distinguished between lower-interest (1.25 per cent per month) loans made for consumption purposes (i.e., probably to the poor) and higher-interest (5 per cent per month) loans made for trade/commercial purposes (Glaeser and Scheinkman 1998: 23)

However, not all religious traditions and pre-modern societies were so accommodating. Other than Muslim scholars, both contemporary and historical, the most consistent and vociferous condemner of interest/usury appears to have been the Roman Catholic Church for most of its history. In the First Ecumenical Council, at Nicaea in 325 CE, the Church forbade its clergy from lending at interest (the original definition of usury) and soon extended that ban to the laity by the end of the century (Rubin 2009: 764–5). This position was reiterated by the Third Lateran Council in 1179 CE that excommunicated usurers (Glaeser and Scheinkman 1998: 24), and again in 1311 by Pope Clement V when he nullified all secular legislation that permitted lending at interest (Visser and McIntosh 1998: 178). As late as the end of the nineteenth century, the Roman Catholic Church still condemned interest/usury, and in terms that gave no room for any doubt in the matter, when Pope Leo XIII in 1891 denounced 'voracious usury … an evil condemned frequently by the Church but nevertheless still practised in deceptive ways by avaricious men' (quoted in Visser and McIntosh 1998: 179). However, this was perhaps the last gasp of the Church's once categorical opposition to lending at interest since it has been almost silent on the topic since then. The only ones left still condemning interest-based finance now are the orthodox Muslim *ulema* and Islamic economists, who continue to do as passionately now as they ever did.

The divine prohibition of *riba*

The rationale for non-interest-based Islamic banking and finance arises out of the prohibition in the Koran on *riba*. There is no question that *riba*[6] (variously translated as 'interest' or 'usury' but with a literal meaning of 'increase' – Ayub 2007/2002: xxxi) is prohibited in the Koran.[7] There are four instances in the Koran where *riba*[8] is mentioned in the relevant economic/financial context[9] and it is clear that it is a progressive prohibition, i.e., *riba* is first mentioned as something that is not viewed favorably by Allah but not explicitly forbidden (Koran 30:39 and 4:161) and then moving on to final prohibition (Koran 3:130 and 2:275–280). Koran 2:275–280 is considered to be the definitive prohibition and clearly contrasts *riba* with *zakat* (the poor tax) and *sadaqah* (charity).[10]

Within the Pakistani legal/constitutional context, the debate on whether or not *riba* was permissible was settled when the 1973 (i.e., current) Constitution was adopted as Article 38(f) stated unequivocally that it was the task of the Government of Pakistan to 'eliminate *riba* as early as possible.' This was only natural as Article 2 of the Constitution had established Pakistan as an explicitly Islamic state: 'Islam shall be the State religion of Pakistan.' Article 227(1) stated that 'All existing laws shall be brought in conformity with the Injunctions of Islam as laid down in the Holy Quran and Sunnah … and no law shall be enacted which is repugnant to such Injunctions.'[11]

The argument over what exactly is banned?

So *riba* is clearly prohibited but what exactly is covered by this prohibition? What is *riba*? The 1962 Constitution had defined *riba* as usury so there was less room for doubt but this had been nullified by the new constitution.

Within Pakistan, the Maximalist or Literalist advocates of Islam hold that as the literal meaning is increase/rise/swell, etc. (Rahman 1964: 2), it is clear 'that any addition to the principal amount' *ipso facto* constitutes *riba* (see e.g., Mawdudi 2011: 145).[12] The Minimalist position in Pakistan was best argued by the Islamic Modernist Fazlur Rahman, appointed in 1963 by the then military ruler, Field Marshall Ayub Khan, as the head of the Central Institute of Islamic Research, who relied on a much more complex argument. Using a contextual interpretation of the term *riba*, Rahman defended contemporary Pakistani banking practices (i.e., conventional banking) against Maximalist charges that bank interest was the same as the *riba* referred to in the Koran.[13]

Rahman, citing the *Muwatta* of Imam Malik,[14] argued that *riba* should not be interpreted literally but must be understood in the context of pre-Islamic Arab moneylending customs. The banned *riba* in the Koran, he argued, refers to a particular custom, *riba al-nasiah* or *riba al-jahaliyah*, where when the debt came due it was traditional to ask the borrower 'Will you pay or will you *riba*?' If the borrower chose the latter, he would be granted an extension on the loan but the amount due would be doubled – hence the *riba*. The catch was, if the borrower then defaulted on the doubled amount, his debt was re-doubled and he was given another time extension: if unable to pay, he and all his possessions could be auctioned off to satisfy his creditors. Thus:

> [T]he initial interest itself was not usurious and was, therefore, not considered *riba*. What made it *riba* was the increase … that raised the principal several-fold by continued redoubling.
>
> (Rahman 1964: 6)

Rahman (1964: 5) explicitly contradicts Maulana Maududi's contention that the initial amount was 'granted free of interest' as no professional money-lender would ever extend a loan, for however short a time period, truly interest-free. It then also follows that if the initial loan was indeed 'interest free,' it was likely made by friends or family of the borrower who were extremely unlikely to raise the amount due many-fold if repayment was not made on time. This then was the context of the Koranic verse (Koran 3:130) that cautioned the faithful, 'O ye who believe! Devour not usury, doubled and multiplied; but fear Allah; that ye may (really) prosper' (Yusuf Ali[15] translation). Rahman's conclusion is that the Qur'an bans extreme usury and so by extension injustice but not interest. This line of thinking closely parallels that set out by the father of Islamic Modernism and the ideological force – South Asian Muslim separatism – that eventually led to the creation of Pakistan in South Asia, Sir Syed Ahmad Khan[16] (1817–98).

Sir Syed, as he is almost invariably referred to in Pakistan, in his extensive *tafsir* (exegesis) of the Koran, characterized *riba* as being usury bordering on injustice and exploitation and thus not applicable to conventional bank finance or modern trade; he also characterized the orthodox view of *riba* as being unsupportable by the Koran and simply the personal opinion of Muslim scholars:

> Therefore it is clearly proved by the context [of 2:273–276: the exhortation to be merciful towards the indebted poor] that *riba* is forbidden which is taken from poor people …. In my opinion, there is no reason to regard the taking of interest from [rich] people to be prohibited by the Qur'an. … In a similar way there are many loan affairs which are arranged in trade and in business … and by which trade, national welfare and prosperity are supported; in the case of those affairs where interest is taken and given, I do not believe that it is a kind of interest forbidden by the Qur'an. Certainly there have been many *fuqaha* (lawyers) who have added many conditions to it on their own authority (*ijtihad*) and deduction (*qiyas*) and whose rules for interest have hindered severely the development of trade. Those regulations, however, cannot be based upon the Qur'an.
>
> (*Tafsir al Quran,* vol. 1 p. 306, translated and quoted in Baljon 1964: 44–45)[17]

However, the orthodox *ulema* did not accept this or any other of Sir Syed's interpretations and his *tafsir* was condemned as being at best *bida* (heretical religious innovation) and more likely *kufr* (outright unbelief). The best that the religiously orthodox could say about his views was succinctly put by A. S. Bazmee Ansari:[18]

> The eccentricities and idiosyncrasies in which some modern self styled '*Ulama*' and interpreters of the Qur'an have indulged cannot be taken to be representative of, or reflecting, the general trend of opinion among the large majority of the Muslims. In spite of his sterling and greatly-admired services to the cause of the Muslims of the Indo-Pakistan subcontinent the fantastic and natural [i.e., naturalistic] explanations put forward by (Sir) Sayyid Ahmad Khan in his various exegetical monographs and other writings are little read by the Muslims of today … The Muslims have shown their disapprobation in unequivocal terms of all such works and rejected them as they failed to conform to the exegetical views of the *Salaf al-Salihin* [19] or what is contained in the authentic (*sahih*) *hadiths* [sayings of the Prophet] and which do not run counter to the agreed beliefs of the Muslims.
>
> (Ansari 1963: 292–293)

The worst was 'a real hurricane of protests and outbursts of wrath from the representatives of the old school … and in every town and village *fatwas* [religious edicts] were issued by the Maulawis [literally Islamic scholars but here village priests] which declared him to be a *kafir* [infidel]' (quoted in Baljon 1964: 108)[20] and he was openly accused of having converted to Christianity (Baljon 1964: 106).[21]

Sir Syed Ahmad Khan's and Fazlur Rahman's interpretation of the difference between 'usury' and 'interest' in the context of *riba* was one shared by other prominent Islamic Modernist *alims* (scholars) such as Muhammad Abduh (1849–1905; Grand *Mufti* – highest-ranked Muslim cleric – of Egypt) and his chief acolyte Rashid Rida (1865–1935; a prominent theorist of political Islam), Abd El-Razzak El-Sanhuri (1865–1971; author of the Egyptian, Syrian, Jordanian, and Iraqi legal codes), Muhammad Asad[22] (1900–92; Director of Pakistan's Department of Islamic Reconstruction of the state, and author of his own translation and extremely well regarded exegesis on the Koran), and Mahmud Shaltut (1893–1963; Grand *Mufti* of Egypt and *Shaikh* – Rector – of Al Azhar[23]).

I shall briefly discuss Asad's and Shaltut's views on *riba*. Asad's because he was an important and influential Pakistani Islamic Modernist who independently came to the same conclusion as Sir Syed regarding *riba* and usury. Shaltut's because he was an Islamic Maximalist who tried to reconcile modernity with Maximalist Islam *à la* Maududi but came to a different conclusion.[24]

Muhammad Asad's analysis is quite similar to Sir Syed's and Fazlur Rahman's in many respects. In his exegesis of the Koran, Asad concludes that:

> Roughly speaking, the opprobrium of *riba* (in the sense in which this term is used in the Qur'an and in many sayings of the Prophet) attaches to profit obtained through interest-bearing loans involving an exploitation of the economically weak by the strong and resourceful. … With this definition in mind, we realize that the question as to what kinds of financial transactions fall within the category of *riba* is, in the last resort, a moral one …. Hence, while the Qur'anic condemnation of the concept and practice of *riba* is unequivocal and final, every successive Muslim generation is faced with the challenge of giving new dimensions and a fresh economic meaning to this term which, for want of a better word, may be rendered as 'usury'.
>
> (Asad 1980: 622–623)

In contrast to these South Asians, Shaltut actually started out as a Maximalist on financial issues. Shaltut's views on interest and *riba* are especially noteworthy as he changed his position entirely; the only occasion in a long and illustrious career when he did so (Zebiri 1993: 74). In a 1951 legal opinion he vehemently condemned interest as *riba* for exactly the same reasons as al Razi and Maududi (discussed later in this chapter). A few years later, Shaltut argued that for purely practical reasons and the fact that modern financial institutions are something completely different from those envisaged in Classical *fiqh*, 'the stipulations laid down concerning those transactions do not apply here' (Zebiri 1993: 76). While Shaltut was referring specifically to the government-owned Egyptian Postal Savings Bank which paid a fixed interest rate to account holders, by analogy the ruling clearly applies to other banks as well and if you can legitimately receive a fixed interest rate, you can pay a fixed interest rate. However, Shaltut's views should not be seen as an unqualified endorsement for interest-based finance as he continued to maintain that the ideal was a truly interest-free economy but practical considerations necessitated otherwise (Zebiri 1993: 77). This is of course in keeping with all the schools of *fiqh* which hold that necessity (*dharura*) makes permissible that which would otherwise be impermissible.

More recently, in 2002 Dr. Muhammad Sayyid Tantawi, then the Grand *Mufti* of Egypt and Rector of Al-Azhar, issued a *fatwa* that essentially reaffirmed Shaltut's ruling when he said that a rate of return of 10 per cent on a one-year time deposit (i.e., 10,000 Egyptian pounds on a deposit of 100,000 Egyptian pounds; the contract specified both the annual rate of return as well as the specific amount of the deposit) held at the International Arab Banking Corporation was permissible. However, this was again a more convoluted case than it might appear at first glance since the ruling held that a time deposit was not a 'borrower–lender' relationship but an 'investor–investee' one, but the essential permissibility of fixed, predetermined interest rates was reaffirmed (see El-Gamal 2006: 139–147 for more details on this case). These are all, however, minority opinions in the current era.[25]

The vanguard of contemporary Islamic orthodoxy, at least as regards *riba* and finance, was led by Maulana Syed Abul Ala Maududi (1903–79) who broke away from his traditionalist Deobandi background to, in effect, espouse his own version of Islamic Modernist Maximalism. Maududi was arguably among the three most influential thinkers and prolific Islamist writers of the Twentieth century and his work has influenced not only Pakistani politics from the creation of the country on but virtually all other Islamic revivalist parties as well. Like his two better known, in the West at least, contemporaries Ayatollah Khomeini of Iran (1900–89) and Sayyid Qutb of Egypt (1906–66), Maududi is usually regarded as more of a political thinker and for his work on the theory of the Islamic state than for his economic writings, but the latter did not escape his incredibly prolific pen.

Maududi's 1941 address, ironically at the Aligarh Muslim University founded by Sir Syed Ahmad Khan to impart Western education and cultural mores to Indian Muslims, on *Insaan ka Maashi Maslah aur aus ka Islami Hul* ('The economic problem of man and its Islamic solution') is generally considered to be one of the founding documents of modern Islamic economics (Nasr 1996: 103–106; Kuran 2004: 84–86)[26] and, indeed, many give Maududi credit for coining the term 'Islamic economics.'[27] Chapra (2004: 173) argues that Maududi was the one who 'who laid down the foundations for the development of this discipline [Islamic economics] in modern times.' However, Maududi's concept of Islamic economics was as merely one component of an integrated Islamic way of life and not as a systematic study of Islam's economic teachings or, indeed, even as something applicable or comprehensible outside of a holistic Islamic way of life:

> [T]he economic problem of man which was, indeed, a part of the larger problem of human life, has been separated from the whole and looked at as if it were an independent problem by itself. … This [has] made its solution infinitely difficult. … if economics is isolated and segregated from the whole way of life of which it is part … and [man's] moral and spiritual aspirations have no reality apart from his economic endeavours, you should not be surprised if chaos and confusion are the final result.
>
> (From *Insaan ka Maashi Maslah* … reprinted in Maududi 1997: 9–10)

In short, Maududi saw Islamic economics 'as a corollary to his discussion of the *din* [faith/religion] and the Islamic state' (Nasr 1996: 103) and therefore 'Mawlana Mawdudi's oeconomic [sic] thought then is better viewed as an inextricable component of this larger social and political vision' (Zaman 2013: 16).

Thus Islamic economics, banking, and/or finance, for Maududi, is best seen as simply another arrow in his quiver. It was a tool that would help him achieve his real goal rather than an end in itself. Since the ultimate goal was the creation of the modern world's first truly Islamic State, the role that Islamic economics, banking, and finance would play in this was to prevent the creation of 'partial Muslims' (Kuran 2004: 85). This is because if Islam were simply relegated to the private sphere, as is now the case of religion in much of the West, the Muslim *ummah* (community of believers) would be rapidly reduced to being merely 'partial Muslims' (Kuran 2004: 84). They would become people for the vast majority of whom their public lives have nothing to do with Islam, in the same way that, for example, most American Christians are 'partial' Christians or most American Jews are 'partial' Jews. By making economics, banking, and finance Islamic instead of secular, continued economic growth and development would *ipso facto* reinforce a Muslim identity and so strengthen Islam rather than weaken it (Kuran 2004: 85).

However, if *riba* equaled usury and it was usury that was *haram* (forbidden) and interest was *halal* (permissible) or *mubah* (neutral) or at worst merely *makruh* (to be avoided if possible but not *haram*),[28] Muslims could safely bank with conventional, Western banks and thus take another step towards becoming the 'partial Muslims' that he detested. But if *riba* equaled interest, then Western-style conventional banking was *ipso facto haram* for Muslims and they would retreat from the disastrous path of irreligiousness followed by the West and back to accepting Islam in all aspects of their lives.

It should be stressed that Maududi was not an obscurantist reactionary like the traditional *ulema* of, say, the great Indian *madrassa* at Deoband who argued that speaking English was if not actually *haram* then at least *makruh*. Quite the opposite in fact as Maududi wanted to reconcile modernity to Islam:

> Although the two had different aims, little separated Mawdudi's position from that of Islamic modernists. … The modernists [e.g., Sir Syed Ahmad

> Khan] wanted to modernize Islam whereas Mawdudi wanted to also Islamize modernity.
>
> (Nasr 1996: 53)

Riba*: interest or usury?*

The difference between a Maximalist and a Modernist/Minimalist interpretation of *riba* is readily apparent when one looks at translations of some relevant passages concerning *riba* in the Koran. The Yusuf Ali translation of verse 3:130 of the Koran, 'O ye who believe! Devour not usury, doubled and multiplied; but fear Allah; that ye may (really) prosper,' stands in sharp contrast to the Maududi[29] translation of the same which reads: 'O Believers, give up the devouring of interest by doubling and redoubling it, and fear Allah: it is expected that you will achieve (true) success.' Similarly, the Yusuf Ali translation of verses 2:275–280 of the Koran translates *riba* as 'usury' while Maududi always translates it as 'interest.' In the crucially important passages (2:275–276) that discuss the permissibility of making a profit via legitimate means (trade) versus illegitimate ones (moneylending), the replacement of 'usury' by 'interest' changes the essence of the passage:

> Those who devour *usury* will not stand except as stand one whom the Evil one [Satan] by his touch hath driven to madness. That is because they say: 'Trade is like *usury*,' but Allah hath permitted trade and forbidden *usury*. Those who after receiving direction from their Lord, desist, shall be pardoned for the past; their case is for Allah (to judge); but those who repeat (the offence) are companions of the Fire: They will abide therein (forever). Allah will deprive *usury* of all blessing, but will give increase for deeds of *charity*: For He loveth not creatures ungrateful and wicked.
>
> (Koran 2:275–276, Yusuf Ali translation, emphasis added)

And Maududi's translation of the same passage:

> But those who devour *interest* become like the one whom Satan has bewitched and maddened by his touch. They have been condemned to this condition because they say, 'Trade is just like *interest*', whereas Allah has made trade lawful and *interest* unlawful. Henceforth, if one abstains from taking *interest* after receiving this admonition from his Lord, no legal action will be taken against him regarding the *interest* he had devoured before; his case shall ultimately go to Allah. But if one repeats the same crime after this, he shall go to Hell, where he shall abide forever. Allah deprives *interest* of all blessing and develops charity; and Allah does not like an ungrateful, sinful person.
>
> (Koran 2:275–276, Maududi translation, emphasis added)

Clearly then, if usury is what is banned by Allah, conventional banking is not forbidden to Muslims since it is not usury. Maududi's translation of the same passage makes an unequivocal equivalence of *riba* with interest and thus bars Muslims from conventional banking which is, of course, interest-based. Finally, in the last line, the contrast between exploitation (*riba*/usury) and benevolence (*sadaqat*/charity) is made clear in the Yusuf Ali translation but the contrast is between 'interest' and 'charity' in the Maududi translation. For Yusuf Ali the opposite of charity is usury; for Maududi the opposite is interest.

To modern sensibilities Maududi's juxtaposition of 'interest' with 'exploitation' is quite jarring. However, the overwhelming consensus among Muslim scholars and most of the *ummah* currently strongly favors Maududi's Maximalist view of *riba*.

Riba *and Islamic finance*

Other than divine prohibition, what reasons did Muslim scholars proffer for continuing the ban on interest/usury when virtually all other religious traditions had, if not accepting it fully, at least become aware of the crucial and irreplaceable function it serves in a modern economy, and become reconciled to it? One of the first systematic modern works on the Islamic view of interest and *riba* was Anwar Iqbal Qureshi's *Islam and the Theory of Interest*, originally published in 1945 in India. While there have obviously been many treatises written by Islamic scholars from the Classical period onwards on the economy and *riba*,[30] this was probably the first by a Muslim economist with extensive formal graduate training and experience in Western economics. Qureshi's PhD in economics was from University College Dublin with an earlier Master's in Economics from the University of London; in the 1950s he worked at the then fledgling International Monetary Fund in Washington, DC (Qureshi 1991/1967: xxix). Thus, unlike pre-modern – whether Muslim, Christian, Hindu, or Jewish – religious scholars or contemporary Muslim scholars steeped in classical *fiqh*, Qureshi was well aware of the role played by interest rates in a modern economy and the central role they have in modern macroeconomic theory. In his analysis, Qureshi explicitly contrasts the Islamic view of interest with several then-contemporary Western (Keynesian, Austrian, etc.) perspectives. He also clearly differentiates between 'interest' and 'usury' as translations/meanings for *riba* but in the end Qureshi's conclusion is a strong restatement of Muslim orthodoxy regarding *riba*/interest/usury and he adopts an Islamic Maximalist position.

Qureshi (1991/1967: 47–48), basing his analysis on the great Twelfth century CE Koranic exegete Imam Fakhr al-Din al Razi's monumental *Tafsir al-Kabir* (*The Large Commentary*, also known as *Mafatih al-Ghayb* or the *Keys to the Unknown*) gives five reasons for the Koranic ban on *riba*:

(I) The interest accruing to the creditor is simply money extracted from the debtor 'without legal consideration or return [and so] This amounts to exploitation and reduces a debtor to poverty which is a colossal inequity.' No compensation is due to the creditor for his inability to use the lent funds himself[31] since the creditor might or might not have made a profit in his own venture but 'this "additional" amount [i.e., interest] from the debtor to the creditor is certain.'

(II) The creditor lives as a rentier and not as a productive member of society: 'He would, thus, loathe engaging himself in some business or occupation which entails labour or hardship.'

(III) The ability to borrow will engender increased, wasteful and/or conspicuous consumption by the debtors and so result in 'squandering money' and the end of 'mutual sympathy, human goodliness, and [mutual] obligation.'[32]

(IV) Since creditors will be mainly the rich and debtors mainly the poor, allowing borrowing at interest will result in 'the rich [endeavoring to] seek the poor people's money more and more.'

(V) Since the Koran (2:275) is the word of God and so unchallengeable by mere humans, no true Muslim should question why one source of profit (trade-based) is permissible while another (interest-based) is not, regardless of the fact that we cannot fathom why one is permitted and the other is not.

Point V is a crucial element in Islamic examinations of the ban on *riba* and one that is repeated by more than one analyst. In fact, there is a tendency, especially among those with training in formal (Western Neoclassical) economic theory, for defenders of the literalist interpretation of *riba* to resort to it in the final analysis, a metaphorical *ultima ratio regum* as it were. The importance of Imam Razi's 800-year-old critique, especially Point V, is demonstrated by the fact that it is still the center-point of the contemporary Islamist critique of interest-based financial systems.[33]

Qureshi (1991/1967: 117–118) in his attempt to discredit conventional banking makes the argument, surprising in a Western-trained economist, that 'Modern banks perform more or less the same functions which moneylenders performed before the banking era' and just as moneylenders – usurers – may:

> [P]erform very useful services in the rural economy of the country and help the cultivators at times of need, but the cost of this help is very disproportionate to the services rendered. It has been very pertinently remarked that this 'credit holds the borrower just as the rope holds the hanged'.
>
> (Qureshi 1991/1967: 147–148)

The first line is of course a neat rephrasing of the Koran: 'They ask thee concerning wine and gambling. Say: "In them is great sin, and some profit, for men; but the sin is greater than the profit" (Koran 2:219, Yusuf Ali translation). As many of Qureshi's Muslim readers would have been familiar with the Koranic turn of phrase, the point was sure to have gone home doubly strongly. Qureshi then concludes with a strong defense of what has become the orthodox Islamic alternative to interest-based finance: 'society should abolish the bonds and debentures (interest-bearing debts) and allow only "shares" (partnerships in which they share profit and losses)' (Qureshi 1991/1967: 181).

Qureshi and other Islamic Maximalists clearly adhere to the Aristotelian view that money is 'barren' and its use by another deserves no recompense since there is no opportunity cost to the creditor of simply letting someone else use her 'medium of exchange.' Money by itself is not productive but if the creditor had lent the debtor some useful tool or other factor of production, then compensation (rent or other payment) was due; similarly if the financier had invested (become a partner) in some enterprise, then she was due her fair share of the profit since she was now risking a loss in the transaction. Obviously the assumption is that a standard, collateralized interest-accruing loan is a 'risk-free' endeavor and Qureshi along with many other Islamic economists disregards the possibility of it accruing losses. Qureshi also makes the curious and indefensible assumption that if interest-accruing loans are made, they will be used for non-productive and/or conspicuous consumption purposes but if 'zero-interest' loans are made, they will be used for productive and/or morally worthy purposes. Finally, Qureshi ignores the likelihood that many of the depositors in a conventional bank, whose funds make lending possible, are likely to be as poor as, if not poorer than, the borrowers; moneylenders of course, whether modern or pre-modern, are likely to be wealthier than most of their clients.

The Maximalist view of interest

Maududi's detailed analysis of interest, *Sood* (Interest), came shortly after Qureshi's work (which in turn had been influenced by Maududi's *Economic Problems of Man …*) and was published in two volumes between 1948 and 1952 (detailed English excerpt in Maududi 1997).[34] Maududi also drew extensively on al Razi's *Tafsir al-Kabir* and gave the Minimalists no quarter in demolishing their argument that *riba* did not equal interest or that it applied only to private-consumption loans made to the poor. While Qureshi's work is now known only to a few specialists in the field, Maududi's analysis has become the *de facto* starting point for the Maximalist position on interest – the current Muslim orthodoxy – not only in South Asia but far beyond as well (Chapra 2004: 173).

Maududi defined 'interest' quite succinctly: 'Interest is the excess amount on the Principal which is received at a fixed rate after a fixed period, both conditions being predetermined' (Maududi 1997: 164–165). The presence of three conditions – (i) 'excess on the Principal,' (ii) the amount of excess being determined 'according to the period of time,' and (iii) 'excess being a condition of the transaction' – renders any financial transaction 'a usurious transaction, regardless of the consideration, whether the loan was taken for productive investment or to meet a private need or whether the debtor is rich or poor' (Maududi 1997: 164).

Maududi like Qureshi held that interest (usury) 'develops miserliness, selfishness, callousness, inhumanity and financial greed in the character of man. … It severs the ties of sympathy and fraternal cooperation between individuals …. [It] diverts the flow of money from the poor to the rich' (Maududi 1997: 165–166). This is of course virtually identical to Qureshi's (1991/1967: 48) restatement of al Razi's argument against interest, and the analysis of all three would support the argument in Chapter Five of this work that Islamic economists see the ban on interest/usury as an explicit mutual insurance/survival mechanism. While such an argument may well have been valid in al Razi's time (the twelfth century CE), it was certainly a very problematic one to make in the mid-twentieth century CE where the major source of credit is the financial system and not idle-rich rentiers lending money at exorbitant interest rates to the peasantry.

Mawdudi further argues that even low rates of interest invariably tend to increase over time and so rapidly become usurious by anyone's reckoning, therefore there is no 'natural and reasonable' rate of interest that can be called non-usurious and, more broadly, 'the first fact that appears before us is that no such thing as a "reasonable rate of interest" has ever existed in the world' (Maududi 1997: 178–179). In addition, interest-based financial systems refuse to fund any project whose internal rate of return does not cover the borrowing costs and so many societally desirable projects remain unfunded because they do not meet this artificial criterion of 'profitable use' of funds, and such financial systems force 'the business-man to use all means fair or foul to keep his profit rate above the interest rate of the money-lender' (Maududi 1997: 187–188). Thus, for Maududi, interest-based financial systems *ipso facto* lead to exploitation and injustice.[35]

Furthermore, interest-based financial systems stifle growth and development by inhibiting profitable economic activity and thus overall economic activity as:

> [T]here is constant conflict instead of cooperation between the capitalist [moneylender] and the entrepreneur. When the entrepreneur wishes to borrow in the hope of productive investment, the capitalist begins to raise the rate of interest, till it reaches a level at which it is no longer possible for the entrepreneur to make profit on his borrowings. Thus when capital investment in business stops … the entire business world is gripped by an acute crisis of depression.
>
> (Maududi 1997: 181)

The counter to this disastrous capitalism is 'a straight and reasonable partnership [by the capitalist moneylender] with the entrepreneur and settle his share in the actual profit of the business on a just basis' (Maududi 1997: 181).

Maududi is of course describing a (presumably pre-modern) scarcity economy where credit is extremely limited and controlled by an oligarchic elite. Most modern economies do not fit this pattern of extreme capital scarcity where those that control it can indulge in near-perfect price discrimination that renders the borrowers' profits virtually zero.

However, for Maududi this is not a description of a particular form of society but of all interest-based economic systems as:

> There is hardly a country of the world in which moneylenders and *banks* are not sucking the blood of poor labouring classes, farmers and low income groups. … Even when they have paid *interest equal to double or treble* of the principal amount, their liability of the principal amount remains intact. … A major portion of the earning of a working man is expropriated by the moneylenders, leaving the poor man with hardly enough money to feed himself and his family.
>
> (Maududi 1997: 192, emphasis added)

While this description of the effects of predatory moneylending no doubt conforms to the conventional view of the North Indian peasantry groaning under the heel of the moneylending *bania* (Hindu merchants who often doubled as local moneylenders), with monumental debts being passed on from father to son,[36] it is hardly an accurate description of a modern conventional banking/financial system. The proverbial 'man on the Clapham omnibus' would not normally describe, say, a 30-year mortgage at 5 per cent interest per annum as exploitation or illegitimate profit-taking by the creditor but he is very likely to so describe a loan from a moneylender at 5 per cent interest per month (i.e., 79.6 per cent annualized). Maududi, of course, explicitly does not differentiate between the two cases and, quite on the contrary, makes a slippery-slope argument that the one inevitably leads to the other (Maududi 1997: 178–179).

For Maududi, as stated earlier, the counter to the interest-based system is the direct equity participation economy where the financier becomes a direct shareholder/investor in the firm (Maududi 1997: 181, 209). Maududi (1997: 188) gives a concrete example of how a direct-equity-investment economy would be superior to a conventional-interest-based economy by looking at how financiers treat societally profitable (affordable low-income housing) versus financially profitable (commercial real-estate) investments: interest-based economies fund the financially profitable while direct-equity economies fund the societally profitable. However, nowhere does Maududi actually explain why, absent Utopian levels of selflessness, every financier in a direct-equity participation economy would fund the societally much more desirable but much less financially profitable 'low-income' housing when s/he has the opportunity to invest in the societally much less desirable 'magnificient cinema hall' that 'holds far better [profit] prospects' (Maududi 1997: 188).

Homo islamicus or the 'New Islamic Man'

The answer to where this selflessness would come from lies in why Maududi and those who followed his lead argued that Islamic economics, banking and finance had to be a part of an integrated whole. An Islamic financial and economic system was nothing other than part of an integrated Islamic way of life in an Islamic state governed by purely Islamic norms. Thus, once all undesirable options have been eliminated, society would naturally gravitate towards the just and more equitable, i.e., Islamic, outcomes. The imposition of a truly Islamic system of governance, which would require declaring charging interest a penal offense with the death penalty being imposed on repeat offenders (Maududi 1997: 199), would increase humanity's natural 'generosity, sympathy, large-heartedness and magnanimity' through continued good examples of 'everyone [lending] generous assistance to a fellow citizen in need, in which the affluent extend considerate help or at least honest cooperation to the deprived sections – in such a society mutual love, consideration and regard will develop and flourish … [and] internal strife and conflict will never find headway' (Maududi 1997: 191).

Thus Maududi is clearly advocating the creation of *Homo islamicus* – the New Islamic Man – who will build a far better world than the one we inhabit today. This is not an isolated aim of just one advocate of Islamic economics but one that echoes and resonates among almost all contemporary advocates and theorists, as opposed to its mere practitioners. For example, Zaman (2008: 28–29) reiterates Maududi's words almost verbatim – that Western economics expects humanity to behave selfishly and so creates the situation where that is the only possible outcome – but buttresses them with references to contemporary cooperative game theory and experimental economics to argue that:

> Instead, since human behaviour responds to expectations and social norms, we are free to choose the type of society in which we wish to live. If we promote that idea that human beings are naturally selfish, and that such selfish behaviour leads to the best social outcomes, human beings will learn to behave selfishly. In fact, Islam teaches us that all children are born in Islam, which is the religion of nature (*deen-ul-fitrah*), but that childhood training causes them to deviate from the 'natural path'. This does not mean that children are naturally cooperative and generous; rather, that the recognition and appreciation of virtuous behaviour is built into their hearts. This makes it easy to train them to be good.[37]

That is, humans respond to incentives and attempt to conform to societal norms and so human nature can, in effect, be transformed if the society is sufficiently virtuous and removes the conditions necessary for intolerant and selfish behavior.

However a minority of Islamic economists take a different, more realistic perhaps, view of the matter. Farooq (2011: 8)[38] concludes:

> So is there no such thing as *Homo islamicus*? Islamic economists argue that there is. However … it pertains to a normative world, where people seek certain ideals motivated by self-interest as enunciated in the Qur'an. However, the Qur'anic values meant for the entire humanity are to be upheld as ideals. They are not necessarily a positive basis for establishing a system.

That is, what Maududi and Zaman see as the ultimate but completely attainable goal of societal development and human progress, Farooq views as a Platonic Ideal that fallible humanity should continually strive towards despite knowing that it will never be achieved. Maududi and other Islamic Maximalists vehemently reject the charge of utopianism levied against them and continually reaffirm the *transformative* nature of Islamic economics.

There is general agreement among advocates of Islamic economics that, as it is an integral component of *Shariah*, Islamic economics' ultimate aim is essentially transformative. Unlike Western economics, which prides itself on positive analysis (an objective description of *what is*), Islamic economics goes beyond even normative policy prescriptions (*what ought to be*) into the transformative realm (*what can be*). That is, rather than being simple normative economic analysis that advocates a desired economic outcome, Islamic economics, being a part of the *Shariah*, is aimed at achieving a 'transformation of human beings from followers of base desires to people concerned with achieving higher goals' (Zaman 2008: 28; see also Chapra 2008; Khan and Bhatti 2008[39]). For its advocates, the transformation of 'base' (i.e., self-centered if not outright selfish) desires into 'higher goals' of peace, human welfare improvement and spirituality is a key difference between Islamic and Western/capitalist economics. Its advocates deny that Islamic economics is utopian wishful thinking since this would mean that the *Shariah* is neither practical nor implementable. Quite on the contrary, as Zaman put it, the task is certainly difficult as it requires a total strategy aimed at all aspects of society but far from impossible:

> A major difficulty faced by Muslim reformers, pointed out by many authors, is that a financial system is an integrated and coherent structure and piecemeal changes towards an Islamic system are quite difficult to devise, manage and implement. Replacement of an existing system by an Islamic system *based on trust, community and no interest* is a difficult job, requiring changes and interventions on several different fronts simultaneously.[40]
>
> (Zaman 2008: 62, emphasis added)

The predetermined conclusion

Maududi's and most other Islamic Maximalists' treatment of interest leads one to the same conclusion as that reached by Gibb in 1947 when discussing the vast majority of Islamic modernists and reformers who 'leave us with the feeling that either the author is incapable of handling his materials or his treatment of them is vitiated by writing to a predetermined conclusion' (Gibb 1975/1947: 64).[41] This is because, as Gibb continues, the issue troubling the Muslim reformers, contrary to the Islamic concept of *ijtihad*, 'is that ultimately they have no trust in the mass of men … but seek to drive them toward a predetermined objective' (Gibb 1975/1947: 115).[42] For Maududi this 'predetermined objective' is the belief that if interest did not equal *riba* and so Muslims could use a conventional bank and partake in conventional finance, they were invariably set upon the path of becoming 'partial Muslims.' Thus a separate Islamic economic system was needed and so had to be created if Muslims were to live a truly Islamic existence. Maududi was certainly successful in this since most current orthodox Islamist critiques of conventional finance are derived, explicitly or implicitly, from Qureshi's and Maududi's path-breaking works whether they realize it or not.[43] These two Keynesian 'academic scribblers' have laid the foundation of modern Islamic banking and finance.

The Islamization of Pakistani banking and finance was then part and parcel of the Islamization of Pakistani society, culture and governance. One could not have the former (Islamic banking and finance) except as a part of the latter (an Islamic society governed by Islamic socio-economic norms). Maududi's agitation for an Islamic form of government for Pakistan under the aegis of an Islamic constitution (as defined by him in his writings) was why any study of the Pakistani experience with Islamic banking has to be perforce a study of Maududi's and other Islamists' attempt to forge Pakistan 'as a new Medina'[44] which would then 'emerge as the leader of the Islamic world in the twentieth century, a laboratory where experiments in Islamic modernity would be successfully conducted *en route* to ushering a new Islamic renaissance' (Dhulipala 2011: 381).

Notes

1 Mishkin also gives a second, more technical definition, one more in line with the standard economic view of the essential purpose of interest in an economic system. The interest rate is the specific discount rate 'that equates the present value of cash flow payments received from a debt interest with its value today' (2013: 70). That is, it is that interest (discount) rate that makes one indifferent between receiving a sum of money now versus a different sum of money at some point in the future since the values of both are equal ('equates'). For example, if the current market interest rate on one year Certificates of Deposits (time deposits) is 5 per cent, I would theoretically be indifferent between receiving \$100 now or \$105 exactly a year from now because I could invest the \$100 now at 5 per cent and receive \$105 in a year's time (ignoring inflation, of course). This example, without going into

the details of present value calculations and mathematical formulae, nicely illustrates the concept of the time value of money.

2 See Chapter Five for instances when this was not always the case historically in many Muslim societies.

3 Pronounced *hadees* in Urdu. These are the sayings and actions of the Prophet Muhammad AS; along with the Koran these form the core of Islamic law (*fiqh*), the earthly representation of the *Sharia* (Divine Path) that all observant Muslims must follow.

4 See also Chapra 2008 (for a more sympathetic) and Kuran 2004 (for a more critical) presentation of the basic tenets of Islamic economics.

5 See also Rubin 2009 and Glaeser and Scheinkman 1998 for more on interest/usury bans.

6 Arabic, being a Semitic language, has an analog to *riba* in modern Hebrew: *ribbit.*

7 There was, at one point at least, some confusion as to which category of Koranic words *riba* falls into. This arises from the fact that many *ulema* are of the view that there are words in the Koran whose meaning has changed over time or is simply unclear (i.e., open to differing interpretations), or is simply unknown (and unknowable?) to us. A discussion of this topic is an extremely difficult and complex one that is far beyond the scope of this work, but see e.g., Kamali 2005 for a reasonably accessible (to the non-specialist) introduction to *Usul al Fiqh* (principles of Islamic jurisprudence). Suffice it to say that some scholars put *riba* into the category of *mujmal* (ambiguous) words. There is a tradition that the second Caliph, Umar, remarked that 'The verse of *riba* (or the verse which forbids *riba*) is among those which were revealed during the last days of the Prophet [Muhammad], peace be upon him. He passed away before explaining its implications' (Meenai 1996: 5; also Asad 1980: 622–623). Meenai categorically dismisses this story as a 'myth' and asserts that there was no doubt as to what was being forbidden (Meenai 1996: 21). Asad (1980: 622) is less categorical in his dismissal and cites the great Fourteenth century exegete Ibn Kathir (1301–70 CE) as stating 'the subject of *riba* is one of the most difficult subjects for many of scholars' precisely for the reason that no further elaboration was given by the Prophet.

8 Most scholars of Islamic finance differentiate between *riba al-nasiah* (*riba* of deferment; also known as *riba al-jahiliyah* – *riba* of the age of ignorance), where the amount repaid over time is greater than that originally lent, and *riba al-fadl* (the *riba* of excess), where two similar goods are traded in unequal amounts, e.g., two pounds of inferior quality dates for one pound of superior quality ones, to use an example from *hadith.* For the purposes of this book, the focus will be on *riba al-nasiah* and general references to *riba* are to it.

9 *Riba* may also be used in a non-financial sense, e.g., 'May your camel herd *riba.*'

10 The Koran is available online, in various translations into English, and in a searchable database format at http://quran.com.

11 The current Constitution and its various amendments are available online at www.pakistani.org/pakistan/constitution (accessed October 8, 2008).

12 This edition of Maududi's (also spelled Mawdudi or Maudoodi) work draws heavily on his detailed treatise *Sood* ('*Interest*', published sometime between 1948 and 1952 in two volumes). Maududi's arguments are very similar to Qureshi's (1991/1967) which is heavily influenced by Maududi's earlier analysis. See later in this chapter for more details on Qureshi.

13 Islamic Maximalism and Minimalism do not easily map onto a conservative–liberal or traditional–modernist categorization. Maududi was certainly an Islamic Maximalist but he was also an Islamic Modernist of sorts and far from a Traditionalist. Fazlur Rahman was an Islamic Modernist but probably a Minimalist, while some Maximalists are quite traditional and conservative.

14 Imam Malik was the founder of the Maliki School, one of the four great Sunni *Madhab* (pronounced *mazhab* in Pakistan) or schools of thought/jurisprudence, in Islam. See also Qureshi (1991/1967: 57–60) for an extensive discussion of other classical sources who describe essentially the same moneylending procedure.

15 Abdullah Yusuf Ali, 1872–1953, was an Indian Muslim whose 1934 translation of the Koran was probably the first by an Indian Muslim, albeit one from a minority Shia sect, into English. Yusuf Ali's work on the Koran has been described as 'monumental' and 'the most widely circulated work of Twentieth century Islamic scholarship' due to his 'accurate rendering of the Qur'anic Arabic, command of English expression and erudition' (Sharif 1994: viii). An accomplished scholar educated at Cambridge and other Western universities, and called to the Bar at Lincoln's Inn, he was one of only two Muslims (along with three Hindus and 60 British) who qualified the extremely competitive Indian Civil Service – the steel frame of the Raj – exam in 1895. Although promoted rapidly in the Civil Service, he resigned in 1914 for personal reasons (marital problems and other family issues) and to pursue his second career as an author; there seems to be no basis for the rumors that he was forced to resign due to British racism.

16 Please see Chapter Two for more on Sir Syed Ahmad Khan and Islamic Modernism in South Asia.

17 *Fuqaha*, plural of *faqih*, is from *fiqh* (Islamic jurisprudence) and is probably better translated as a scholar of, or an expert in, Islamic jurisprudence rather than simply 'lawyer;' probably the more common contemporary usage would be *alim* (from *ilm* – knowledge; also a scholar of Islamic jurisprudence, plural *ulema). Ijtihad* (usually translated as 'consensus of the community of believers,' and best understood as the consensus of the *fuqaha/ulema*) and *qiyas* (deduction by analogy) are two of the four main sources of Islamic law after the Koran itself and the Sunnah (sayings and actions) of the Prophet Muhammad. Baljon, writing originally in 1949, is perhaps using a very old fashioned usage/translation, perhaps analogous to referring to *ulema* as doctors of Islamic law.

18 Ansari was the founding editor of the influential Pakistani journal *Islamic Studies* and on the Executive Board of, and a contributor to, the second edition of the authoritative, some would say definitive, *Encyclopedia of Islam* (Leiden: Brill) published in several volumes between 1954 and 2005.

19 'Pious Ancestors' or the first three generations of Muslims; reputed in a *sahih hadith* of the Prophet to be the 'best' of Muslims and so venerated by ultra-orthodox Muslims as those whose practices embody 'correct' Islam. All of the founders of the four great schools of Sunni Muslim jurisprudence – Hanafi, Hanbali, Maliki, and Shafi – and of the Twelver Shia school fall in this category.

20 The quotation is from the 1901 biography of Sir Syed Ahmad Khan, *Hayat e Jawid*, by his friend the famed Urdu poet Altaf Husain Hali (1837–1914). One *maulvi* went so far as to travel to Mecca and obtained a *fatwa* against Sir Syed Ahmad Khan that condemned both him and his attempt to bring modern education to Muslims (Baljon 1964: 109). So great was the uproar against him by the traditional *ulema* that, when approached by a destitute young man to use his connections with the British colonial administration to get the young man a job, Ahmad Khan told him, 'It is not my habit to give recommendations, but I think the best thing to improve your income will be to write and publish a polemic against my Quran *tafsir*; God willing, it will be a good seller, and you will become a rich man' (quoted in Baljon 1964: 105).

21 Since apostasy in Islam is usually regarded as being punishable by death, in effect his critics called for him to be declared *wajib ul qatl*, i.e., permissible for any true Muslim to kill.

22 Asad is one of the fascinating characters that come along every now and then in history. Born Leopold Weiss into a long line of Jewish rabbis (although his father

broke tradition to become a lawyer) in Lvov in the Polish part of the Austro-Hungarian Empire, Asad converted to Islam in 1926 in Berlin and then went on Haj to Mecca where he lived for six years polishing his Arabic. In the process he became a close confidante of and advisor to King Ibn Saud of Saudi Arabia and his son Faisal, the future King of Saudi Arabia, on foreign affairs and may have carried out some delicate political and espionage work for them as well. Asad was an amazing polyglot who, in addition to his native German (and presumably Yiddish), was extremely well versed in Arabic, Aramaic, English, French, Hebrew, and Persian. His autobiography, *Road to Mecca* (first published in 1954 and continuously in print since then), is one of the great accounts of spiritual awakening. Asad's *Message of The Qur'an* (1980) is rightly considered one of the great exegesis of the Koran and is a masterpiece of Islamic modernism and rationality. Despite his extremely close ties to the Saudi monarchy, Asad's views were far removed from and indeed antithetical to Saudi Wahhabism and his exegesis was officially banned in Saudi Arabia in 1974 during the reign of his old friend Prince Faisal, now King. Asad was personally very close to Allama Sir Muhammad Iqbal, who shared his views on interest versus usury/*riba* (Iqbal 1930), whom he met when he visited India in 1932 and it was Iqbal who persuaded Asad to stay on there. Asad moved to Pakistan after 1947 and joined government service. Asad's last government positon was as Pakistan's Ambassador to the United Nations which he resigned in 1952, after official permission was refused for him to marry a non-Pakistani, in order to write his great exegesis on the Koran. A prolific writer all his life, Asad was later twice (at least) asked to assume further official positions in Pakistan as personal advisor to two different presidents on Islamic affairs, both of which he politely declined in order to continue to write books on Islam.

23 Founded in 970 CE, Al Azhar University is one of the world's oldest Sunni Muslim *madrasah* and arguably among the greatest seats of Islamic learning in the world. Zebiri (1993: 1) and many others describe the position of *Shaikh* of Al Azhar as 'the highest religious office in Sunni Islam.'

24 This makes Shaltut extremely difficult to categorize easily as either a Modernist or a Traditionalist but he certainly was not a Minimalist.

25 See Farooq 2009 for an extensive discussion of the contending views of *riba* in Islam.

26 A compendium of Maududi's extensive writings on economics is available in English (Maududi 1997).

27 See Zaman (2013) for an extensive discussion of the origins of the term 'Islamic economics.' Unlike both Kuran (2004) and Nasr (1996), Zaman contends that Maududi never used the exact term '*Islami mashiat*' or its English equivalent 'Islamic economics' in his extensive writings on the subject but instead referred only to '*maashi nizam*' (economic order) or '*nazm i mashiat*' (organization of the economy).

28 In common usage Muslims consider that most actions or items are either *halal* (permissible) or *haram* (forbidden). In *fiqh*, however, there is a finer division usually called the *al ahkam al khamsa* (the fivefold ordering) that gives a finer distinction of permissibility and repugnance for all acts and items rather than the simple *haram/halal* binary. These are *wajib* (obligatory), *mustahab* (recommended), *mubah* (neutral), *makruh* (detestable), and *haram* (forbidden/sinful). The expectations are that observant Muslims will of course perform any act that falls in the first two categories and avoid any that falls in the last two.

29 Maududi's translation and extensive commentary on the Koran is available in a searchable format at: www.englishtafsir.com.

30 See Chapra (2008) or Ghazanfar (2003) for more details on Islamic economic thought in the Classical period. Their work is in part a direct refutation of the great Harvard economist Joseph Schumpeter's (1996/1954: 74) fatuous claim in

The History of Economic Analysis that 'So far as our subject [economic analysis] is concerned we may safely leap over 500 years to the epoch of St. Thomas Aquinas (1225–74) …' This is Schumpeter's 'Great Gap' thesis which argues that there was nothing of any importance written in the Eighth through the Thirteenth centuries CE on economic analysis!

31 In contemporary economic usage, no compensation is due to the creditor for the opportunity cost of capital.

32 Here Qureshi is implicitly laying out the argument, developed in Chapter Five, which argues that the ban on lending at interest in pre-modern societies should be seen as a mutual obligation/insurance/survival mechanism; hence Qureshi's use of terms such as 'mutual sympathy, human goodliness and [mutual] obligation.'

33 See, for example, Algaoud and Lewis's 'Islamic critique of conventional financing' in the authoritative *Handbook of Islamic Banking* (2007), probably now the standard reference in the field.

34 Because it was originally published in Urdu and earlier Urdu publishers did not always adhere to Western norms of publication details in their editions, it has been quite difficult to determine the exact publication date of this important work. Chapra (2004: 163) gives the date of the first Urdu edition as 1951.

35 Maududi's argument here is similar to that of Structural Marxism: the individual bourgeois employer and exploiter of labor may not be a reprehensible person but the reprehensible system forces him to behave as one.

36 See Desai *et al.* (1984) for a detailed analysis of agrarian power dynamics in South Asia, and especially Ludden (1984) for a more nuanced view of the role of moneylenders in South Asian agrarian economies.

37 Most Western economists would argue that the correct term here is not 'selfish' but 'self-interested.' That is, most people put their self's interest (and that of their family, immediate associates, etc.) above that of a theoretical societal interest, but self-interest in no way rules out altruism or generosity or any other societally desirable trait. Maududi's and Zaman's criticism of contemporary Neoclassical (orthodox) economics is one that is shared by many Western critics of orthodox economics as well.

38 See Farooq (2011), Head of Research in Islamic Finance at the Bahrain Institute of Banking and Finance, for an extensive discussion and critique of the utopianism inherent in the concept of *Homo islamicus.*

39 For example, Khan and Bhatti (2008: 102) argue that the real answer to preventing or even reducing financial fraud and other related crimes and undesirable behavior does not lie in better laws or better enforcement of existing laws, but 'The real solution to this problem requires the adoption of a moral and motivational approach – teaching the individual and society to adhere to Islamic moral codes in their all dealings [sic].'

40 Perceptive readers will have immediately realized that *Homo islamicus*, aka the New Islamic Man, is the Islamic analog to *Homo sovieticus*, the satirical and derogatory way of referring to what the ideologues of Marxism–Leninism in the Soviet Union referred to as the New Soviet Man. *Homo islamicus* is usually used in a non-satirical and non-derogatory fashion by those Islamic economists who believe in the transformative nature of Islamic norms of governance and economics. For those who have less faith in the transformative nature of these norms, it is used in the same sense as the original *Homo sovieticus*: a satirical and derogatory way of reference.

41 Sir H. A. R. Gibb, the great Scottish Orientalist scholar of Islam, argued that the writings of most Islamic Modernists, far from heralding a Reformation of Islamic thought, merely 'turn out to be apologetic works, composed with the object of defending Islam and demonstrating its conformity with what their writers believe to be present-day thought' (Gibb 1975/1947: ix). In an otherwise scathing critique

of most Islamic modernists, Gibb singles out the Indian Muslim philosopher Sir Allama Mohammad Iqbal, famous for his path-breaking *Reconstruction of Religious Thought in Islam* (2004/1934) and his Urdu and Persian poetry, as being 'the most outstanding in intellectual life between 1910 and his death in 1938' (Gibb 1975/1947: ix, 59) and Iqbal's *Reconstruction* … as being the 'first (and so far the only) thoroughgoing attempt to restate the theology of Islam in modern immanentist terms' (Gibb 1975/1947: 59–60).

42 Islamic Maximalists would of course say the same about this work: that it is arguing to a predetermined conclusion. Following where the facts lead is undoubtedly in the eye of the beholder.

43 See Zaman (2008) for a comprehensive discussion of Islamic economics.

44 Medina (properly *Al Medina Al Munawarra*, the radiant city) was then called Yathrib but was renamed by the Prophet Muhammad (pbuh) who established the first Muslim society there after leaving his native Mecca in 622 CE to escape persecution at the hands of his enemies. The Islamic calendar dates from the *hijra* (migration) from Mecca to Medina.

5 The new orthodoxy of 'old' Islamic financial norms

The purpose of this chapter is to lay out the view of contemporary Islamic finance theorists on how Islamic finance should function, to consider whether or not Islamic financial norms allow for the time value of money, and to provide an alternate explanation for why early Islamic and other pre-modern societies may have banned charging interest on loans. It shall also show that the current belief that Islamic financial norms prohibit charging interest on loans is not supported by historical Muslim financial practices, although there were always those who opposed the charging of any rate of interest.

Contemporary Islamic finance and views on interest

Most contemporary advocates of Islamic banking and finance who insist that theirs has to be an interest-free system rarely start their argument from al Razi's fifth point (that *riba* is forbidden because God said so) but they often end on it. Much of their argument is, implicitly or explicitly, derived from al Razi's early analysis of why charging interest is forbidden (usually via Maududi's or Qureshi's reinterpretation), whether this debt is formally acknowledged or not.

It is on these lines, for example, that Presley and Sessions (1994: 586) argue that because 'All income should be commensurate with work effort' and 'money does not create a surplus value by itself' is why interest is forbidden in Islam. Some (e.g., Ayub 2002: 12) argue that money has zero opportunity cost and thus does not require any compensation for use; however, when combined with other resources, money becomes capital and so deserves 'just' compensation. That is, an investor in an enterprise requires compensation but a mere lender does not.

In a related vein, some more conservative scholars (usually those without formal training in modern economics) argue that Islam does not recognize the concept of time value of money, i.e., a dollar now is worth more to the beneficiary than a dollar a year from now. Maududi (1997: 176), for instance, explicitly rejected the concept and held that, in the case of a man borrowing 100 rupees from a money lender but returning 103 rupees a year later,[1] the extra 3 rupees 'represents the difference between the psychological (not economic) value of the present and future wealth … [because] the difference that has been pointed out between the psychological values of the present and the future is nothing but an illusion.' His argument is that people in an interest-based economy have been conditioned to selfishness and thus demand an 'excess' return for whatever help they may extend to one another. Following Maududi's lead, the eminent Islamic finance expert, Deobandi scholar, and Pakistani jurist M. Taqi Usmani (2002b: xvi), known for his relatively conservative interpretation of the *Shariah* with regards to Islamic finance,[2] stated flatly that 'in *Shari'ah* there is no concept of time value of money.' Thus, according to Fahim Khan (1991: 35)[3] of the Islamic Research and Training Institute in Saudi Arabia, in Islam 'the prohibition of interest which can be considered as sort of a denial of time value of money.'

The view that Islamic *fiqh* rejects the concept of time value of money across the board has, however, been hotly contested by others who cite classical sources to show that it was normal for the spot price of a commodity to be less than the deferred credit price, i.e., time had a monetary value (El-Gamal 2000: 12). Others, though, have argued that this not a universal application of the time value of money concept as it applies only to the sale/purchase of actual goods and 'not in the exchange of monetary values or loans or debts' (Ahmad and Hassan 2006: 85–86). This same view is supported by Ayub (2007: 440) who argues that time-value concepts apply only to tangible items which is why the spot (cash) price for a commodity is allowed to be lower than the future (deferred payment) price; these practices are referred to as *bay' mu'ajjal* and *bay' salam*.

The classical authorities for these views on the time value of money applying to tangible goods are quite impeccable. For example, Abraham Udovitch, one of the earliest and most widely respected Western scholars of Arab commerce and finance, quotes the great *alim* of the Hanafi *fiqh* Muhammad ibn Ahmad al-Sarakhshi (died 1090 CE) as stating unequivocally that 'A thing is sold on credit for a larger sum than it would be sold for in cash' (Udovitch 1970: 80). Similarly, an even earlier eminent Hanafi *alim*, Muhammad ibn al-Hasan al-Shaybani (died 805 CE), whose *Kitab al Asl* (*Book of Principles*) is one of the oldest extant Muslim legal compendiums, endorses the sale of goods on credit as an essential way of doing business (Udovitch 1970: 78). There is apparently no classical source that will allow the time value of money concept to be allowed for a purely financial transaction.

The usual grounds for not applying the concept of time value where a loan is concerned (i.e., where 'money' is the 'commodity' being 'purchased' or 'sold') is that money is viewed solely as a medium of exchange and so is seen as being 'barren' in the Aristotelian sense of not being able to reproduce itself. This view among Islamic scholars is akin to the Christian Scholastics', especially St. Thomas Aquinas' (1225–74) heavily Aristotle-influenced, view of the sole 'natural' function of money being a medium of exchange so charging interest would distort this function since more would be returned in the future than was borrowed – i.e., the standard used in exchange would be violated.[4]

Thus a shirt may cost you $10 if paid for on the spot or $11 if paid for next month but I may not lend you $10 to buy the shirt now on the condition that you pay me $10.50 next month. The inability to puzzle out why the one is permitted but not the other bothered Qureshi (1991/1967) who was intellectually honest enough to admit that the rationale for this was beyond his understanding. It is for exactly this reason that some contemporary Islamic economists have also concluded that the reason for allowing the one but not the other is knowable only to God.

Thus writing in 2000, over five decades after Qureshi's (1991/1967) 1945 path-breaking work first appeared, the prominent Islamic economist (and vocal critic of contemporary Islamic finance) Prof. Mahmoud Amin El-Gamal[5] voiced the same sentiments that al Razi had done many centuries earlier:

> The permissibility of the first [trade] and the prohibition of the second [usury/interest] are both quite clear and unequivocal. ... Why one is permitted while the other is forbidden can only be fully known by Allah and whomsoever he gave such knowledge. As a practical matter, we should know what is permitted and use it to our advantage, and what is forbidden and avoid it.
>
> (El-Gamal 2000: 12–13)

Why the ban on interest/usury?

Is there a reason for the banning of usury/interest more comprehensible to modern sensibilities than a simple 'God said so?' A possible reason for the prohibition on interest/usury in many pre-modern societies is that the ban could be viewed as an early attempt to deal with a missing-markets situation and/or a simple risk-amelioration mechanism.

Given the absence of effective financially-based insurance mechanisms in the pre-modern world, it is now a 'stylized fact' in the social, behavioral, and biological sciences that cooperation among small-group members is a highly desirable trait from the perspective of both individual and group survival. That is, whether the issue is the survival of an individual or a group, cooperation improves the odds of survival and success. Whether this cooperation takes the form of several hunters (in a hunter-gatherer band) joining forces to bring down a larger prey animal or a more successful hunter sharing his catch with a less successful one, cooperative groups are much more likely to survive than non-cooperative ones.

Starting from Axelrod and Hamilton's (1981) path-breaking paper 'The evolution of cooperation' and Axelrod's (1984) book of the same name, there have been literally thousands of academic papers written on why, how, and under what circumstances humans (and occasionally primates and other animals) cooperate to achieve a more desirable joint outcome than would be possible if each individual were to go it alone. Similarly, from a purely selfish and self-interested perspective, it is to an individual's benefit if others cooperate (share with her) but she does not have to cooperate (share with them). That is, she is a free-rider. This way she would gain the benefits from her own and others' resources without having to share her own resources with them. While this may be desirable from her own (selfish) perspective, it is clearly undesirable from that of other members of her group. Sigmund *et al.* (2002) provide an excellent and easily accessible survey of research showing that fairness is a universal norm across cultures, and excessively 'unfair' or 'selfish' (however defined) behavior elicits a strong emotional response (moral outrage) and a desire to punish the offender, often at substantial cost to the punishers. Furthermore, Sigmund *et al.* (2002: 85) argue that the evidence increasingly indicates that these emotions (a sense of morality and outrage at unfair behavior) were the result of 'millions of years of living in small groups, where it is hard to keep secrets.' Since cheaters threatened the survival of cooperators, the latter punished the former. This research on cooperation essentially confirms Wilson's (1993: 229) earlier argument in *The Moral Sense* that our 'moral senses are … to some important degree innate.' A key difference between this analysis and that of the 'cooperation as an individual/group survival mechanism' group is that Wilson posits a moral basis for various aspects of this cooperative endeavor, especially such aspects as equity, fairness, reciprocity, and so on. But how does this connect with Islam's 'ban' on usury and, according to many, interest?

It is precisely this moral facet, especially the equity aspect, that contemporary Muslim *ulema* and economists argue is the key reason why interest is forbidden in Islam: an interest-based financial system is inherently immoral because it is unjust and it is unjust because it is inequitable. The inherent inequity arises from the 'fact' that a standard debt contract, i.e., an interest-bearing loan, is treated by both *ulema* and Islamic economists as being a risk-free transaction from the lender's perspective since he will either receive his principal plus interest or, in case of a default, keep the collateral offered by the borrower: in short, heads the lender wins and tails the borrower loses. This then, for Islamic economists of the past and present, creates a vicious rentier class that thrives on the misery of the poor and so perpetuates a system designed to enrich the few at the expense of the many (Ayub 2007: 8).[6]

Of course, as the 2008 subprime financial crisis has shown, even AAA-rated collateral is often insufficient to ward off lender losses but this possibility is almost never considered by Islamic economists who consider a 'collateralized loan' to be a *de facto* 'risk-free asset.' Thus, since a collateralized loan *ipso facto* carries no risk of loss for the lender, 'one is entitled to profit only if one bears the risk of loss' (Ayub 2007: 438). A simple lender is not morally entitled to any return on her money. The financier is not subject to injustice or inequity by being forced to accept the riskier profit-and-loss-sharing arrangement since it is assumed that his greater wealth and resources make him far better able to handle adverse outcomes.

The Council of Islamic Ideology reports on *riba*, banking and interest

Along with researchers, academics and analysts writing in Western publications, many if not most contemporary *ulema* also hold that not only is Islam's ban on interest unchangeable, it is still needed as much today as it was when it was first imposed in the Seventh century CE. There is no distinction made between, say, a bank loan that carries a 10 per cent nominal annual interest rate and a moneylender charging 10 per cent a month: both transactions are equally morally repugnant and equally damaging to society. The fact that the bank loan has an effective annual interest rate of 10.47 per cent if compounded monthly while the moneylender's annual interest rate works out to 213.84 per cent is irrelevant to the *ulema* as there is no distinction made between usury and interest. The reports of Pakistan's official Council of Islamic Ideology (CII), among 'the most important documents on Islamic banking' (Algaoud and Lewis 2007: 45), reflect this: 'There is complete unanimity among all schools of thought in Islam that the term *riba* stands for interest in all its types and forms' (Council of Islamic Ideology 2006: 9). This understanding of *riba* also excludes indexing for inflation since that too would constitute an increase in the amount repaid and so would violate the CII's interpretation of the Koranic ban.

The direct precursor of the CII, the Advisory Council of Islamic Ideology, was established as an integral part of the Government of Pakistan and its role was specified under the military-created 1962 Constitution, the least religious of Pakistan's three official constitutions. This Advisory Council was given its current name and its importance reiterated by again giving it official status under the 1973 (i.e., present) Pakistani Constitution. As per Article 230 of the 1973 Constitution, the task of the CII is to advise the Pakistani Government 'as to whether a proposed law is or is not repugnant to the Injunctions of Islam' and 'to make recommendations as to the measures for bringing existing laws into conformity with the Injunctions of Islam and the stages by which such measures should be brought into effect.'[7]

Accordingly, since all three (1956, 1962 and 1973) of Pakistan's formal constitutions contain several explicit Islamic provisions, and all three mandate the abolishment of *riba*, in 1969 and 1980 the CII issued detailed reports on the Islamization of the Pakistani economy. The first formal request by the Government of Pakistan (GoP) to the CII on financial matters was in March 1963 when the GoP asked the CII to give its expert opinion on whether standard government debt issues (i.e., bonds that pay a fixed coupon – interest – rate) constituted the forbidden *riba* of the Koran and *Sunnah*. In January 1969 – just weeks before the fall of the tottering Islamic Modernist Ayub Khan regime that had asked the original question and its replacement by another military regime friendlier to traditional Islam – the CII gave its opinion that government coupon bonds were indeed *riba* and thus forbidden. The CII expanded on its original opinion in December 1969 when it found that all forms of interest-based transactions were forbidden in

Islam and that any positive rate of interest constituted *riba*; this finding was reiterated in the 1980 CII Report.

The CII ruling was a direct slap in the face to the former director of the Central Institute of Islamic Research (CIIR)[8] Prof. Fazlur Rahman. Rahman (1964), a member of the board of the CII, had argued that contemporary bank interest was not the forbidden *riba* and, indeed, that the *riba* referred to in the Koran went far beyond simple usury: it was a particularly heinous form of pre-Islamic moneylending where a debtor unable to make repayment would have his loan rolled over but at the cost of doubling (and then redoubling again if another time extension was granted) the original amount outstanding. Haque and Kamzi contend that this was not simply an academic article offering one scholar's opinion but 'an official statement of the Institute' in response to the initial government query in 1963 (Haque and Kazmi 1993: 939–940). As Rahman's article was published in the journal of the CIIR, it may have been an attempt by him (and the government?) to send a clear signal to the more orthodox of the CII's *ulema* as to what their answer *should* be. Furthermore, since Rahman's article was originally published in the Institute's Urdu journal, it was clearly aimed at a larger and more conservative audience than if it had been published in the English journal – it is highly doubtful that the majority of the members of the CII would have been able to read it in English.

The pressure, if there actually was any, on the CII was successful in that it issued its official opinion – that coupon bonds did constitute the forbidden *riba* – to the government after six years when Fazlur Rahman had left the country and a sick Ayub Khan was no longer really in charge of Pakistan. Despite the new military regime being more sympathetic to traditional Islam than Ayub's, the CII findings were studiously ignored by it and no change in either government or commercial practices ensued for over a decade. In 1977 Pakistan's third military regime, that of Gen. Zia ul Haq, and by far Pakistan's most overtly Islamist government, asked the CII to prepare a more detailed study of the issue. The CII established a panel of fifteen distinguished Pakistani bankers, economists, and *ulema* who submitted their report to it in February 1980. The CII, on the basis of this, issued its own report, *The Report on the Elimination of Interest from the Economy 1980*, later that year. The CII Report was a powerful restatement of Islamic orthodoxy, albeit with a small nod towards pragmatism in that it envisaged a phased transition to an Islamic system over five years or so, and it reaffirmed and greatly expanded upon the findings of the 1969 report.

The 1980 Report contained detailed instructions, including numerical examples, on how Islamic modes of financing were to be implemented in industrial and retail trade and agricultural financing, as well as instructions on how the Pakistani government could initiate the transition out of its interest-based foreign loans. The Report determined that the primary alternative to an interest-based financial system was profit-and-loss sharing (i.e., direct equity participation by the lender; exactly as advocated by Maududi and Qureshi) but that, as a secondary and less desirable alternative when direct equity participation was not feasible, banks could use leasing, 'normal rate of return' lending, hire-purchase, sale and buyback (i.e., *murabaha*), time-multiple counter-loans,[9] and so on. For longer-term financing, the CII proposed participation term certificates (essentially unsecured debentures with a variable rate of return). However, the CII determined that service charges and indexing loans and deposits to the inflation rate were not permissible under Islam.[10]

The CII Report, as discussed in detail in the following section, was an explicit negation not only of Islamic Modernism but of generations of Muslim usage and custom supported by the *fatwa* of respected *ulema* that held low rates of interest to be acceptable, non-usurious, and not *riba*. More conservative *ulema*, in the minority, of course disagreed with these findings and practices. Even though Pakistani Muslims are overwhelmingly of the Hanafi *madhab*, the CII Report was also a clear rejection of the financial clauses of the Ottoman Empire's attempt to turn classical Hanafi *fiqh* into a usable legal code: the *Mejelleh al Ahkam e Adliya* (the *Manual of the Rules of Courts*; commonly referred to simply as the *Mejelleh*) of 1876. The *Mejelleh* was the product of almost a decade of work by a large team of scholars (including highly respected *ulema*) and was the greatest Islamic *fiqh* endeavor for several centuries. It was the first successful attempt to render the until then haphazard, 'poorly classified,' 'difficult to use,' and scholastically exclusive Hanafi *fiqh* (hitherto accessible only to *ulema*) into a modern legal civil code comprehensible to the many instead of just to the learned few (Kamali 1999: 150). Since the *Mejelleh* was approved by the Ottoman Sultan Abdul Hamid II in his capacity as the *Amir ul Momineen e Khalifa ul Rasul e Rub al Alamin* (Commander of the Faithful, Deputy of the Prophet of the Lord of the Universe; i.e., the Sunni Caliph of Islam) and Indian Sunni Muslims had accepted the Ottoman Sultan as the Caliph, the CII in effect overruled the Caliph and his *ulema* in favor of their own interpretation. While the *Mejelleh* in Turkey did not outlast the Ottoman Sultanate and Caliphate, abolished by Mustafa Kemal Ataturk in 1922 and 1924, respectively, it continued as the legal code of the Ottoman successor states in the Middle East and North Africa for many decades afterwards.

The attitudes displayed in the 1980 CII Report were exactly what Sir Muhammad Iqbal, the ideological father of Muslim separatism in South Asia and lauded posthumously as Pakistan's national poet, had decried about the attitude of South Asian *ulema*. In his extremely influential *The Reconstruction of Religious Thought in Islam*, Iqbal had condemned the attitudes of many South Asian *ulema* towards their religion when he lamented the rigidly dogmatic and reflexively reactionary attitude of Islamic, especially South Asian, scholars to any change or innovation. Universally referred to as Allama[11] Iqbal in Pakistan now, Iqbal (2004/1934: 131) wrote that the 'intellectual attitudes' of the *ulema* 'has reduced the Law of Islam practically to a state of immobility.' *Bidah* (heretical innovation) is of course a sin in Islam but the orthodox *ulema* seemed to hold that any innovation was heretical.[12] Earlier, Iqbal (1930) in his Presidential Address to the annual meeting of the All-India Muslim League in 1930 had cited approvingly the fact that Muslim princely states in India did not restrict modern banking or attempt to impose some sort of 'Islamic' concept of interest-free financial transactions.

Rigidly dogmatic views such as the *ulema*'s were the source of Evelyn Baring (Lord Cromer)'s, (in)famous proclamation on Islam's opposition to change and innovation. Baring, an influential Orientalist scholar who also served as the *de facto* British ruler of Egypt from 1883 to 1907, observed that 'it should never be forgotten that Islam cannot be reformed; that is to say, reformed Islam is Islam no longer; it is something else' (Baring 1908: 229). While Lord Cromer's observation may be disregarded by some as High Orientalism at its worst, it is difficult to so cavalierly dismiss the same rueful lament from Iqbal, a man almost universally acknowledged as 'India's most important Muslim thinker' of the Twentieth century CE (Devji 2013: 110),

The CII's powerful counterblast against Islamic modernism and the overtly pragmatic views of its leading advocates such as Fazlur Rahman was not an isolated instance of the counterattack of Islamic orthodoxy. The subsequent development of Islamic banking and finance globally, or at least its apparent development as Chapter Six will show, was very much along the lines set out by the CII reports.

Historical practices of Islamic finance

Contrary to what many may think, the Islamic Modernists were not actually advocating a real rethinking of historical Islamic financial practices. Quite the opposite is true as it was actually the Maximalists who were introducing innovation in historical practice. Surprising as it may seem, the preoccupation with ensuring an 'interest-free' banking environment for Muslims is mainly a post-World War II phenomenon. Traditionally, in Islamic societies financiers (and not just village moneylenders) operated on an explicitly interest-based basis and financial transactions were never characterized by the predominance of direct-equity participation.

Jennings (1973: 184, 187), after analyzing Seventeenth century CE Ottoman *Shariah* court records from the town of Kayseri, concludes that interest rates below 20 per cent 'were accepted by the entire religious community as in accordance with the *Shariah*' and offering collateral or third-party guarantees for loans was also common practice. Similarly, Gibb and Bowen (1960/1950: 301) in their study of Eighteenth century CE Egypt find that trade between it and the Barbary States was normally financed at rates varying from 7–12 per cent per annum and 'that to take interest over 10 per cent was regarded as usurious.' More recent research concurs in the assessment that it was not charging interest that was condemned, but usury. In Sixteenth century CE Ottoman Turkey it was only charging rates above the normal 10–20 per cent that invited community censure and all the financiers and moneylenders in

Aleppo, then a major trading center, were Muslim (Faroqhi 1997: 492–493). Indeed, Mehmet Ebusuud Efendi (1490–1574), the Ottoman Empire's *Shaikh ul Islam* (the senior-most Islamic cleric of the Ottoman Empire), went so far as to issue a *fatwa* decreeing the permissibility, on purely pragmatic grounds, of interest-based lending for Islamic *auqaf* (charitable foundations) (Faroqhi 1997: 492).

Interest-based lending continued unhindered in the Muslim Middle East for centuries after Mehmet Efendi's ruling. In 1840 the cash-strapped Ottoman Empire began paying its bills half in cash and half in what were, in effect, treasury notes paying 12.5 per cent annually; these proved so popular among the finance houses and the public that the Ottoman government was able to reduce the interest rate to 10 per cent in 1843 and 6 per cent by 1844 (Cizakca 1996: 187–189). Four decades later, the 1887 Ottoman '*murabaha* ordinance,' a part of the *Mejelleh*, set the maximum interest rate at 9 per cent (Kuran 2004: 310).[13]

Nonetheless there remained a tension between praxis and religious orthodoxy, and some pious Muslims shied away from such professions even if on occasion they were clients (Gibb and Bowen 1960/1950: 301). Kinalizade Ali Efendi (1510–72), an influential Ottoman political theorist and Islamic moralist (Uysal 2007) and contemporary of Mehmet Ebusuud Efendi, in his trifold (noble, neutral, inferior) categorization of professions placed 'usury and the entertainment professions' firmly in the 'inferior' category but conceded that 'for the good order of the world, all these professions are necessary' (Inalcik 1995: 44–45). The Ottoman Empire's *ulema* implemented the Sultan-Caliph's *firmans* (imperial decrees) regarding finance but apparently there was always doubt among some, the ultra-orthodox, as to the true validity of the Sultan's *firmans* (imperial decrees) since 'it was in the form of a legal trick that usury received legislative recognition by the Caliphs of Turkey, as the commentator of Dur i Mukhtar informs us' (Khan 1929: 244). They however consoled themselves with the:

> [C]omforting theory [that it was] the duty of the judges [i.e., *ulema* acting as *qadis* – judges] to carry out the law laid down by the Sultan. Beyond this they kept a discreet silence – discreet because the implication is plain that the Sultan, if he thinks it necessary in the public interest, can pass a law which violates the law of the Koran, if not in form … certainly in effect and intention.
>
> (Khan 1929: 244)[14]

This is of course referring to a literalist interpretation of *riba*. After the Eighteenth century CE it appears that the main bankers and financiers in the Eastern Middle East were 'Jewish and Christian bankers … Greeks also engaged in the money business [but] it was only in the Turkish period that they were joined by Armenians' (Gaudefroy-Demombynes 1968/1950: 191).[15] This was probably because these non-Muslim minorities were more willing to adopt the new financial techniques and practices introduced by Europeans than their Muslim counterparts, who had hitherto enjoyed a more privileged position in the now-decaying Ottoman Empire. Even Ottoman officials issuing the treasury notes in the 1840s were concerned about their religious implication and some fretted that they 'have the perpetual harm of usury' (quoted in Cizakca 1996: 189); these notes were eventually withdrawn in 1851, though probably for fiscal and not religious reasons.

The situation was very different in South Asia. Whereas Muslims were a large majority of the population in the Asian and North African parts of the Ottoman Empire, in South Asia Muslims constituted a (sometimes ruling) minority of the population. It appears that Muslims were usually absent from most finance-related fields (i.e., mainly moneylending) until the Twentieth century CE. Tripathi, in his encyclopedic *Oxford History of Indian Business* (2004), mentions only three (very small) Muslim groups, Khoja, Bohra, and Memon traders, as being involved in banking or finance, which was an overwhelmingly Hindu and British preserve. However, Tripathi (2004: 21) adds 'they were converts from Hindu trading castes and still retained some of their pre-conversion customs and trading practices including usury.' Chandavarkar (2003: 56) concurs in the assessment that Khojas and Bohras, who were 'mere converts and sometimes persecuted as heretics' by the orthodox Shia and Sunni *ulema*, 'applied local usages regarding usury' rather than 'the constraints [of] orthodox Islamic law' and flourished as traders and moneylenders.

Perhaps it is because Muslims were a minority (albeit a large one) in South Asia, and because Indian *ulema* felt that their religion was under constant threat from the British colonial rulers and the Hindu majority, explains both the rise of contemporary Islamic economics there and Pal's observation regarding the orthodox rigidity of South Asian *ulema* that infuriated Iqbal. Pal (2006: 86) wrote that South Asian '*ulema* are ultra-traditionalist and much more conservative than the conservative *ulema* in the Middle East' and condemn un-Islamic practices such as *riba* even more vociferously and unqualifiedly than do their Middle Eastern counterparts. Accordingly, explicitly interest-based finance was probably less acceptable for South Asian Muslims than it was for many Muslims in the Middle East.

Making the new old again

Given the earlier discussion of pre-modern societies, it should also be obvious that the prohibition of interest/usury in all pre-modern, and not just Muslim, societies is a simple and effective risk-mitigation mechanism for small borrowers that cannot afford the down-side risk inherent in financial transactions. Similarly, as societies developed economically and became more complex and sophisticated, such a risk-mitigation mechanism was dispensed with as insurance markets developed and average income increased.

By adhering to a literal interpretation of *riba*, many of the current *ulema* of Islam – unlike their Christian and Jewish counterparts – have rolled back centuries of Muslim financial practices and in effect have invented a new orthodoxy that purports to harken back to a purer form of Islamic finance. Instead of Muslim religious law coming into alignment with actual practice, as happened over the centuries with Christian and Jewish interpretations of the distinction between usury and interest, actual practice was forced into (apparent) conformity with what appears to be a very strict interpretation of divine command.

So what then is the preferred form of Islamic finance? How is an interest-free financial system supposed to operate? And does the practice of Islamic finance actually follow its own rules? Or does praxis differ from theory? Since a fully collateralized, interest-based loan is apparently not permissible, how is business to obtain its essential credit? How is an Islamic bank supposed to operate?

Notes

1 This example is itself illustrating. It is extremely doubtful that any moneylender in history has ever charged a 3 per cent annual interest rate in the normal course of business but it suits Maududi's purpose to show that even such a low rate is moneylending and so by definition unjust, exploitative, and hence forbidden.

2 See Chapter Six of this work for his ruling on *sukuk*, Islamic bonds, for an example of his relative conservatism.

3 Fahim Khan, PhD in Economics from Boston University in the USA, is one of the few Islamic economists who hold such a view. He has had a long affiliation with the Islamic Research and Training Institute (IRTI), serving as Head of Research and then Director, of the Islamic Development Bank, Saudi Arabia. The Institute is the best funded and probably the largest and most influential Islamic banking and finance (IBF) 'think tank' in the world. It promotes a fairly restrictive version of IBF and is the research wing of the Islamic Development Bank, the regional multilateral development agency for the Muslim world, akin to the Asian Development Bank or the Inter-American Development Bank.

4 See Ghazanfar 2003 and Saeed 1996 for more on the affinity between the medieval Scholastic and contemporary Islamic view of the nature and function of money, and what constitutes usury.

5 El-Gamal, who has a PhD in economics from Northwestern University and an MS in statistics from Stanford University, is Professor of Economics, Statistics and Islamic Finance and Management at Rice University. In an interesting coincidence, like Qureshi he also served a stint at the International Monetary Fund in Washington, DC.

6 It is not simply religious scholars untrained in anything other than classical *fiqh* or semi-literate laypersons wholly ignorant of a century plus of modern economic theory who hold such patently medieval views of debt-based finance. In 2007, Ayub, with graduate degrees in modern/Western economics, was Director of Training, Development and Shariah Aspects for the Institute of Islamic Banking and Insurance in London, the oldest and most important training and research institute on Islamic finance in the West. Previously he was a Senior Research Economist at the State (i.e., central) Bank of Pakistan and a senior research associate on the Commission on the Transformation of the Financial System established by the Bank in

1999 to map out the complete transformation of Pakistan's financial system along Islamic lines; however, the *Shariat* Appellate Bench of the Supreme Court decision to reconsider its 1999 ruling in 2002 rendered this work moot (see Chapter Seven for more details). Of course, after the 2008 financial crisis, there are probably many in the West as well who would agree with the contention that modern finance is nothing but a system that enriches the few at the expense of the many. In any case, the 2008 financial crisis was not caused by the standard debt contract *per se.*

7 Details on the CII are available from its website, www.cii.gov.pk/aboutcii.aspx.

8 The Advisory Council of Islamic Ideology (CII) and the Central Institute of Islamic Research (CIIR) were both established under the 1956 Constitution and reaffirmed by the 1962 Constitution. The main task of the CII was to assist the government in determining whether or not legislation was in conformity with Islam, while the CIIR was to act as a pure research institute and so assist the CII in its deliberations. In 1980 the CIIR was subsumed into the International Islamic University in Islamabad, Pakistan, as its Islamic Research Institute.

9 Time-multiple counter-loans is a theoretical concept developed by Shaikh Mahmud Ahmad, another early Islamic economist and advocate of interest-free banking, in the early 1960s, as a way of getting around the key role played by interest in a modern financial system. Suppose a bank customer wants a loan of $100,000 for one year. In order to obtain this loan she would agree to deposit $10,000 at the bank for a period of ten years or $20,000 for five years or some such combination that totaled 100,000. This way, Ahmad argued, there was no need for interest to be charged since the time-multiple of the monetary amounts exchanged was equal. If the customer did not have, say, $10,000 to deposit, the bank would lend her $110,000 but she would only withdraw $100,000 of it. The remaining funds would stay as her 'loan' to the bank. Presumably if the customer wanted $500,000 for five years, she would have to deposit $100,000 for 25 years or some such combination. To the best of my knowledge, for reasons that are immediately obvious, no Islamic bank has ever actually implemented such a proposal, not even on a limited trial basis. The State (central) Bank of Pakistan rejected his proposal outright when Ahmad presented it to a Bank committee on Islamic finance in the late 1970s. Some advocates of Islamic banking and finance, however, keep proposing it as an Islamic 'alternative' to interest-based finance despite the fact that even ostensibly fully Islamic banks have refused to consider it even in principle.

10 The preceding details on the activities of the CII are drawn from Council of Islamic Ideology 2006, which includes the 1980 Report in its entirety, as well as excerpts from the 1969 Report and various State Bank of Pakistan, the central bank, directives through 1985 to implement the transition.

11 *Allama* is an honorific that denotes that the person has attained the highest level of Islamic knowledge and scholarship.

12 Iqbal was commenting on a very longstanding view in Sunni Islam that 'the Gates of *Ijtihad*' are closed. That is, no further discussion, analysis or reinterpretation of the Koran and *fiqh* is needed or, indeed, possible. *Ijtihad*, one of the four sources of Islamic jurisprudence along with the Koran, *hadith*, and *qiyas* (deduction from analogy) derives from the same root as *jihad* or struggle. It is the process by which scholars, after a thorough study of the Koran and *Sunnah*, arrive at an independent decision as to whether or not an act or policy is permissible. However, as the main Islamic *madhabs* formalized their teachings and succeeding Muslim generations became further removed from the first three that would have known the Prophet personally, the consensus grew by the early tenth century CE that Muslim jurisprudence's 'creative force was now spent and exhausted [and] the right of *ijtihad* was replaced by the duty of *taqlid* or "imitation"' (Coulson 2007/1964: 80). That is, an extreme form of *stare decisis* had become the norm in Islamic societies. Contrary to the views of some, mainly Western, Muslims about the possibility of

an *ijtihad* by the mass of ordinary Muslims, Islamic tradition holds that a *mujtahid*, one capable of performing *ijtihad*, had to be an acknowledged *alim* of great learning and probity who had devoted his life to the study of the Koran, the *hadith*, classical Arabic, and *fiqh*.

13 Such an explicitly stated fixed interest rate would now be anathema for most present-day *ulema* and Islamic bankers.

14 Although he confusingly and quite irritatingly does not contextualize it in his article, Khan (1929) is referring to the extensive discussion by the eminent Hanafi *alim* Muhammad Amin Ibn Abidin (1783–1836 CE, the chief *alim* of Damascus and so probably the most important Muslim cleric in Ottoman Syria) in his authoritative commentary on earlier works of Hanafi *fiqh* (*Dur i Mukhtar*, 'The Choicest Pearls') regarding the various legal opinions issued on the permissibility of overtly *ribawi* (*riba*-based) contracts. Abidin is particularly important in South Asia, especially among non-Deobandi *ulema*, where he is usually referred to as Abidin al Shami (Abidin the Syrian).

15 See Kuran 2004 and Warde 2000, esp. pp. 48–50, for more details on the acceptance and prevalence of *de facto* interest-based transactions in Muslim societies and the various stratagems employed to disguise interest; Warde also details how some of these stratagems were used by medieval Europeans to get around the Catholic Church's ban on usury.

6 The nuts and bolts of Islamic banking worldwide

The purpose of this chapter is to lay out the preferred form of Islamic finance and compare it to how Islamic banking and finance (IBF) is actually carried out both in Pakistan and worldwide. Accordingly, it will look at the range and type of financial products offered, the impact of information asymmetry, adverse selection and moral hazard on the functioning of Islamic banking and finance institutions, the key differences between the more liberal Malaysian and more restrictive Gulf/Pakistani forms of Islamic finance, and whether or not Islamic banking lives up to its claims.

The preferred form of Islamic finance

The form that IBF is supposed to take was succinctly summarized by a publication of the Islamic Research and Training Institute of the Islamic Development Bank as follows:

> The most important feature of Islamic banking is that it promotes risk sharing between the provider of funds (investor) on the one hand and both the financial intermediary (the bank) and the user of funds (the entrepreneur) on the other hand. … In conventional banking, all this risk is borne in principle by the entrepreneur.
>
> (Iqbal *et al.* 1998: 15–16)

That is, venture capitalism. Islamic financiers should take a direct equity stake in suitable ventures. In short then, 'In Islam, one does not lend to make money, and one does not borrow to finance business' (El-Gamal 2000: 33).

So the preferred form of Islamic finance is equity participation in which the financier takes a direct stake in the project and shares the same risk as the initiator of the project (who may provide only expertise and no actual monetary investment). The consensus among the *ulema* is that the sharing of profits/losses among the participants should be roughly commensurate with their investment of capital and/or time, and that no monetary losses can be charged to someone who has contributed only his expertise/time (see e.g., Usmani 2002: 7–10). If the venture succeeds, the financial investor receives a larger return than a predetermined interest rate would allow (Usmani 2002: xiv) as profits and losses are shared in a pre-decided ratio. Equity finance, as originally argued by Maududi (1997: 181) during the early 1950s in the modern IBF context, would make more financial resources available to small businesses, make it more difficult to accrue 'unearned' income, and generally promote an ethos of equity and justice in society since all deserving ventures would be financed, not just the ones with excellent collateral or well established credit histories.

This line of reasoning is still strongly argued by most advocates of IBF who hold that such a 'risk-sharing' financial system would lead to greater equity, allocative efficiency, financial system stability, and GDP growth (see e.g., Iqbal and Molyneux 2005: 31–34).[1] For its most partisan advocates, an equity-participation-based Islamic system, once fully implemented, would automatically give us a world where 'no inflation, no unemployment, no exploitation and no poverty exist' (Ahmad El Nagar, quoted in Warde 2000: 21).[2] In a more sober vein, early IBF advocates envisaged 'Islamic banks as predominantly risk-taking institutions committed to long-term productive investment on a partnership or equity basis' (Mills and Presley 1999: 51) since profit-and-loss sharing (i.e., equity participation) 'is at the core of Islamic banking' (Zaher and Hassan 2001: 161). Thus, exactly as advocated by Maududi several decades earlier, Islamic banks are supposed to act as venture capital providers, investing in worthy firms and financing promising ideas in exchange for a share of the profits, rather than lending on the basis of cash-flow and collateral, and forcing firms into liquidation to recover loans that had gone bad through no fault of the borrower.

Islamic banking and finance: critics and defenders

As discussed in more detail in this chapter, virtually every advocate of IBF has argued for the immense superiority of equity participation over the standard, interest-based debt contract that forms the backbone of conventional finance worldwide. The more enthusiastic of its advocates argue that equity participation as the basic of finance is a new paradigm that will truly revolutionize the way financial markets work and help usher in an era of greater equity, efficiency, and economic justice. Nonetheless, contemporary IBF practices have not been without their critics (e.g. El-Gamal 2006; Kuran 2004; Zaman 2002; see Nomani 2006 for an excellent summary of the debate) who often charge that IBF is merely a change of terminology (e.g., substituting 'profit rate' or 'markup rate' for 'interest rate') in what is essentially a standard debt contract. This, they argue, gives IBF a *de jure* distinction that is without a *de facto* difference.

One of the earliest and severest critics of contemporary IBF has been the Turkish-American economist Timur Kuran (2004, 1993).[3] Kuran, in his voluminous work on the subject, has argued that in its Twentieth century CE incarnation IBF arose in colonial India and was part of a broader movement designed to replace Western (i.e., Christian) leadership and structures in all areas of Muslim life. In other words, as discussed extensively in Chapter Four, the aim of Islamic economics was not to provide a viable alternative to conventional economics but to strengthen a threatened Islamic identity: to prevent the creation of a generation of 'partial Muslims,' in Maududi's phrase. The Kuran thesis flowing directly from this is that 'Islamic economics was primarily a vehicle for reasserting the primacy of Islam and secondarily a vehicle for radical economic change' (Kuran 2004: 5) and 'Islamic economics' would help counter the danger that 'Westernization was weakening the control that religion [Islam] exerted on personal worldviews and interpersonal relationships' (Kuran 2004: 88).

The current secured, interest-based debt contract that is the basis of conventional banking evolved over centuries of operation in an asymmetric information environment. Therefore Islamic banks, which also operate in an asymmetric information environment, would inevitably be 'sticking so closely to the techniques of conventional banking' that they would be indistinguishable from the latter (Kuran 1993: 311). Since in this case form does follow function, there should be nothing surprising in Islamic banking being virtually indistinguishable from conventional banking once one accounts for the completely different – classical Arabic instead of Western – terminology favored by IBF advocates.

A counter to the Kuran thesis was offered by Ahmad (1993: 59), a leading early advocate of IBF, who argued that the apparent similarity between conventional and Islamic banking was simply a phase in the transition away from conventional banking as IBF's clients had to be offered products they were immediately familiar with, and that 'evidence suggests that the significance of *murabaha* is declining in the overall financing operations of Islamic Banks.'[4] Ahmad (1993) was writing well over a decade after the establishment of major Islamic banks in many parts of the world (e.g., United Arab Emirates 1975, Saudi Arabia 1978, Pakistan 1981, and Iran and Malaysia 1983) but many quite justifiably still viewed IBF as being a relatively new financial innovation that would take time to wean its clientele away from conventional banking practices.

A decade after Ahmad, IBF's advocates were still defending it from the same charges. Yousef (2004: 63–64) while conceding the 'predominance' of what he terms the '*murabaha* syndrome,' i.e., Islamic banks closely mimicking conventional banking practices, holds that this does not provide valid grounds for arguing against IBF as an alternative to conventional finance since this criticism has been severely overplayed and merely serves as a convenient tool to unfairly condemn all of IBF outright.

So which is it? Is the Kuran thesis a valid criticism of IBF, or is Ahmad correct in arguing that Islamic banks are transitioning away from mimicking conventional banks? A legitimate question to ask, therefore, is what are the *desired* characteristics of an Islamic banking system and do *actual* IBF practices differ from their desired characteristics to the extent that contemporary IBF is functionally indistinguishable from conventional banking?

It seems that almost four decades after IBF was first introduced as a major financial innovation, the Kuran thesis is still a valid characterization of IBF. Current IBF practice conforms in almost all key respects to the conventional banking norm and IBF practice does not resemble what its advocates say IBF is supposed to be. Thus Ahmad's (1993) defense of IBF is increasingly untenable and unconvincing, and even some of IBF's staunchest advocates condemn how it is currently practiced. Consequently, as this chapter will show, the '*murabaha* syndrome' is a valid charge to levy against IBF.

So what is IBF supposed to look like?

Making banking 'Islamic'

As discussed in more detail in Chapter Four, the contemporary *ulema* of the various schools of Islamic *fiqh* (law/jurisprudence) have concluded that, along with *riba*, all practicing Muslims must also avoid financial transactions that involve *gharar* (uncertainty; i.e., where the outcome is extremely uncertain), *maysir* (outright gambling), and *haram* (religiously forbidden) products. Engaging in trade is encouraged but, ideally, profits must be the result of assuming a proportionate share of the risk involved in the transaction by taking an equity stake in the business venture; profits must not be earned 'risk-free' by making a collateralized loan.

Whereas Maududi (1997), Qureshi (1991/1967) and others defined Islamic finance in broadly religious terms with some limited, at most, attempts at analyzing its implementability, others have attempted a more practical – read 'implementable' – definition. For example, El-Hawary *et al.* (2004: 5) defined IBF as a system that adheres to the following four principles.

- *Risk-sharing*: the terms of financial transactions need to reflect a symmetrical risk/return distribution for its participants; no-one may benefit disproportionately to the risk s/he takes.
- *Materiality*: all financial transaction must have 'material finality,' i.e., be directly linked to a real underlying economic transaction; thus options and most other derivatives are banned.
- *No exploitation*: neither party to the transaction should be exploited.
- *No financing of sinful activities*: transaction cannot be used to produce goods banned by the Koran (e.g., alcohol, pork products, gambling).

Thus the current relatively strict interpretation of the *hadith* relating to trade and commercial transactions would ban not only speculative financial transactions such as options and futures but also, for example, hedging by forward sale, interest-rate swaps, and any transaction involving items not physically in the possession of the seller (e.g., short sales) and all other forms of derivatives, i.e., financial securities that have no underlying 'real' transaction (see Venardos 2005 and Usmani 2002 for more details). Warde (2000: 140–141) takes a more nuanced approach to derivatives and other financial instruments but generally considers them to be violating Islamic norms. Similarly, if a strict Maximalist interpretation is followed, activities such as bill discounting and government debt issue with a fixed coupon rate (the basis of modern open market operations by central banks and financing the national debt), inflation indexing, securitized debt obligations, and foreign exchange dealings would also be prohibited unless cumbersome intervening steps reminiscent of the medieval *contractum trinius* are undertaken.[5]

It should now be apparent that IBF is more than just the 'interest-free' banking that some commonly think it to be. However, since virtually all financial instruments involve the interest rate in some way or form, 'interest-free' operations have become the *sine qua non* for any bank calling itself 'Islamic.' How then is IBF actually carried out and how 'interest-free' are its operations?

Islamic banking in theory

At its most basic, there are only two ways to finance any commercial venture if one's own resources are insufficient for the task: take on a partner or borrow money. The advocates of IBF contend, as discussed in Chapters Four and Five, that equity finance is preferable to interest-based debt finance because if the venture fails, the borrower does not bear the entire cost alone or lose the collateral. Similarly, if the venture is a success, the financier gets a larger share of the profits for herself.

However, equity participation is not the sole means of Islamic financing available. Islamic banking may be done on the basis of something other than equity participation. There are actually two types of IBF: profit-and-loss sharing (PLS) and non-profit-and-loss sharing (non-PLS) (Sundarajan and Errico 2002: 20). Non-PLS is now more commonly referred to as 'trade-based financing' since the non-PLS designation does carry a somewhat pejorative connotation of being less 'Islamic' than its alternative. Thus the financier may choose to be a direct participant in the venture (a direct equity stake or a partnership) and share in the enterprise's profits or losses (PLS), or she may choose to be non-participatory (non-PLS) and not take an equity stake, and be content with a potentially lower return. Obviously the non-PLS would also have a lower down-side risk (i.e., lower chance of making a loss) but this aspect is almost never mentioned in the literature.

Virtually every IBF advocate argues that equity participation is the desirable alternative, and non-participatory finance is acceptable (theoretically at least) only as an interim measure or for situations where participatory finance is clearly unsuitable, such as very small or personal consumption loans (Usmani 2002b: 42; see also Kuran 2004; Ayub 2002; Sundarajan and Errico 2002; Zaher and Hassan 2001, and especially Warde 2010 and 2000). Striking a dissenting note, El-Gamal (2000: 15) argues that there is no Koranic justification for preferring one permissible mode of financing over another; the perceived religious desirability of one over the other arises out of the personal inclinations of the observer.

The main participatory and non-participatory forms of Islamic financing are as follows.

Main participatory forms:

- *mudaraba*: a 'sleeping' partner contributes capital and another expertise/knowledge;
- *musharaka*: the financier takes a direct stake in the venture;
- *sukuk*: an asset-based bond.

Main non-participatory or trade-based forms:

- *murabaha*: 'markup' or cost-plus sale;
- *ijara*: lease;
- *bai salam/istisna*: deferred delivery of goods;
- *bai muajjal*: deferred payment, credit sale;
- *jo'alah*: service fee;
- *qard-e-hasana*: a charitable, interest-free loan payable when and if able.

Box 6.1 summarizes these major Islamic financing modes. While there are other forms possible, these constitute the overwhelming majority of Islamic financing forms. In fact, four forms of financing effectively constitute IBF, as is shown by an analysis of the 1994–96 financing patterns of the then ten largest Islamic Banks: *ijara*, *mudaraba*, *murabaha*, and *musharaka* accounted for over 87 per cent of all financing provided.[6]

Box 6.1 Major Islamic financing modes

Main forms of participatory (profit-and-loss sharing) Islamic finance

- ***Mudaraba***: 'trustee finance contract' or passive partnership; one party provides funds while the other provides expertise and management; profits accrued are shared on a pre-agreed basis; losses are borne only by capital provider.
- ***Musharaka***: 'equity participation contract' providing for profit/loss sharing in the joint business; bank provides a portion of the total funds and all partners may participate in management; profits are distributed in pre-agreed ratios but losses are borne strictly in proportion to respective capital contributions. A 'declining *musharaka*' may be used for installment purchase of, for example, a house with the buyer paying *pro rata* 'rent' to the financer.
- ***Sukuk***: Islamic bonds, generally paying a 'Libor + *x* per cent' rate but may have a fixed rate if backed by *ijara* or *murabaha* transactions; must

be asset-backed and *Shariah*-compliant; sometimes also referred to as *musharaka* term finance certificates, with a nominal equity component.

- **Direct equity investment**: for example, purchasing shares on the open market.

Main forms of non-participatory (non-profit-and-loss sharing) or trade-based Islamic finance

- ***Murabaha***: markup sale, i.e., a sale on mutually agreed profit; client requests the bank to purchase an item for her; bank resells it to the client for a predetermined ('marked up') price usually paid in installments.
- ***Ijara/ijara wal iqtina***: lease/lease purchase.
- ***Bai salam*** (including ***istisna***): deferred delivery purchase; only items that can be fully specified in terms of quantity, quality, attributes, etc., are eligible; monetary instruments are specifically excluded.
- ***Bai muajjal***: deferred payment/credit sale, also known as *Murabaha muajjal*, where seller informs buyer of cost, selling price and the final payment date (may be installment or lump sum); spot price may be lower than deferred payment price.
- ***Musawamah***: normal market sale with no cost disclosure obligation.
- ***Jo'alah***: service charge, consultancy fee, placement fee, etc.
- ***Qard-e-hasana***: zero-interest beneficience loans; repaid when/if able.

El-Gamal (2000); Ayub (2002); Sundarajan and Errico (2002). See Ayub (2002) or Usmani (2002b) for extensive discussion of these and other forms of Islamic finance.

Islamic banking in practice

Given the extensive critique by IBF advocates of debt-based/interest-based financing that constitutes the overwhelming majority of conventional finance, one would expect equity participation/direct investing to dominate the trillion-dollar IBF market. Unsurprisingly, this is not the case. *Murabaha* and *ijara* predominate.

So how exactly does a *murabaha* operate? Say a firm needs to upgrade its existing machinery. It would approach an Islamic bank to obtain the machinery on its behalf, with a concomitant agreement to purchase the machinery on a marked-up basis from the bank. If the bank's purchase price was $100,000, it might resell the machinery to the firm for $110,000, payable in, say, twelve equal monthly installments. The bank retains ownership until the last installment is paid and so the bank's position is fully secured. This is accepted as fully *Shariah*-compliant by many authorities (e.g., Usmani 2002b: 52–54; Warde 2000: 133) because the agreement is based on a real transaction and the rate of cost-plus or markup is (theoretically) not a function of the time taken to repay the bank (Mills and Presley 1999: 17). The *murabaha* is Islamically permissible since the bank has had actual ownership of the machinery and so has borne some risk; a simple loan for $100,000 at 10 per cent interest, secured by the machinery, is not.

The *murabaha* can also be used for personal loans. In that case it is usually referred to as a 'reverse *murabaha*' or '*tawarruq*' (converting to silver, i.e., monetizing). For example, many Saudi banks keep a stock of gold or some other commodity on hand for personal loans (UNCTAD 2006: 9). The bank 'sells' these to a customer for, say, 25,000 riyals with payment to be made monthly over one year; the customer then immediately 'sells' the gold back to the bank or to a dealer for, say, 23,000 riyals spot cash. It is, however, a relatively cumbersome process to sell to a dealer so it is usual for the customer to appoint the bank her sales agent, and it is now very rare for any actual commodity to ever change hands; all that changes hands is papers being signed and then handed back. This is technically a *Shariah*-compliant transaction despite the 8.7 per cent implicit annual interest rate, although more conservative scholars tend to frown upon it as they consider it an obvious *hiyal* (ruse or legal stratagem) designed to get around the letter of the ban on *riba* (Warde 2010: 144). The State Bank of Pakistan, Pakistan's central bank, requires prior approval from it before any Pakistani Islamic bank can carry out a *tawarruq* transaction (SBP 2008b). To counter the obvious violation of the spirit of the *riba* ban here, some Islamic financial regulatory agencies require that a legitimate *tawarruq* must involve four parties: two additional commodity brokers in addition to the customer and the financier (Warde 2010: 144).

The 'reverse *murabaha*' or *tawarruq* is also used as a basis for issuing *Shariah*-compliant credit cards, for example, by the Saudi British Bank. If the outstanding balance is paid in full no *tawarruq* transaction takes place, but if the balance is not fully retired then the bank 'sells' the purchased product to the customer for higher price at a predetermined markup rate (Saudi British Bank n.d.). It is also used occasionally to finance home purchases, for example, by the Malaysian Bank Islam (Bank Islam n.d.), although Islamic mortgages are more usually done on a declining *musharaka* basis (see later in this chapter for details). In this case, since the customer actually wants the house, 'material finality' does obviously exist and there is no *hiyal* involved but the Bank Islam also issues *tawarruq*-based credit cards.

These sort of *hiyal* are nothing new to Islamic finance. Far from being a recent innovation to make Islamic finance functionally indistinguishable from conventional finance, as Prof. Noel Coulson[7] has pointed out, these are actually centuries-old practices. Coulson argues that even if explicitly interest-based transactions were not utilized by financiers or borrowers, all schools of Islamic *fiqh* from the very beginning of Islam availed such *hiyal* extensively as legal stratagems 'designed to achieve purposes fundamentally contrary to the spirit of the Shari'a' (Coulson 2007/1964: 139).

However, there do appear, at first glance, to be some exceptions to this preponderance of non-PLS financing. Some Islamic banks, for instance in Sudan and Kuwait, apparently have a substantially larger share of their assets in PLS transactions. A closer examination shows that they, too, fall far short of the participatory ideal.

In Sudan between 1998 and 2002, the shares of *musharaka* and *mudaraba* in total financing averaged 29.8 and 4.6 per cent, respectively, versus 43.5 per cent for *murabaha* (Ibrahim 2006: 60); however the impetus for this was not a desire for greater Islamic financial authenticity but rather Sudanese 'government pressure' that forced the banks to reduce non-PLS lending (Stiansen 2004: 160). Furthermore, the Sudanese Islamic banks were not providing PLS finance on truly objective criteria – assessing the projects' social desirability or business plan – but the banks' 'major shareholder and the members of the board(s) of directors [had] monopolised the banks' available capital resources' (Stiansen 2004: 163–164). So in effect you have here a 'house bank' taking an equity stake in a 'house company' – an outcome hardly true to the PLS spirit advocated by the proponents of Islamic banking.

The Kuwait Finance House (KFH), the second largest bank in Kuwait and established by royal decree in 1977, was exempted from direct Central Bank regulation for much of its history. It could therefore invest in residential and commercial property and firms (e.g., automobile dealerships) outright, participate directly in *musharaka* financing of corporations (now done through wholly owned subsidiaries), and generally act more like a holding company than a bank. In this way the KFH was able to avoid some of the risk issues involved with being a financing partner with limited managerial decision-making powers. However, despite these wide-ranging investments and KFH's direct managerial control over enterprises, the large majority (78.4 per cent) of KFH's total assets were non-PLS (Khan 2010b: 811).[8]

This pattern of non-PLS financing dominating Islamic banking holds true even for non-profit-making, non-commercial, multilateral development agencies. The Islamic Development Bank, founded in 1975 and based out of Jeddah, Saudi Arabia, is the Muslim world's equivalent of the Asian Development Bank, the African Development Bank, or Latin America's Inter-American Development Bank. Its Islamic Research and Training Institute is the world's largest and best funded IBF 'think tank' and probably among the most vigorous promoters of Islamic banking throughout the world.

An analysis of the Islamic Development Bank's asset portfolio for 1976–2004 showed that 91 per cent of its financial transactions were non-PLS (Islamic Development Bank 2004); by 2006–07 this had changed somewhat as 11.3 per cent of its current portfolio was now direct equity participation, but 92 per cent of its income was still derived from non-PLS sources (Islamic Development Bank 2007). Indeed, the Islamic Development Bank makes no bones about the importance of conventional market interest rates for its income generation as its 2005–06 Annual Report makes clear:

> The income from commodity placements increased by 107.6 percent over the previous year. This rise is attributable to the increased level of liquid funds placed in these assets as a result of proceeds from issuance of *Sukuk* and Short-term *Murabaha* with higher yields in an environment of rising Libor-linked rate of returns.
>
> (Islamic Development Bank 2007: 102)

Libor is of course the London Interbank Offered Rate, one of the world's key benchmark interest rates and a bedrock of conventional finance. 'Commodity placements' (or 'commodity *murabaha*') are themselves nothing other than the Islamic Development Bank placing surplus funds with other, usually conventional financial institutions for their own use or to lend out to customers. This is due to the 'excess liquidity' problem inherent to all contemporary Islamic Banks (Ahmed 2001) since they lack many clearly *Shariah*-compliant short-term investment opportunities available to conventional banks (e.g., Treasury bills, or commercial paper, or even the overnight interbank market) to park their short-term excess funds and reserves.[9]

In 2004, 94 per cent of the Islamic Development Bank's placements were with non-Islamic banks and both a minimum return and the principal were guaranteed by the borrowing bank; these 'placements' accounted for almost 31 per cent of the Bank's operational assets (Standard and Poor's 2004: 5). Ostensibly the use of these funds is supposed to be restricted to *Shariah*-compliant purposes (i.e., financing trade in Islamically permissible commodities) but there is no effective check on how these funds are actually utilized as the user/borrower simply affirms that it will not use them for any non-Islamic purpose. It would be remarkable if non-Islamic banks could find more *Shariah*-compliant investment opportunities than could Islamic ones. It is practices such as this that led Al Nasser (2008) to conclude that 'the Shariah authorities demonstrate excessive confidence in their subjects when it comes to dealing with parties in the industry,' so regular, external *Shariah* audits (akin to independent external financial audits) are needed 'to bring about transparency and ensure that they [IBF institutions] deliver what they have committed to their customers' and to 'prevent the exploitation of religion for financial gain and [the] straying away from its regulations.' When external *Shariah* audits have been carried out, 'many of these auditors frequently complain about the amount of violations that they witness and cannot discuss since they [the records] have been tampered with' (Al Nasser 2008). M. R. Zaman (2008: 9) concurs with Al Nasser's assessment and argues that this is often the only way for many IBF institutions to remain profitable.

Too close to conventional banking for comfort?

If the time period, 'purchase,' and 'sale' prices are known, calculating the implicit interest rate is a trivial mathematical exercise. This is why *murabaha, ijara*, and other non-PLS/trade-based forms are viewed by most conservative *ulema* and

IBF scholars as weakly Islamic at best since the similarities to a standard bank debt-finance contract are immediately obvious. For example, Siddiqui, one of the earliest and most prominent theorists of contemporary IBF, considers *murabaha* and other non-PLS or trade-based forms of financing as '*weak* Islamic forms in contrast to the *strong* Islamic forms based on *sharing of returns*' (Siddiqui 2002: 175, emphasis added). Siddiqui, however, goes on to argue that the weak forms are also Islamically permissible as long as there is some, however infinitesimal or inconsequential, sharing of risk between the two parties, even if the risk is predominantly borne by the customer rather than the financier (Siddiqui 2002: 175). Some analysts (e.g., El-Gamal 2006; Kuran 2004) of contemporary Islamic banking practices go further and argue that *murabaha*, like other *hiyal*, is merely legalistic sophistry, that is, an Islamic version of the old medieval *contractum trinius*, designed to fulfill the same functions albeit at a higher transaction cost.

This is not a minor quibble over a small part of IBF, as *murabaha* and *ijara* are still *the* dominant mode of Islamic finance: globally 'profit-and-loss sharing transactions … only account for about five per cent of the operations of Islamic financial institutions' (Warde 2000: 240) and 'In a typical Islamic bank, [non-PLS forms] dominate the assets portfolio and can exceed 80%' (El-Hawary *et al.* 2004: 15). A breakdown of the 1994–96 financing pattern of the world's then ten largest Islamic banks confirms these observations: of the US$8.56 billion of financing during this period, PLS accounted for less than 14 per cent of the total, with *murabaha* alone accounting for 65.66 per cent (Iqbal et al 1998: 30, 28). By 2010, Warde still conceded that 'rather than disappearing, murabaha and comparable sale-based products grew significantly and today they constitute the bulk of the activity of most Islamic Banks … [despite not fulfilling] the stated objectives of Islamic banking – to share risk with the customer and achieve social and developmental goals' (Warde 2010: 141).

It was in keeping with the view of *murabaha* as simply 'disguised interest' that the Pakistani Federal *Shariat* Court and the *Shariat* Appellate Bench of the Supreme Court[10] ruled against the existing system of Islamic banking in 1991 and 1999, and mandated a conversion to full equity participation by the banking system. This ruling was overturned on final appeal in 2002 and the case referred back to the lower courts for further study and deliberation but a new ruling has yet to be issued.[11]

However, in response to these rulings, the State Bank of Pakistan bifurcated the Pakistani banking system and so implicitly agreed with the original court rulings that there was nothing 'Islamic' about the country's ostensibly Islamic banking system. What had hitherto been termed 'Islamic banking' was re-designated as 'conventional banking' (but care is usually taken to avoid using terms such as 'interest rate' and to use either 'profit rate' or 'markup rate') and orders were issued that only 'Islamic banks' would be given new banking licenses. That is, all new banks would have to be truly Islamic and no new conventional banks would be allowed. Accordingly, a spate of new Islamic banks such as Meezan Bank and Al Baraka Islamic Bank set up operation. The distinguishing characteristic of these banks is that their operations are now supposed to be completely *Shariah*-compliant and each bank has its own *Shariah*-board to oversee its activities and ensure that its operations are indeed fully Islamic.

Non-participatory finance and other deviations from the Islamic banking ideal

The predominance of interest-based financing is still the norm in Islamic Banks, the main difference being that now it is no longer explicitly identified as interest-based finance and the business is no longer dominated by non-Muslims. The older evidence cited earlier is not anomalous and the '*murabaha* syndrome' has not diminished.

Khan (2010b: 811) determined that the world's major Islamic banks were all operating on an overwhelmingly non-PLS basis – ranging from between 99.5 and 78.4 per cent non-PLS. These banks (Khan 2010b: 811) included Al Rajhi Bank[12] (the world's largest Islamic Bank, operating almost exclusively in Saudi Arabia with a few branches in Kuwait); Kuwait Finance House (Kuwait's largest Islamic bank, operating mainly in Kuwait, Turkey, and the Persian Gulf region, with a small presence in Malaysia); the Dubai Islamic Bank (the largest Islamic bank in the UAE, with a small presence in the rest of the Middle East and Pakistan); and the Bank Islam Malaysia (Malaysia's largest Islamic bank, operating mainly in Malaysia with a small presence in the UK).

El-Hawary *et al.* (2004: 16–17) also gives another important divergence between Islamic banking theory and actual practice. Although ostensibly accepting deposits on a PLS basis since no preset 'interest' rate is permissible, no Islamic bank has ever written-down the value of its depositor's accounts when it has written-down the value of its non-performing assets. In other words, bad debts are not translated into 'losses' for depositors. On the contrary, Islamic banks have declared market-competitive returns for depositors (obviously to avoid deposit outflows and a loss of faith in Islamic banking) even when running into financial difficulties themselves.

Many central banks also implicitly guarantee Islamic bank deposits in a manner not consonant with Islamic risk-sharing principles. For example, a run on the Dubai Islamic Bank in 1998, following reports of a massive embezzlement scandal, resulted in the withdrawal of US $138 million, 7 per cent of its total deposits, in one day; such a large withdrawal would have caused the Bank's collapse if the Dubai Central Bank had not stepped in as the 'lender of last resort' and effectively guaranteed all deposits (Warde 2000: 155–156). This attitude of 'backstopping' Islamic banks was reinforced recently when the head of the Bahrain-based Accounting and Auditing Organization for Islamic Financial Institutions (AAOIFI), one of the two international standards-setting bodies for IBF institutions, was quoted as stating unequivocally that 'If you let banks share losses right and left, the whole system will collapse in any downturn' (Wigglesworth 2009). While this is certainly true, and was carried out in no uncertain terms by many Western governments in the recent financial crisis for their banks, it is wholly contrary to the spirit and the ostensible rules governing IBF.

Why non-PLS is the dominant mode of Islamic financing

There is a long-established consensus in conventional economics on how best to resolve the debt-finance versus equity-finance question in the presence of non-trivial information asymmetry and hence costly state verification: the standard debt contract is superior to equity financing.[13] That is, in environments where the financier cannot accurately determine the credit-worthiness of the borrower or her intentions *vis à vis* the credit extended, and attempting to do so is both time-consuming and expensive, a secured interest-bearing loan is much more desirable than taking an equity stake. Therefore Islamic bankers' preference for non-PLS financing is an eminently rational response to the information asymmetry problems inherent in all financial transactions.

Given information asymmetry, there is a risk of two types of problem. The *ex ante* problem is adverse selection when loans/investments are made to/in a poor credit risk. The *ex post* problem is moral hazard when loaned/invested funds are misused and/or utilized in inappropriate ways. Naturally the degree of information asymmetry and the resulting adverse selection and moral hazard problems depends upon the amount and quality of information flows between lender or investor and borrower. Institutions such as credit rating bureaus improve information flow and reduce the likelihood of adverse selection, while civil, criminal, and possibly societal sanctions reduce the moral hazard dangers. However, in the absence of effective institutions to mitigate the information asymmetry issue, fully collateralized debt-finance would be the financing mode preferred by banks to minimize their risk.

Warde (2000: 155–157) confirms this serious problem when he details a long list of 'Islamic moral hazard' problems. These ranged from depositors demanding higher returns but a guaranteed principal amount, to borrowers challenging the permissibility of financial penalties and late fees, to Pakistani borrowers in a high-inflation environment cheerfully repaying only the principal of the loan on the grounds that interest is forbidden.

Given the relatively poor quality and quantity of financial information flows in most countries that have substantial IBF operations (El-Hawary *et al.* 2004: 35), the resulting information asymmetry problems would make standard debt contracts secured by excellent collateral even more preferable and equity participation even less desirable. Banks are reluctant enough to lend on a fully collateralized basis to any but the bluest of blue-chip customers in such environments; financing on an equity participation basis is even more problematic and fraught with risks that very few professional bankers would willingly take on.

The poor quality of financial information can be gauged by the following examples. Kemal (2007: 28) estimates the 2005 incidence of tax evasion in Pakistan as being between 5.7 and 6.5 per cent of GDP and the size of the unofficial/underground economy as between 54.6 and 62.8 per cent of GDP, among the world's highest; other estimates give a lower bound of 38.7 per cent in 2002–03 but steadily increasing since the late 1990s (Schneider 2006: 24). This was in sharp contrast to the 2002–03 averages for the Organization for Economic Cooperation and Development (OECD) country unofficial/underground economy of 16.3 per cent, Asian economies of 30.4 per cent, and African economies of 43.2 per cent (Schneider 2006: 23, 24, 27). Tedds (2010) found in that in Africa and the Middle East, 38 per cent of firms surveyed did not report at least 30 per cent of their sales to government tax authorities, while for OECD countries only 14 per cent of firms indicated the same degree of sales underreporting. Jalali-Naini (2000: 11) reports 'widespread tax evasion in both the formal and informal sectors' of the Middle East and North African (i.e., Arab) countries. Similarly, Transparency International's *Corruption Perceptions Index* rankings for 2013 showed that the highest-ranked Muslim country was the United Arab Emirates but it was only the 26th least corrupt country in the world (out of 175 surveyed) and that the majority of the world's Muslim countries were in the lower (more corrupt) half of the survey (Transparency International 2013). This gives an indication of the low quality of financial information available to IBF institutions in Muslim countries and the resulting more severe moral hazard and adverse selection issues. Therefore, for credit providers, collateralized, conventional debt contracts are vastly preferable to direct equity investment in firms characterized by severe information asymmetry issues.

Indeed, even some IBF advocates implicitly agree with the above assessment even if they refuse to follow it to its logical conclusion. For example, Iqbal *et al.* (1998: 50) argue that higher 'due diligence' costs associated with taking an equity stake versus fully collateralized conventional lending make equity participation much less desirable. However, they refuse to go the next step and acknowledge that conventional bank finance is the superior alternative for banks operating in a very poor financial environment – such as that where most Islamic banks are to be found – where the 'due diligence' costs of taking an equity stake would be excessively high.

These sorts of issues are, of course, not confined solely to Muslim or low and lower-middle-income economies. Even in advanced financial systems with sophisticated credit-rating systems, seemingly advanced and competent financial regulatory authorities, and broad and deep financial markets, the information asymmetry problems are so severe that the vast majority of financial transactions are debt-based and not equity-based.[14] Thus it is really a question of the *degree* of information asymmetry and the *amount* of adverse selection and moral hazard that is present and not whether it exists since it is an indisputable fact that they do exist. For example, the United States market for venture capital and investment, among the largest and most sophisticated in the world, was only $27.1 billion in 2012, down from $29.6 billion in 2011 (National Venture Capital Association n.d.). This was a massive drop from the pre-financial crisis heyday of venture capitalism in the US when it was $59.9 billion in 2004 (Euromonitor International 2005). However, even in its glory days, venture capitalism in the United States was absolutely trivial compared to bank lending: US banks as a source of corporate financing are worth several trillion dollars and most debt is fully collateralized (Mishkin 2013: 164–165, 214, 281–282). Although, as the US subprime mortgage crisis showed, even ostensibly 'fully collateralized' AAA loans are not immune to information asymmetry issues and the resulting problems.

In addition to the moral hazard and adverse selection issues involved in financial activities in asymmetric information environments, El-Gamal argues that the Islamic product has to be clearly functionally identical to the conventional financial product since otherwise it would not be approved by banking regulators in both Islamic and non-Islamic countries (El-Gamal 2006: 20–21). So IBF institutions are forced to conform to conventional norms, whether they want to or not, by government regulations that favor conventional banks. This does not, however, explain why Islamic banks in Malaysia, Pakistan, Sudan, and Iran, whose governments all favor Islamic banking over conventional, rely on non-PLS financing forms. That is, regardless of whether or not the country has a separate Islamic banking system or is wholly IBF, the regulators treat Islamic financial institutions as being the functional equivalent of conventional ones. One could debate as to why this is the case: were Islamic banks forced to mimic conventional ones or did they naturally gravitate to the conventional model? Given the earlier discussion of form following substance, it seems more likely that the latter is the case since otherwise, over the past few decades, regulations for Islamic financial institutions would have diverged in those countries with wholly Islamic financial systems or those where IBF enjoys a privileged position. This is not the case. On the contrary we see that:

> When it comes to the manner in which Islamic securities are offered, the process and rules for such offerings, even in those jurisdictions with special licensing regimes, are, in effect, the same. (For example, the rules governing the listing of Islamic bonds issued by the Securities and Commodities Authority of the United Arab Emirates are almost identical to the rules governing the listing of conventional bonds save for the use of [*sic*] word 'profit' instead of 'interest'.)
>
> (Henderson 2009: 378)

Some IBF advocates have proffered other rationalizations for Islamic bankers' preferences for products, especially *murabaha*, that closely mimic standard banking transactions. This, they argue, is due to:

- their being Islamically permissible as long as the bank has ownership for any length of time (Henry and Wilson 2004: 3–4), i.e., no justification is actually necessary as the financial transaction is Islamic;
- the weak property rights and high expropriation-risk levels found in most Muslim countries (Yousef 2004: 73);
- their being a 'hangover' from the conventional banking industry (where most Islamic bankers originally started their careers) which sees banks as liquidity/credit providers rather than investment vehicles (Ahmed 2002: 28);
- the tax advantages of debt financing over equity stakes (Iqbal *et al.* 1998: 51);
- their simply being an initial necessary step in the 'early stages of the development of Islamic Banks' as they seek to establish themselves as viable competitors to conventional ones (Ahmad 1993: 59).

Since IBF has been around for almost four decades now and many if not most Islamic bankers have served their entire careers in Islamic financial institutions, the 'hangover' argument becomes increasingly less tenable as the explanation for why Islamic banks shy away from direct equity participation.

With regard to taxation issues, the situation is quite complex. Initially some Islamic financial products, especially home purchases, were very often at a taxation disadvantage *vis à vis* conventional products but this is no longer the case in most jurisdictions. While the situation, as is often the case with the vast majority of taxation issues anywhere, is far too complex to deal with briefly and without getting bogged down in minutiae and obscure technicalities, Amin[15] concludes that most Muslim-majority countries do not treat Islamic financial products adversely from a taxation perspective, as is the case with several but not all Western countries:

> The treatment of Islamic finance transactions in computing business income may or may not need specific legislation. Muslim majority countries may not need legislation, illustrated by Egypt, or may choose to legislate to put the tax treatment beyond doubt as in the case of Malaysia. In the case of Western countries, if the tax system looks primarily to the substance of a transaction as with the Netherlands or the USA, specific legislation may not be needed. Conversely, if the tax system looks primarily to the legal form as with the UK, then specific tax legislation will be needed to ensure that Islamic finance transactions receive the expected tax treatment.
>
> Amin (2009: 376)

And the UK has already taken extensive steps to change the tax treatment of Islamic financial products in keeping with its government's decision to make it an IBF hub: removing double taxation of Islamic mortgages for both individuals and corporations as well as favorable tax treatment of Islamic debt issuance (UK Trade & Investment 2013). Baele *et al.* (2014: 7) determine that while Pakistan treats Islamic and conventional financial products similarly, in

Malaysia Islamic financial products actually enjoy favorable tax treatment *vis à vis* the conventional alternative. It seems unlikely then that government regulations forced Islamic banks to 'copy' the conventional model; rather it seems that Islamic banks naturally converged on it, as Kuran had predicted.

Thus Ahmad's (1993: 59) confident prediction about the declining role of *murabaha* in IBF was to say the least premature and overly optimistic. *Murabaha, ijara* (leasing) and other Islamic forms (e.g., installment, deferred payment, or deferred delivery sales) that very closely mimic conventional debt-finance overwhelmingly dominate current IBF practices (over 99 per cent in the most extreme case) for the world's largest and most important Islamic banks (Khan 2010b: 813). Even in Malaysia, widely considered 'to have the most developed Islamic financial system in the world,' PLS forms barely 0.5 per cent of total Islamic banking assets (Chong and Liu 2009: 130, 133).

Sometimes the IBF institutions simply lie in their accounting and report conventional banking/finance transactions as being wholly Islamic. For example, the President of Faisal Islamic Bank of Egypt, the sixth largest Islamic bank in the world at the turn of the century (Iqbal and Molyneux 2005: 81), revealed that the bank was buying conventional government bonds and reporting the income as 'religiously legal operations' (Soliman 2004: 281). Sometimes they do not lie in their financial statements but simply choose not to highlight their conventional activities. An examination of the Annual Report of Al Baraka Islamic Bank of Pakistan shows that 12.75 and 19.65 per cent of its 2006 and 2005 gross financings were in the form of conventional (i.e., explicitly interest-based) export finance.[16]

Thus there is no Islamic bank that has any meaningful level of true PLS investment. Furthermore, in some cases the Islamic banks' aversion to equity participation has led them to develop novel ways of appearing to be carrying out a PLS transaction while actually doing nothing of the sort.

When participatory is not participatory

Clearly a *mudaraba* partnership is PLS financing: one partner contributes capital and another contributes expertise/managerial skill. *Musharaka* financing should also be PLS since there is actually a direct equity stake taken by the financier but this is often simply misleading terminology. Often when an Islamic bank appears to have taken a direct equity stake, it has actually done nothing of the sort. It is the extent of 'non-participatory participation' in Muslim countries that underscores the strength of the Kuran thesis and the weakness of IBF's claims that it represents an alternative to conventional banking for Muslims.

For example, one common way of structuring an Islamic residential mortgage is as a 'declining *musharaka*.' In this arrangement, the financier purchases the house on behalf of the eventual owner (with or without a down payment) and then rents it out to her on a 'rent-to-own' basis. The monthly payment contains two distinct components: 'rental' for the financier's 'share' of the house and a 'buyout' component for its 'purchase' (El-Gamal 2000: 16). The contract ends when the entire financier portion of the house has been purchased. As El-Gamal (2000: 16) notes, the entire process looks:

> [V]ery much like a conventional mortgage schedule [and] it is trivial to calculate the equivalent interest rate which would make the conventional mortgage payments identical with the diminishing partnership payments.

In a confirmation of El-Gamal's (2000: 16) observation regarding Islamic versus conventional home financing, Khan (2010b) compared Rammal's (2004) detailed example of a $150,000 house purchased as a 15-year diminishing *musharaka* transaction with the Islamic bank financing 80 per cent ($120,000) of the house value and a conventional 15-year, $120,000 mortgage financed at an 8 per cent interest rate. He found that the differences between the two were so minimal as to amount to less than $100 *in toto* over the 15-year period. Thus the differences between actual Islamic banking practices and conventional debt-finance with an interest rate charge are often minimal at best.

In theory, the 'rent' charged should be based on comparable homes in the area but in practice the 'rental rate' invariably varies according to the prevailing mortgage interest rate (e.g., see Islamic Bank of Britain 2007: 13). Preliminary indications are that the implicit mortgage rate charged Islamic borrowers in the US is at least 25 basis points higher than that of comparable conventional mortgages (Healy 2005), an extra $6,271 over the life of a 30-year, $150,000 mortgage. However, Islamic mortgages often entail additional closing costs for the buyer so total costs are often far higher than a conventional mortgage's (Healy 2005). One anonymous mortgage broker in the US cynically justified this as: 'The price for getting into heaven is about 50 basis points [above a conventional mortgage]' (quoted in Morais 2007: 132).

Some ostensibly Islamic Banks do not even make a pretense of attempting to disguise the role of market interest rates in a 'diminishing *musharaka*' and how the 'rental' rate is directly derived from conventional interest rates and not from any imputed 'fair market rent.' For example, the Islamic Bank of Britain, proudly calling itself 'the UK's first fully Sharia'a compliant bank,' offers home mortgages on a declining *musharaka* basis and states in its official consumer's guide to home finance that:

> The monthly instalment of Rent will be calculated by reference to the relative ownership shares. ... In this example, the rent was calculated by the Bank at a rate equivalent to 6% p.a.
>
> (Islamic Bank of Britain 2007: 7)

The brochure goes on to state that the Islamic Bank of Britain's 'rental rates' are 'benchmarked' to commercial rates 'such as Libor plus a further profit margin' and so the rental amount will vary but that Islamic scholars 'have permitted Islamic finance providers to refer to an interest rate benchmark for determining Rent' (Islamic Bank of Britain 2007: 13). The UK was the only Western country to have a developed Islamic mortgage market and even there it was fairly small, under £0.5 billion, although it grew at about 40 per cent annually (Oakley 2007) until the financial crisis of 2008. After that, major British banks pulled out of the Islamic mortgage and Islamic finance market completely, leaving it to small Islamic banks as a niche market product (Knight 2010), and the once ebullient British financial press started casting a skeptical eye on the growth potential of Islamic financial products in the UK (Moore 2013). Islamic mortgages are also available as a niche financial product from boutique financial services firms in the US and Canada but are still relatively uncommon outside of Muslim countries.

In Pakistan, for example, Meezan Bank Limited, the country's largest Islamic Bank, offers home mortgages on a declining *musharaka* basis but using a straight-line amortization schedule instead of a conventional mortgage amortization schedule. This divides the amount financed by the Bank into equal monthly units (so 180 equal units for a 15-year mortgage; 240 for a 20-year mortgage and so on) where the home owner purchases a unit each month until she owns them all. Despite the Islamic *musharaka* terminology, a straight-amortization schedule is also an explicitly interest-based transaction that is widely used in conventional financial calculations. However, Meezan Bank is careful to use 'profit rate' instead of 'interest rate' in its documentation and there is minimal mention of Kibor (the Karachi Interbank Offered Rate that forms the basis for the rate charged the customer) in much of its documentation.[17] However, it does state explicitly that it benchmarks to the conventional mortgage rate and that its product is an adjustable-rate mortgage.

> Meezan Bank's Profit margin is correlated to the conventional mortgage market trends. At Meezan Bank, the profit margin is directly correlated to market trends to provide a competitive product to our customers. Shariah allows the use of any conventional market factor as a benchmark to determine the profit rate of a particular product. *The mere fact that the applied profit rate of our product is based on similar factors used in determining the applied rate of interest of a mortgage does not render the transaction or the contract invalid from the Shariah perspective, and neither does it make the transaction an interest-bearing one.* On the other hand, it is the underlying structure of the product that determines its Shariah compliance. [and] Profit rates will be revised annually on Account Anniversary.
>
> (Meezan Bank n.d., emphasis added)

Quite often the extent of non-participatory participation extends all the way to the top as financial system regulators themselves dictate how the participatory form is to be belied by the conventional substance. The State Bank of Pakistan is the country's central bank and ostensibly fully committed to the promotion of Islamic banking. Its Islamic export refinance scheme, designed to promote exports by making subsidized credit available to firms that secure export orders, shows how unparticipatory *musharaka* financing can be. In the conventional export refinance scheme, banks borrow from the State Bank at 6.5 per cent and lend to firms at 8 per cent, i.e., the bank's margin is statutorily set at 1.5 per cent on an annualized basis (SBP n.d.). However, these predetermined interest rates are clearly unIslamic in the current orthodoxy. Therefore, since the country also has dedicated Islamic Banks, the State Bank of Pakistan has established an Islamic export refinance scheme on a *musharaka* pool basis where the firm seeking export credit is to be charged the financing bank's average profit rate based on the rate earned on financing offered to ten 'blue-chip' bank corporate clients.

The State Bank has issued thirteen pages of detailed instructions on how this *musharaka* pool is to be established and what criteria are to be used to determine 'blue-chip' status. This is, however, all irrelevant since:

> The Islamic Commercial banks shall have to ensure that the effective cost of funds to the exporters does not exceed the rate declared by the State Bank under its Export finance Scheme, besides ensuring that there is no negative spread on their portfolio under the Scheme.
>
> (SBP 2005: 2)

That is, the State Bank of Pakistan sets the rate charged by Islamic Banks so the '*musharaka* pool' and 'setting profit rates' is simply rigmarole designed to give a semblance of Islamic risk-sharing on what is effectively a straight interest-based, conventional finance transaction since the 'pool' has to be structured in such a way that the 'profit rate' has to equal the refinance lending rate set by the State Bank of Pakistan.

This type of non-participatory participation is the norm in other parts of the Pakistani banking system as well. Utilizing essentially the same fundamental concept as a *tawarruq*/reverse-*murabaha*, Pakistan's Meezan Bank has pioneered the provision of an Islamic running finance facility (i.e., a line of credit for a firm's working capital needs) on an ostensible *musharaka* basis to its corporate customers. This overcomes a major problem that had plagued Islamic banks for a long time. Since a *murabaha* is meant as a product-based financing vehicle (i.e., it is real), unlike a straight line-of-credit extended to a firm by a conventional bank, it technically cannot be rolled over immediately upon expiry. Thus the firm cannot be provided seamlessly continuous funding and firms had to resort to alternative – and usually quite expensive, albeit very short term – bridge financing mechanisms between the end of one *murabaha* and the initiation of a second; or the firms had to ensure that they had a series of staggered ending-period *murabahas*, with concomitant increases in transactions costs for the firm.[18]

This Islamic running finance facility extends the firm a line of credit that it may draw upon as needed on a daily basis; the firm also deposits its sales proceeds into the same account. The firm's net (negative) position at the end of the day is viewed as the bank's contribution or 'investment' (hence the justification for calling it *musharaka*) to the firm on a daily basis. 'Profit' is accrued to the bank daily on its net contribution using the Karachi Interbank Offered Rate plus a bank-set margin (i.e., Kibor+) as the pricing basis. This is of course exactly the same as a conventional line of credit on a daily product basis.[19]

It is not just Islamic banks that utilize non-participatory participation. The multi-billion-dollar Islamic bond market also uses the same basic principles in its transactions.

Islamic bonds

A *sukk* (plural *sukuk*) is a generic term for an Islamic financial certificate, an 'Islamic bond.' *Sukuk* are corporate or public debt instruments, usually with a variable rate of return tied to a commonly accepted market indicator rate (usually Euribor or Libor) and must have an underlying 'real' transaction basis to be *Shariah*-compliant. The AAOIFI (one of two international regulatory bodies for IBF) has issued *Shariah*-compliance standards for the issuance of 14 different types of *sukuk* (Gassner 2005). Thus the typical *sukk* is in effect a 'floater' bond (i.e., with a variable coupon – interest – rate, Libor + margin) type of asset-backed security with some restrictions as to what it may be used to fund (no activity forbidden by Islam).

In November 2008, Maulana Justice M. Taqi Usmani, formerly of the Pakistan Supreme Court's *Shariat* Appellate Bench and now head of the AAOIFI's *Shariah* Advisory Board, issued a ruling that shook the *sukuk* market when he decreed that most *sukk* transactions mimicked conventional bonds too closely and so were unIslamic. This affected roughly four-fifths of the US$80 billion outstanding *sukuk* issue but the ruling was not to be applied retroactively.[20]

The most common type of Islamic bond now, and one not affected by Usmani's ruling, is the *sukk al ijara*, essentially a conventional lease-revenue bond. Here the borrower's tangible asset is 'sold' to the financiers and then 'leased' back to the borrowers, who make regular payments to the financiers from the income stream generated by the asset. This tangibility and its related income stream is what makes the transaction 'Islamic.' General revenue or general obligation bonds issued by governments or corporations are not Islamically permissible since they are not asset-backed securities (there is no direct connection between the security and the income stream accruing to the financiers) and are backed by nothing more than faith in the government's/corporation's credibility and ability to service its debt.

A typical *sukk al ijara* transaction, the most common type of *sukk* offering, might be structured as follows. A special purpose vehicle (SPV) is created by X-Co, which then 'sells' to the SPV some of X-Co's physical assets (e.g., manufacturing plant) for, say, US$500 million, with a concomitant agreement to lease the assets from the SPV for a specific time period, say five years, and a specific lease payment, say Libor + 1.5 per cent. X-Co also agrees to buy back the assets from the SPV at the specified sale price at the end of the agreed-upon time period, after which the SPV is dissolved. The SPV, in turn, sells shares of itself to investors who are assured a (*pro rata*) share of the lease payment, and uses the proceeds from this sale to pay X-Co. The lease payment may include an amortization component, or X-Co may set up a separate sinking fund for the buyback from the SPV.

As this is essentially a lease-revenue bond, there is nothing particularly 'Islamic' about this financial transaction. While there is no doubt some implicit connection between overall market interest rates (as an indicator of economic conditions) and corporate sector profitability, there is unlikely to be a direct short-term, cash-flow or revenue link between, say, Libor and the profitability of an offshore oil platform in the Gulf. Thus the return to the investor is very unlikely to have any direct connection to the actual profitability of the ostensible underlying physical asset.

Islamic capital markets have been relatively underdeveloped until very recently but, while growing extremely rapidly, are still small compared with regular bond issues. Gassner (2005) estimated the entire 2004 *sukk* volume to be under US$7 billion; by 2006 *sukk* issuance was $10.8 billion, 44 per cent of new market debt issue in the Persian Gulf, and world *sukk* outstanding had grown to approximately US$22 billion (Fitch Ratings 2007: 4). The phenomenal *sukk* market growth rate ensured that, by end 2008 the worldwide market had grown to US$80 billion (Oakley 2008) and by June 2013 to US$245 billion. The global financial crisis of 2008 caused a massive decline in new issuance (to only US$20 billion in that year) but 2012 was the best year ever for *sukuk* as new issuance totaled almost US$130 billion (Malaysian International Islamic Financial Centre 2013).

The continuing popularity of *sukuk* for investors can be judged by the fact that a US$1 billion *sukk* offering in February 2013 by the Dubai Electricity & Water Authority was five times oversubscribed (Zaheer and van Wijnbergen 2013: 4). This is not a new phenomenon as a January 2006 US$3.5 billion offering by Dubai Ports Corporation (the largest *sukk* offering to date) was 325 per cent oversubscribed and news reports indicated that several Persian Gulf countries were considering massive (US$50–65 billion) petroleum projects financed by *sukk* issue because of the extremely attractive rates (for the borrower) resulting from the high demand for them as almost all *sukk* 'offerings are hugely oversubscribed' (AMEinfo 2006). These reports proved to be somewhat premature as the market suffered a sharp decline in the 2008 global financial crisis but this popularity led to some offerings being listed on the London Stock Exchange in 2006 and assigned credit ratings by Standard and Poor's (AMEinfo 2006).

In addition, Dow Jones created the Dow Jones *Sukuk* Index (DJSI) to track *sukk* issues and serve as a benchmark performance index for 'Global U.S. dollar-denominated investment-grade bonds that are screened for Shari'ah-compliance' (Dow Jones Sukuk Index 2013). As of December 31, 2012, the DJSI listed only 39 investment-grade *sukk* with a market value of some $32.6

billion. It is obvious, given the size of the total *sukuk* market, that most *sukk* offerings are considered below investment grade (i.e., 'junk' status in common parlance). Many governments have taken advantage of this high demand for *sukuk* to issue foreign currency debt that no mainstream Western investor would contemplate purchasing.[21] Thus the biggest issuer of *sukuk* are governments (65.6 per cent of the total), followed by power and utility companies (13.6 per cent) (Malaysian International Islamic Financial Centre 2013).

As the oversubscription shows, there is clearly a massive demand for *Shariah*-compliant debt, but this debt continues to be plagued by serious unsettled legal issues. Fitch Ratings, one of the three original financial ratings agencies (along with Standard and Poor's and Moody's) recognized by the US Securities and Exchange Commission, has indicated its concerns about the degree to which the asset sale underlying most *sukk* issues have been 'validly transferred … [so that] in the event of an insolvency of the originator … the underlying collateral must remain completely separate from the originator/parent company' and 'Fitch has not reviewed any transaction to date that would satisfy these requirements' (Fitch Ratings 2007: 3). Therefore it is Fitch's policy to not rate individual *sukk* issues separately but to assign them the same issuer default rating as the originator. Moody's concurs with this assessment: an exhaustive analysis by it of the Persian Gulf's *sukk* market indicated that 'The sukuk investors would have no first-lien or prior ranking or security above any other unsecured creditor' (Howladar 2009).

The validity of these concerns was underscored by the Chapter 11 bankruptcy of East Cameron Partners (ECP) LP in 2008, the world's first *sukk* default. East Cameron had originated a US$165.67 million, CCC+ rated (i.e., below investment grade) *sukk* in 2006, but in bankruptcy court its US lawyers argued that the *sukk* was not a true sale but merely a secured loan and so the *sukk*'s assets belonged to ECP and not to the *sukk* holders (Howladar 2009). The final decision in this case did not clearly resolve the issue since the settlement approved by the Court allowed the investors full rights to the revenue stream from the asset as the *sukk* 'holders invested in the sukuk certificates in reliance on the characterisation of the transfer of the royalty interest as a true sale' (quoted in Zaheer and van Wijnbergen 2013: 18), but the Court then revised its ruling to allow the assets to revert to ECP once the *sukk* principal had been repaid after ECP filed a revised lawsuit and then settled out of court with its investors (Zaheer and van Wijnbergen 2013: 18). Thus it is still not clear that *sukk* 'sales' are true sales or merely give the investors first claim on an asset's revenue stream while the asset itself belongs to the *sukk* originator. That is, in financial parlance, is the *sukk* 'asset-backed' or merely 'asset-based' (Warde 2011). If they are asset-based, then we have essentially the same non-materiality problems that led most IBF scholars to consider *tawarruq* ('reverse *murabaha*') to be a highly suspect transaction from a *Shariah*-compliance perspective.[22] An asset-based *sukk* is then functionally indistinguishable from a general revenue bond (used to fund the construction of, e.g., water treatment plants, airports, power plants, toll roads, etc.) since presumably general revenue bonds will repay investors from the earnings stream of the issuer's assets, just as an asset-based *sukk* does.

Given the recent worldwide financial crisis, it is unsurprising that IBF has also been hit with a spate of defaults and bankruptcies. Between 2008 and 2010 alone there were at least 21 substantial *sukuk* defaults (Khnifer 2011: 25). This is not counting gigantic near-defaults, such as when the Government of the Emirate of Dubai asked the major creditors of Dubai World (where Dubai's ruler had a majority stake) to accept a six-month 'standstill' on debt repayment after its finances had been severely overextended by a massive and extremely ill-conceived acquisitions binge; a major financial crisis was narrowly averted when Dubai's oil-rich neighbor the Emirate of Abu Dhabi stepped in and provided a loan to stave off default (Warde 2011). This was literally a last-minute reprieve as US$10 billion was transferred to Dubai World on the same day that a US$4.1 billion payment – the reason for the 'standstill' request – was due (BBC 2009); given that Dubai World's debts totaled over US$26 billion, a default of this magnitude could have had catastrophic knock-on effects in the Persian Gulf and world *sukuk* markets.

In reviewing the recent spate of cases involving IBF defaults and bankruptcies, Siddiqui[23] concluded that:

> Through reading many cases that have so far been litigated in courts around the world, I have found that in almost all cases, *the courts have struggled to reconcile the substance and form of the contract*. Was it a sale, lease, construction or partnership contract or a financing arrangement between the parties?
>
> (Siddiqui 2011, emphasis added)

In short, there is no evidence to suggest that Islamic bonds are actually participatory financial instruments in any meaningful way or that they are anything but Islamic clones of conventional financial instruments.

Malaysia's innovative approach to Islamic finance

Asset securitization is further constrained by the fact that not all Islamic scholars are in agreement about what constitutes a *Shariah*-compliant financial instrument. For example, Malaysian *ulema*, adherents of the more progressive (in financial matters at least) *Shafi* school of Islamic *fiqh*, have *Shariah*-certified securitizing Islamic private debt securities (IPDS), i.e. corporate accounts receivable, thereby allowing corporations to raise funds by selling their debts.[24] However, scholars in Pakistan, India, and the cash-flush Persian Gulf have held that IPDS are not *Shariah*-compliant since the underlying transaction is a sale of debt and not a tangible asset: there is no material finality. This is, according to their interpretation of the *hadith*, *riba*.[25] Therefore the largest national Islamic corporate debt market, approximately US$34 billion in 2012 (Krasicka and Nowak 2012: 4), is not 'Islamic' enough for investors in most of the Muslim world.[26] Nevertheless, both the Islamic Development Bank and the Abu Dhabi Islamic Bank, in contravention of general *Shariah* rulings applicable to them, have quietly 'sold' assets, i.e., securitized prior 'real' financings, as repos in order to generate funds and service fees (Fitch Ratings 2007: 3).

The comparatively liberal approach followed by Malaysian Islamic banks is a direct result of the Islamic Modernism of Mahathir Mohammed, Prime Minister of Malaysia from 1981 to 2003. In 1997 Mahathir established the National *Syariah* [*Shariah*] Board 'to harmonize financial practices and review the compatibility of new financial products with religion' (Warde 2010: 127). That is, there is only one official (and hence only one permissible) interpretation of *Shariah* regarding financial issues in Malaysia;[27] this runs counter to centuries of Sunni Muslim custom that holds that a ruling by a *faqih* (jurist) is binding only to the extent that people respect his (and it is invariably a 'he') learning and knowledge, trust his judgment, and are willing to voluntarily abide by his considered opinion.

The Board was given its marching orders by Mahathir who declared that 'Only when Islam is interpreted so as to be relevant in a world which is different from what it was 1,400 years ago can Islam be regarded as a religion for all ages' (quoted in Warde 2010: 127). This is of course encapsulating the key point of Islamic Modernism in one sentence. The *ulema* were further 'asked to adopt a more innovative approach' to financial matters and to seek a new *ijtihad* (consensus) on financial matters and not 'to interpret the Koran too literally' and to avoid being 'too harsh' and reminded that 'religion [was to be] at the service of development goals' and not *vice versa* (Warde 2010: 127).[28]

Unsurprisingly, this approach has drawn considerable criticism from many non-Malaysian *fuqaha* and *ulema* even as major Arab Islamic banks have quickly opened Malaysian subsidiaries after the Malaysian financial services market was opened up to foreign firms. In 2006 some of the world's largest Arab Islamic financial institutions, the Kuwait Finance House, Saudi Arabia's Al Rajhi Bank, and the Asian Finance House (a consortium of Gulf investors led by Qatar Islamic Bank) were licensed to operate subsidiaries in Malaysia although 51 per cent ownership must be with a Malaysian partner (Warde 2010: 130). In yet another major departure from 'traditional' IBF practices, the Al Rajhi Bank subsidiary offers such innovative Islamic services as deposit accounts with predetermined returns (ostensibly made possible by a 'profit reserve account' which covers 'fluctuations in its profit and losses') (Warde 2010: 130). This smacks of a *hiyal* (legal ruse) at par with the State Bank of Pakistan's Islamic Export Refinance Scheme's '*musharaka* pool' for determining the rate charged to corporate clients by Islamic banks and is of course simply mimicking a practice that conventional banks have been providing for many decades: certificates of deposit whose return is set beforehand.

Islamic derivatives?

A derivative is, of course, an instrument that derives its worth (price) from that of an underlying financial asset. Derivatives are invaluable in risk-hedging for firms (e.g., financial futures options to hedge foreign exchange transactions for importers/exporters) but are now used mainly for speculating on the direction of future price movements since the notional value of derivative contracts is many multiples of the actual underlying economic transactions. Thus derivatives fail both the 'materiality' and 'no speculation' test for IBF and almost all conservative *Sharia* scholars have ruled that 'when applied to modern financial contracts, the prohibition of *gharar* eliminates futures, options, and some life assurance contracts' (Mills and Presley 1999: 5; see also Ayub 2002: 35). However, some argue that if there is an actual underlying economic transaction being hedged (e.g., in a forward contract), then some derivatives may be legal (Ayub 2002: 35; Warde 2000: 139–141).

Until quite recently most scholars had held that a short-sale was strictly forbidden since it violates the materiality and no-speculation provision. However, some *Shariah*-compliant hedge funds have created an Islamic-short sale that is *Shariah*-certified if the shorter puts a 'down-payment' towards the shorted stock to establish ownership of the item being sold (Morais 2007: 131). Since short-selling in the US, for example, requires that a substantial margin be put up by the seller, an Islamic short sale is functionally equivalent to a conventional one. El-Gamal (quoted in Morais 2007: 131) characterizes the substantially higher fees charged by these Islamic funds as preying on 'the gullible who don't really understand the structure' since 'both the sophisticated investors and the ultrapuritans will see through this.'

El-Gamal (2006: Ch. 5 and 7) outlines several ways in which IBF institutions have now 'synthesized' Islamic versions of short and long sales as well as put and call options. For example, call options (i.e., where the buyer has the right but not the obligation to buy in the future at a preset price) are known as an *urbun* (down-payment) sale where the buyer has the right to cancel the sale by forfeiting her down-payment (El-Gamal 2006: 181). The down-payment here obviously serves the same function as the premium on a conventional call option and the preset price functions as the strike price. A put option (i.e., where the seller has the right but not the obligation to sell at a preset price by some point in the future) is, of course, simply a 'reverse *urbun*' (Ayub 2007: 209–210).

Again unsurprisingly, synthesizing options is extremely controversial among 'traditional' IBF scholars even if there are many Islamic finance professionals who want to partake of them. Ayub (2007: 116–117), after extensive study of classical *fiqh*, concludes that Imam Malik (founder of the Maliki school of Islamic jurisprudence – *madhab* – in the Eighth century CE) considered it invalid and that of the four great Sunni *madhab*s 'only the Hanbali school considers Bai' al 'Arbun [an option] a legal contract' and they rely mainly on a single report where a junior official concluded a conditional agreement with a merchant to purchase a building for 4,000 dirhams; the condition being that if the Caliph Umar (the second caliph of Islam, died 644 CE) did not approve the transaction, the merchant would be given 400 dirhams for his troubles. Thus a legitimate use of *urbun* is restricted to, at most, a down or advance payment on a purchase agreement 'in actual sale transactions' which if not concluded by the buyer 'within so many days' would be forfeit to the seller. No legitimate extension of the *urbun* principle to synthesizing put or call option is possible.[29]

It seems an inevitable conclusion that IBF appears to be so functionally equivalent to conventional finance as to be conventional finance cloaked in Islamic terminology. So is Islamic finance 'Islamic' in any meaningful way?

So how Islamic is Islamic banking and finance?

El-Hawary *et al.* (2004: 5) gave the four defining characteristics of IBF as risk-sharing; materiality; no exploitation; and no financing of sinful activities. How well has contemporary IBF practice lived up to this?

- *Risk-sharing.* Given the overwhelming use of non-PLS financing modes, IBF cannot be said to be risk-sharing in any meaningful sense. IBF transactions mimic conventional, collateralized debt contracts very closely, often right down to actually using current market interest rates as pricing benchmarks.
- *Materiality.* As shown by *tawarruq*, commodity *murabaha*s, Malaysian Islamic private debt securities, and the Islamic short-sale example, contemporary IBF often has no meaningful underlying material transaction. Similarly, the sale and lease-back of existing physical assets, common in many *sukuk* transactions, is a fictional materiality in that either no new asset is being financed or there is no actual title transfer; this is a convenient vehicle to circumvent the fact that conventional bonds are not *Shariah*-compliant in the current orthodoxy.
- *No exploitation.* Insofar as the higher fees associated with Islamic mortgages and investment funds for doing nothing more substantial than mimicking conventional banking/finance products are exploitative, IBF institutions fail on this criterion as well. Given that IBF institutions try to convince pious Muslims that they are truly *riba*-free, they are guilty of exploiting the pious here as well.
- *No financing of sinful activities.* Here as well IBF institutions are sometimes guilty of not being *Shariah*-compliant, as the Faisal Islamic Bank of Egypt and Al Baraka Islamic Bank of Pakistan examples have shown. Furthermore, commodity placements usually rely on the simple word of the borrowing bank/firm that the funds will not be used for 'sinful' activities and rarely are *Shariah*-audits performed to ensure this. This is the IBF equivalent of 'don't ask, don't tell.' It cannot, therefore, be unequivocally said that there is no financing of 'sin.' There is no way of

knowing how many other IBF institutions are similarly fudging their reporting.

Thus it seems clear that, vociferous rhetoric to the contrary notwithstanding, IBF is virtually indistinguishable from conventional banking and finance. All that makes it Islamic is what El-Gamal (2006: 20) calls 'Shariah arbitrage,' carried out by the bank's *Shariah* board which earns its fees by 'finding an appropriate [classical] Arabic name for the Islamic analog product' and using it to 'justify and lend credibility to the Islamic brand name.'

Each IBF institution has a '*Shariah* board,' usually comprised of between one and three respected *ulema* who certify that the IBF institution's financial products are *Shariah*-compliant. How then can these institutions certify that these practices are 'Islamic' when they do nothing more than replicate, using Islamic terminology, standard, interest-based banking products? There are two possible answers to this.

The first is the Kuran thesis of IBF's origins. In its current incarnation, IBF arose in colonial India and was part of a broader movement designed to replace Western/Christian leadership and structures in all areas of Muslim life. Therefore 'Islamic economics was primarily a vehicle for reasserting the primacy of Islam and secondarily a vehicle for radical economic change' (Kuran 2004: 5).[30] As such, then, it had no choice but to replicate Western (i.e., interest-based debt contract) forms in asymmetric information environments if it was to function at all, and there is nothing surprising in the fact that it looks very similar to conventional banking. The *Shariah* scholars are then satisfied if the IBF institutions convince their customers that they are partaking in something exclusively Islamic, something that reinforces the borrower's 'Islamic identity,' rather than in ensuring that the financial products on offer provide a real alternative to conventional finance.

A second possible explanation for why the *Shariah* boards regularly certify these IBF financial offerings as *Shariah*-compliant is that accommodating scholars are actively sought after by multinational and national financial institutions eager to gain the imprimatur of *Shariah* certification. And these firms are willing to pay top dollar. For example, Morais (2007: 122) reports that there are only 20 or so 'rock star' *Shariah* scholars worldwide who have the necessary stature to certify something as *Shariah*-compliant; these scholars sit on 40–50 *Shariah* boards each and earn between US$20,000 and $30,000 per board annually. Other reports indicate that some scholars have earned US$150,000 to $500,000 to *Shariah*-certify large transactions, sometimes by serving as simple translators, in that technical financial terms in complex Western financial instruments are simply given a classical Arabic equivalent and then certified as being 'Shariah compliant.'[31]

Malaysia, in response to the common perception of *Shariah* boards being mere rubber stamps, has prohibited scholars from serving on more than one *Shariah* board at a time (Bloomberg 2013); in contrast, the Persian Gulf countries are virtually unregulated and some *Shariah* scholars have strongly resisted any attempt at regulating their activities (*Asiamoney* 2006). Naturally the more accommodating the scholar, the more business he will get; those known to be particularly strict in their interpretation are not likely to be much in demand.[32]

Thus a vicious cycle is set up. Pious Muslims try to avoid *riba* by avoiding the standard debt-contract, but this is not possible in most situations. Major banks wish to cash in on this desire but cannot provide truly *Shariah*-compliant vehicles. Therefore they look for scholars willing to certify conventional instruments as being *Shariah*-compliant. Barring a reinterpretation of current *fiqh* to allow a more progressive view of the ban on *riba* and greater latitude in financial transactions, Islamic banking will continue as it currently is: providing a fairly wide range of financial products and services that closely mimic conventional ones. The major difference between it and conventional banking and finance will continue to be the additional layer of transaction costs needed for *Shariah* certification.

There have thus been two broad categories of critic of the current version of IBF: the Islamic Modernist/Minimalist position, and the Islamic ultra Orthodox/Maximalist one. The Modernists/Minimalists argue that since *riba* equates to usury and not to interest, no change is necessary or needed, and contemporary IBF is nothing but disguised conventional banking. The ultra Orthodox/Maximalists agree with the Modernist/Minimalist criticism that contemporary Islamic banking is indeed nothing but disguised conventional banking but do not, of course, advocate for conventional banking. They agitate for a truly Islamic banking and financial system. It was precisely because of mimicry so close that it verged on functional indistinguishability that the Pakistani courts, dominated by ultra-Orthodox/Maximalist jurists, ruled against the then current form of Pakistani Islamic banking in 1991 and 1999.

Notes

1 See also El-Gamal 2006: 138; Kuran 2004; Usmani 2002b; Iqbal *et al.* 1998 among others for more details; see Mills and Presley 1999: Ch. 2 ('The Islamic critique of interest') for an excellent summary of the current Islamic critique of the conventional view of interest.

2 Although Warde does not contextualize the quotation, El Nagar founded Mit Ghamr Savings Bank, probably the first 'Islamic' bank in the world, in Egypt in 1963.

3 Currently Professor of Economics and Political Science and the Gorter Family Professor of Islamic Studies at Duke University in North Carolina; prior to this he was the King Faisal Professor of Islamic Thought and Culture at the University of Southern California in California. Starting in 1983, Kuran's work on Islamic economics, banking and finance spans over three decades and dozens of books, journal articles, and chapters in edited volumes, far too many to list here, but I include some representative works. A full bibliography is available from his webpage http://econ.duke.edu/people/kuran.

4 A *murabaha* is a 'cost plus' contract between client and financier that essentially replicates a standard, interest-based debt-finance contract and is held to be, at best, weakly Islamic by most analysts and condemned by more conservative ones as

being simply disguised interest. See Box 6.1 and later in this chapter for more details on how it functions.

5 The *contractum trinius* was a complicated series of three separate transactions, all of which were permitted by canonical law, to evade the medieval Catholic Church's ban on usury (El-Diwany 2006; see also El-Gamal 2003).

6 Calculated from 'Table 6: Financing by modes, 1994–1996 averages' in Iqbal *et al.* (1998: 28).

7 Prof. Coulson was probably the leading authority on Islamic law in the West till his death in 1986 (*Arab Law Quarterly* 1985–86). In his obituary in *Arab Law Quarterly* (1985–86), Coulson's monumental work *An Introduction to Islamic Law* was described over two decades after it first appeared as still 'the best introduction to the subject' and was translated into Arabic in Kuwait in 1982.

8 See Smith 2004 for more details on the extremely privileged position enjoyed by the Kuwait Finance House there for much of its history and the role played by it in the Kuwaiti financial system.

9 Iqbal and Molyneux (2005: 75–76) assert that 'excess liquidity' is not a correct way of characterizing IBF institutions since they cannot turn to the interbank market or the central bank to borrow short-term funds in case of a temporary liquidity crunch because these are interest-based transactions; therefore IBF institutions have to have greater liquidity than non-IBF ones; in any case, IBF institutions are only slightly more liquid than non-IBF ones from the same countries. However, this is contradicted by Iqbal's earlier work (Iqbal *et al.* 1998: 77) where, of 60 IBF scholars surveyed, only six said that 'excess liquidity' was 'not a problem' for Islamic Banks and 28 of 60 felt it was a 'serious problem' for some or all Islamic Banks. A decade and a half later, actual Islamic bankers, as opposed to Islamic banking theorists and ideologues, were still saying the same thing: Pakistan's largest Islamic bank, Meezan Bank (2014: 46), stated flatly that 'Limited opportunities for investment of surplus liquidity' was a major problem for it.

10 Those sections of the Pakistani judicial system charged with ensuring that all laws and practices in the country are in strict conformity with *Shariah/fiqh*.

11 See Chapter Seven in this text for more details on this.

12 Al Rajhi Bank has a large proportion of its net investments in what it terms *mutajara* trading. *Mutajara* is essentially a *murabaha*-type transaction used for short-term trade or other financing. *Mutajara* often resembles a repo trade in that it is a matched 'sale and repurchase' agreement, and a substantial portion of Al Rajhi's *mutajara* investments are with the Saudi Arabian Monetary Agency, the country's central bank. Al Rajhi does not give a detailed breakdown in its annual reports for its *mutajara* trading, reporting only gross aggregates. See Moody's Investor Services 'Credit Opinion: Al Rajhi Bank' (2008) for more details.

13 See e.g., Williamson (1987); Stiglitz and Weiss (1981); Townsend (1979).

14 See Mishkin 2013, especially Chapter Eight, for a detailed discussion of financial structure in the US and elsewhere.

15 Mohammed Amin, now an independent consultant, was a tax partner with PriceWaterhouseCoopers LLC (one of the world's largest multinational financial services consulting firms) for 19 years and specialized in taxation issues, especially those involving Islamic financial products. During 2007–10 he was on the British Government's official advisory board for Islamic finance. Further details on taxation issues regarding Islamic financial products, an extremely complex subject, can be obtained from Amin's detailed website: www.mohammedamin.com/index.html.

16 Calculated from Note 11 of Al Baraka Islamic Bank's 2006 Annual Report; see the next section for more details on how export refinance works in Pakistan.

17 See Meezan Bank's online mortgage calculator (www.meezanbank.com/ihomecal.aspx) for sample mortgage payments at a preset 'profit rate.'

18 Personal communication to the author from a senior corporate banking officer of a Pakistani Islamic bank, June 2008.

19 See Usmani 2002a: 189–193 and Khan 2008b: 71–72 for more details, especially an extensive justification for why *ijtihad* (here translated as 'innovation') is good innovation in this case.

20 See Oakley 2008 for more details.

21 For example Pakistan's whose credit rating was lowered to Caa1/CCC+ in 2012, i.e., 'substantially risky' and well below investment grade (Anwar 2012).

22 See Wouters 2012 for a detailed analysis of the 2011 US$2 billion Goldman Sachs *sukk* issue for a discussion of whether it was a legitimate *sukk* or a now-banned *tawarruq* transaction; he concludes that it merely met 'formal Shari'ah compliance only' and that 'De facto however, this resembles strongly' the most controversial type of *tawarruq* transaction.

23 At the time of writing, Siddiqui was Head of Islamic Finance for SR Denton (Dubai), one of the world's largest law firms and a major force in legal aspects of Islamic finance.

24 Malaysian details from Parker 2006.

25 See, for example, Warde 2010: 129 and Haron and Ahmad 2000: 157. Most IBF advocates carefully avoid any extended discussion of the split between Malaysian and non-Malaysian interpretations of *Shariah* rules regarding IBF, usually contenting themselves with just casually mentioning that Malaysian rulings are rarely followed outside the country and that most non-Malaysians take a more restrictive view of what is permissible under Shariah.

26 Krasicka and Nowak (2012) is an excellent example of why a little knowledge is a dangerous thing. Nowhere in their laudatory analysis of the Malaysian Islamic finance experience do they mention that Shafi *fiqh* interpretations of *Shariah* that happily allow securitizing debt are anathema to both other Sunni *fiqh* (Hanafi, Hanbali, and Maliki) and Shia (Ithna Ashari) *fiqh* in this case.

27 After 2006 the Malaysians allowed non-Malays to serve on the *Shariah* boards of Malaysian banks but presumably these scholars also have to abide by the rulings of the National *Syariah* Board.

28 Despite decades of 'democratic' governance since independence from Great Britain in 1957 (and various territorial amalgamations through 1963), any knowledgeable observer of Malaysian politics and Prime Minister Mahathir's extensive use of Malaysia's draconian colonial-era 'Internal Security Act' would know that 'suggestions' from him were not to be taken lightly, much less ignored.

29 Another way to synthesize an option, one that is even more controversial than the *urbun* payment method, is by the double *wa'd* (reciprocal promise) method. Among other things, the *wa'd* can be used as a *de facto* interest rate swap as well. Unsurprisingly, the *wa'd* is especially popular in Malaysian Islamic finance. See Firoozye 2009 for more details, including links to articles criticizing it.

30 See Chapter Three for more on this.

31 See *Asiamoney* (2006) and Tett (2006) for more details.

32 The situation here is very similar to that of the pre-financial crisis US ratings agencies that regularly certified all sorts of often quite questionable financial assets as being not just investment grade but AAA.

7 'Rebooting' Islamic banking in Pakistan to make it more Islamic

The purpose of this chapter is to provide an overview of the changes made by Gen. Zia to the Pakistani legal system that set the stage for the 1991, 1999, and 2002 Pakistani court rulings. The 1991 and 1999 judgments threatened to completely overturn the existing Pakistani financial system in favor of establishing the world's first 'truly Islamic' and '*riba*-free' system. The 2002 judgment restored the *status quo* but paved the way for the 2002 'reboot' of the Pakistani version of Islamic banking. My aim is to provide the reader with both a 'big picture' overview and what I feel are some crucial 'in the weeds' details of the Pakistani Islamic banking sector. Accordingly, the chapter includes the changes to the Pakistani judicial system instituted by Gen. Zia and the 1991, 1999, and 2002 Federal *Shariat* Court (FSC) and *Shariat* Appellate Bench (SAB) rulings that changed the nature of the Pakistani Islamic banking landscape. It will also include a brief discussion of the 2002 'reboot' of Pakistani Islamic banking.

Really Islamizing the state

While Pakistan nominally became an Islamic state shortly after Independence and all of its three official constitutions (1956, 1962, and 1973)[1] have promoted Islam, the actual 'Islamization' of the Pakistani financial system was a very slow process. This process was greatly speeded up after Gen. Zia ul Haq's military *coup d'état* in July 1977 and his changes to the Pakistani judicial system that allowed the orthodox (mainly Deobandi) *ulema* a formal role in the Pakistani judiciary, something which every Pakistani government till then had assiduously avoided doing. That is, by creating this role for the *ulema*, Gen. Zia converted Pakistan into a *de facto* neo-theocracy.

Traditional *ulema* sitting on the apex (the SAB of the Supreme Court of Pakistan) and penultimate (the FSC[2]) benches in the Pakistani judicial system for Islam-related matters meant that, for the first time in Pakistan's history, there was actually a way for the *ulema* to enforce key Islamic provisions of the current (1973) Constitution rather than simply urge the government to do its constitutional duty. The aim of the orthodox *ulema*, in the context of the Pakistani financial system, was to effect a radical restructuring of the Pakistani economy by transforming its financial system along ultra-Islamist lines. Two key rulings, the first by the FSC in 1991 and the second by the Supreme Court's SAB in 1999, represent the most wide-ranging attempt so far to engineer an actual transformation of the Pakistani economy along Islamic lines. They were the logical culmination of the Islamization process that, as detailed in Chapter Three, began shortly after Pakistan's independence from the United Kingdom in 1947.

Some key Islamic provisions of the 1973 Constitution[3] bear repeating. These are:

> Article 2: 'Islam shall be the State religion of Pakistan.'
>
> Article 38(f): 'The State shall eliminate *riba* as early as possible.'
>
> Article 227(1): 'All existing laws shall be brought in conformity with the Injunctions of Islam as laid down in the Holy Quran and Sunnah, in this Part referred to as the Injunctions of Islam, and no law shall be enacted which is repugnant to such Injunctions.'

Given the unequivocal nature of Articles 38(f) and 227(1), the Pakistani state had to act. But how were these articles to be implemented? How were these lofty aims to be realized?

The Islamic State's now (partially) Islamic judiciary

In 1980, on Gen. Zia's orders, the 1973 Constitution was amended to provide for a five-member Federal *Shariat* Court which had the power 'to declare invalid any law' it deemed un-Islamic (Khan 2001: 640). Membership of the FSC was initially restricted to judges of the provincial High Courts – hitherto the penultimate courts in the Pakistani judicial system. All of these judges would have been trained almost exclusively in the Indo-British Common Law system and not as traditional Islamic *alims* or *fuqaha* (although the occasional judge was an acknowledged Islamic scholar as well). A subsequent (1981) amendment to the Constitution allowed for the nomination by the president of up to three *ulema* to the FSC Bench after the Islamist parties and *ulema* complained that the High Court judges lacked Islamic knowledge and were 'too western-educated and West-oriented' (Khan 2001: 641). At first only the Supreme Court of Pakistan was empowered to review FSC rulings but in 1982 a separate *Shariat* Appellate Bench of the Supreme Court, consisting of three regular (i.e., with *de jure* tenure) Supreme Court judges and two *ulema* (*ad hoc* members) was established to review FSC rulings (Khan 2001: 662). It is in the composition of the FSC and the SAB, the formalization of the role of the *ulema* in interpreting Pakistani laws and implementing the Islamic nature of the 1973 Constitution, that the neo-theocratization of Pakistan lies.

In 1980 the Zia government had ordered the implementation of the 1980 Council of Islamic Ideology (CII) report (often referred to as the Tanzil ur Rahman Report after its author, then chairman of the CII and later Chief

Justice of the FSC during 1991–92) 'on the elimination of interest from the economy' (Kennedy 2004: 102). Subsequently all commercial banks in Pakistan were ordered to open 'profit-and-loss-sharing' (PLS) accounts (Khan 2001: 663). This measure was to allow Muslims to invest their savings in an ostensibly *Shariah*-compliant manner by sharing in a bank's profits rather than receiving a fixed rate of interest on their deposits. At the same time, Pakistani banks were instructed by the government to phase out conventional (i.e., Western, interest-based) banking by 1985, and become fully Islamic in their operations (Khan 2001: 665).

The CII had recommended in 1969, and again in 1971, that *riba* be abolished and the banking system overhauled but thus far these suggestions had been studiously ignored by successive administrations, whether civilian or military. Nevertheless, for all his ostensible commitment to Islamization, General Zia explicitly exempted financial matters from the FSC's purview until 1990 by amending the 1973 Constitution (Kennedy 2004: 106); this clause was successively amended three times to continue exempting the financial sector from the FSC's purview.[4]

This delayed the FSC's scrutiny of Pakistan's financial sector for several years but once the third financial exemption had expired it moved quickly against the existing financial system and ruled that 'real' Islamic banking should be introduced. This was because the form of Islamic banking that came to be adopted in Pakistan in 1985 was not greatly different from Western banking as it was overwhelmingly *murabaha* (cost-plus sales) and *ijara* (leasing) transactions. As has been extensively discussed in Chapter Six, these transactions are functionally equivalent to conventional banking. So while 'interest rate' may have been replaced with 'markup rate,' it was strictly business as usual for the Pakistani banks post-1985 as there was no change in actual banking practices (Nomani 2003: 51; Hassan and Azfar 2001: 18).

The banking sector was therefore willing to go along with the government's policy, to become '*Shariah*-compliant' in the current usage, for it made little real difference in the way they conducted their business, especially since any loans they offered would be fully collateralized by the usual hypothecation agreements. All that had happened was that there had been 'a shift in nomenclature' (Hassan and Azfar 2001: 18).[5] Indeed the standard college-level text on money and banking used in Pakistan today states unequivocally that 'The change over from "interest" to "markup" based transactions is thus merely a cosmetic one' (Meenai 2004: 222) and these markup-based transactions constituted Pakistani banking in the 1980s and 1990s.

As discussed in Chapter Four, most Islamic scholars and analysts agree that participatory finance (profit-and-loss-sharing in the Pakistani terminology) is *the* desired mode of Islamic financing and that non-participatory ('trade-based,' to use current terminology) financing should be used only as an interim/transition measure or for small loans not suitable for participatory finance. However, all Islamic banking systems, including Pakistan's, essentially operate according to non-participatory principles. One could therefore characterize the form of Islamic banking implemented in Pakistan as being only at best weakly Islamic since it permitted disguised interest. Clearly then the spirit, if not the letter, of the Islamic injunctions was being violated by most Islamic banks but thanks to the financial sector exemption, the FSC was barred from questioning the country's banking laws until 1990.

Eliminating *riba* by judicial decree

The expiration of the financial sector exemption coincided, or perhaps it was deliberate, with the appointment of an activist Islamic Maximalist as the new Chief Justice of the FSC.[6] In late 1990, President Ghulam Ishaq Khan appointed Dr. Tanzil ur Rahman, former chairman of the CII from 1980 to 1984 and author of the 1980 CII report on the abolishment of *riba*, as the new Chief Justice of the FSC. President Ghulam Ishaq Khan, a Zia loyalist, had served as the chairman of the Senate (Pakistan's upper legislative house) and thus *de facto* vice-president under Gen. Zia's military regime. Dr. Rahman had served as a judge of the Sind High Court in the Zia government from 1980 to 1990 and in that capacity he had argued (unsuccessfully) that the Objectives Resolution was 'supra-constitutional' (Kennedy 2004: 104) and thus overrode exemptions to the country's financial laws. Not surprisingly the new chief justice immediately announced that the FSC would now entertain petitions challenging the existing financial laws. Within a short time 'it was swamped by such petitions' (Kennedy 2004: 106).

In November 1991 the FSC made a sweeping ruling that essentially turned 115 petitions challenging twenty key financial laws into a class-action suit that threatened to destroy the entire Pakistani financial system (Hassan and Azfar 2001: 22).[7] It held that the Pakistani financial system, officially Islamic since 1985, was still effectively *riba*-based and so un-Islamic and thus *ipso facto* unconstitutional. How did it come to this conclusion? First, relying on 'the work of Islamic jurists of the classical period,' it rejected outright the contention that *riba* referred not to interest but to usury (Hassan and Azfar 2001: 19). Second, the FSC determined that *riba* meant any 'addition, however slight, over and above the principal' (Kennedy 2004: 107). Third, it ruled against inflation indexing on the grounds that indexing automatically increased the amount repaid. By taking this stand, the FSC ensured that (at least in theory) virtually the entire Pakistani financial system would collapse on 1 July 1992 when the twenty laws it had rejected as unconstitutional would 'cease to have effect' (Hassan and Azfar 2001: 20).

Prime Minister Nawaz Sharif, who had succeeded Benazir Bhutto as prime minister in November 1990, dependent upon the parliamentary support of Islamist parties as well as being constrained by his own public declarations in favor of more and faster Islamization, simply encouraged understandably anxious Pakistani bankers to file an appeal against the FSC's ruling with the Supreme Court's SAB. Appeals were duly lodged. Meanwhile, banking practices continued as before (Kennedy 2004: 108).

Despite a change in government (the Nawaz Sharif government fell and was replaced by Benazir Bhutto's second administration in October 1993) and new appointments to the Supreme Court, the appeal lodged by the banks was conveniently forgotten and languished in limbo for five years. Clearly no-one other than committed Islamic Maximalists was interested in speeding up the appeals process and threatening the extremely rickety applecart that was the Pakistani financial system.

However, Prime Minister Nawaz Sharif's attempt in his second term[8] to severely restrict the powers of the Supreme Court, especially those of Chief Justice Sajjad Ali Shah, and to appoint several new members to the Bench led the Chief Justice to suddenly move the appeal to the head of the docket.[9] Despite frantic attempts by the government to prevent it, the hearing of the appeal started in February 1999. In December 1999, after 44 days of sittings, during which 40 witnesses were heard and 12 depositions were lodged, the SAB in a unanimous 106-page-long decision[10] (Jafar 2000) dismissed all 55 appeals from the banks against the original 1991 FSC ruling (Kennedy 2004: 109).[11]

However the SAB did not just uphold the FSC's earlier interpretation. It went further and ordered all the country's banks to convert themselves into venture capital funds. Banks in Pakistan after 1999 were to be 'primarily financial intermediaries through equity participation or partnership [or] holding companies,' though 'where feasible,' they could 'also directly engage themselves in commercial, industrial, agricultural and other enterprises and businesses' (quoted in Jafar 2000).

The SAB ruling expanded upon the original FSC ruling in several key aspects. It held that *all* transactions *must* be real: 'No purely monetary transactions should be made because such transactions lead to opening the door of Riba' (Hassan and Azfar 2001: 27). This ruling banned, for example, foreign exchange dealings unless purchase/sale of gold was used as an intermediate step. Furthermore, employing a literal definition of *riba*, the SAB also held that creditors could not be awarded punitive or compensatory damages in case of a loan default; however, damages could be levied if they were then given to charity, i.e., did not accrue to the original creditor (Hassan and Azfar 2001: 43–44). The SAB gave the government until June 30, 2001 to effect the most important of these changes, with earlier deadlines for some relatively minor laws (Jafar 2000).

The SAB did acknowledge that converting lending banking to investment banking might involve practical problems: information asymmetry, corruption, and the like. Accordingly, it noted that eliminating *riba* would require 'strenuous efforts [by the government] on a wide front to inculcate in society basic virtues such as the fear of Allah, honesty, trustworthiness, sense of duty and patriotism' (quoted in Jafar 2000). For the rest, however, some of its prescriptions for reforming the Pakistani financial sector verged on the absurd given the time frame involved: reduced dependence on foreign loans, land reform, debt-equity swaps to convert earlier loans into equity, a national credit-rating bureau, overhaul of audit/accounting systems, all politicians and bureaucrats to make a full accounting of their assets, and so on (Jafar 2000). Jafar (2000) ends his analysis of the 1999 SAB ruling by concluding that 'what is being envisaged is nothing less than the emergence of a new breed of men ... Homo Islamicus,' and understandably wondered how likely was this to occur by the SAB's June 2001 deadline to the government?

On a more practical note, the SAB later also laid out a detailed timetable for the substitution of '*Shari'ah*-compliant' processes (Kennedy 2004: 110). This seems to have been a response to criticism by the government of the Court's ruling when in the appeals process the Attorney-General had presented a formal petition asking for 'authoritative answers' as to how exactly *riba* was to be eliminated from the economy (Kennedy 2004: 109).

A military coup replaced the Islamist sympathizer Nawaz Sharif with the relatively liberal (by Pakistani standards) General Pervez Musharraf in October 1999. Despite this, it seemed as though the Pakistani government was intent on implementing the FSC ruling. The Ministry of Law drafted an ordinance prohibiting *riba* (Kennedy 2004: 112) while the State Bank of Pakistan (the country's central bank) and the Ministry of Finance established a joint working committee to plan the transition (Meenai 2004: 220).

Reverting to business as usual

In June 2001 the government changed course. It sided with a major Pakistani bank, United Bank Limited, in its petition asking the SAB to revisit its 1999 ruling. Moreover, the new military government indicated that it would not stop at just joining United Bank in its petition but actually threatened the SAB. Referring to Kelsen's 'Doctrine of Necessity,'[12] on July 11, 2001 the military government's Attorney General curtly informed the SAB that the national budget-making process was too important for the government to allow the court to endanger it by refusing to grant a further extension of the deadline for the government to implement a *riba*-free financial system (Dawn 2001). Presumably the point being made here by the Attorney General was that, since the *status quo* would be totally disrupted by the changeover to a fully Islamic system, the government could not estimate its total tax revenues or expenditures and so could not formulate a national budget, in which case the government would have no choice but to take some severe action against the justices of the SAB.[13]

The SAB would not back down. It could not consider the government's petition, the presiding judge explained, since it only had three members and not the constitutionally mandated five; therefore it could not issue an extension. The Bench's strength had been reduced by the forced retirement of two judges who had refused to swear a new oath of office affirming the legality of the military government's Provisional Constitution Order validating the most recent (October 1999) military coup (Dawn 2001). At this point the Pakistani Supreme Court stepped in. On July 14, 2001, three days after the Attorney

General's threat, the full Bench of the Court (composed of judges who had sworn the new oath) extended the deadline imposed on the government until June 30, 2002. One could construe this as a victory of sorts for the Supreme Court and its SAB since the government had demanded an extension until 2005 (Ali 2001).

With the extension on the deadline ticking away, the Pakistani government acted again. On May 24, 2002 President Gen. Pervez Musharraf ordered the removal of *ulema* Justice Mohammed Taqi Usmani from the SAB; the SAB was reconstituted with two new *ulema* judges, and a third Supreme Court judge was appointed to bring its strength up to the mandated five (Dawn 2002a).

The reconstitution of the SAB was controversial as Justice Usmani, a son of the founder of the *Jamia Dar ul Uloom* (Pakistan's first and largest Deobandi *madarassah*) and a graduate of it as well, had initially been appointed by Gen. Zia to the FSC in the 1980s (Raja 2003), was a member of the Bench that wrote the 1999 decision, and earlier had served on the CII panel that had recommended the abolition of *riba* in 1980 (Kennedy 2004: 114). Given his involvement in the 1980 CII report and the 1999 SAB judgment, he was unlikely to vote for overturning his earlier decisions and now rule in favour of United Bank. With hearings on the United Bank appeal scheduled to get under way on June 6, 2002, the removal of Usmani on May 24, 2002 made it clear that the government wanted him replaced with a more amenable judge. The official reason given for his removal, after the fact and after some public outcry about it by the Islamist parties, was that Justice Usmani was on the *Shariah* Advisory Board of several banks in Pakistan and thus had a monetary conflict of interest in ensuring that all banks were now forced to become completely Islamic (Ali 2002).

Then in August 2002, shortly after the SAB ruling had been delivered, the Pakistani Government raised the mandatory retirement age for judges from 65 to 68, thereby giving all three non-*ulema* members of the SAB a further three years of service (Dawn 2002b).[14] Finally, the salaries and allowances of Supreme Court (and hence also SAB) justices were raised by 30 per cent even though there was supposed to be a pay freeze on all civil servant wages (Dawn 2002b). The sole possible conclusion to be drawn from all this is that the government was using a none-too-subtle 'carrot-and-stick' approach to ensure that a favorable ruling was delivered on the United Bank appeal.

In contrast to the earlier SAB proceedings which had dragged on for over two years with dozens of witnesses called and hundreds of *amicus curiae* briefs (both pro and con) filed, the 2002 hearing on the United Bank appeal was a model of efficiency, speed and brevity. On June 24, after just six days, the SAB delivered its 22-page decision. It found that the 1999 SAB ruling had been fatally flawed in several key aspects:

i the SAB did not properly distinguish between 'usury,' '*riba*,' and 'interest';
ii the directives made by the SAB in the 1999 ruling were not 'practical' or 'feasible' and, if implemented, would 'pose [a] high degree of risk to the economic stability and security of Pakistan';
iii the SAB had failed to distinguish between the 'legal and moral aspects' of *riba*;
iv the court had misread the commentary of various eminent jurists who had different views regarding the nature of *riba*;
v the SAB had wrongly applied its decision to non-Muslims;
vi indexation is not repugnant to Islam;
vii Tanzil ur Rahman (Chairman of the CII in 1980 and main author of the 1980 report that laid the framework for the Islamization of the financial sector) had approached the 1991 case in a 'predetermined' state of mind and the SAB should have taken this into account when forming its decision in 1999;
viii the SAB did not fully consider 'all of the jurisdictional issues related to the implementation of its directives'; and
ix the SAB did not make sufficient allowances for the effects of inflation in determining what constituted *riba*
(See Kennedy 2004: 112–113 for more details)

As Oscar Wilde's *bon mot* has it, 'Consistency is the last refuge of the unimaginative,' and Pakistani courts are nothing if not imaginative.

The wording of the ruling clearly indicates that the Bench had rejected its earlier reliance on a classical interpretation of *riba* in favour of a more Modernist one, and furthermore that it understood *riba* to require a degree of duress and exploitation not found in common banking transactions (Supreme Court of Pakistan 2002). In line with this interpretation, the SAB ordered the original ruling 'set aside' and remanded the case back to the FSC for a 'definitive finding on all the issues … after thorough and elaborate research and comparative study of the financial systems which are prevalent in the contemporary Muslim countries of the world' (Supreme Court of Pakistan 2002). That is, to re-hear the case *de novo*. Nonetheless, the FSC has not scheduled any new hearings on the issue since 2002 and there appears to be no popular demand for it to do so. So while the Pakistani banking and financial system remains safe for now, was the SAB ruling merely a tactical retreat by the forces of Orthodoxy and Islamic Maximalism or was it a return to the Islamic Modernist *status quo* of the 1960s?

Merely a swing of the pendulum?

The Pakistani courts' conclusion in 1991 and 1999 not only that all interest-based transactions were unlawful in Islam but that eliminating *riba* required the restructuring of Pakistani society and economy was based on the strictest possible definition and broadest possible interpretation of *riba*. These rulings were a complete triumph for an Islamic Maximalist interpretation conforming to the narrowest possible interpretation of classical *fiqh* and were strictly in line with Maulana Maududi's views on *riba* and the need for a truly participatory Islamic financial system expressed over five decades earlier. In short, 1991 was a defeat for the Islamic Modernists and Minimalists and 1999 had been their complete and utter rout. Pakistani Islam was now no longer moderate, Modernist, or Minimalist. Or was it?

Until his removal from the SAB in 2002, the career of Justice Usmani exemplified the collapse of the Aligarh School of Islamic Modernism in Pakistan and the triumph of its great rival, the highly orthodox and decidedly illiberal *Madrassa Dar ul Uloom* Deoband. Justice Usmani was a member of the Pakistani government's Council of Islamic Ideology that issued the 1980 report calling for the abolishment of *riba* from the Pakistani economy, a judge of the FSC (1980–82) and the SAB of the Supreme Court (1982–2002). Usmani is also a son of the founder, as well as a graduate, and currently a Vice-President, of the *Dar ul Uloom* Karachi *madrassa*.[15] The *Dar ul Uloom* Karachi is the oldest, largest, and most influential Deobandi seminary in Pakistan; with strong links to Saudi Arabian Wahhabism, it is the chief promulgator of an extremely narrow and restrictive, if not outright reactionary, Maximalist version of Islam. Progressive, or even pragmatic, interpretations of Islam which had held sway in the 1950s and 1960s were completely absent from government-sponsored think-tanks, advisory panels and the like in the 1980s and 1990s.

Thus while seemingly a swing of the pendulum towards moderation and Islamic Minimalism, the 2002 SAB ruling is actually nothing of the sort since the FSC ruling was not overturned but merely sent back for further study. It is, therefore, a tactical setback for the ultra-Orthodox Maximalists and not their full-fledged rout. This is because the SAB's 2002 decision, far from resolving the issue once and for all, has merely forced them to wait until a more favorable opportunity for asserting their agenda appears. There is nothing to prevent the FSC from coming back after 'suitable' study and reaffirming its original ruling. There is also no reason to assume that yet a third SAB would not uphold it. Given the weakness, inability, and unwillingness of post-Zia governments (whether civilian or military) to challenge the fundamental changes to Pakistani social, cultural, economic, and financial life implemented (even if not initiated) by General Zia, it is not surprising that the Pakistani court system is capable of issuing rulings that, if implemented, would literally destroy Pakistan's financial structure. However, it must be said that the Pakistani judiciary is often discreet to a fault: rulings that the government does not like are few and far between.[16]

When a Pakistani court has ruled against a government, it has usually only been after the government has already fallen, or is commonly perceived as being on its last legs. For instance, the Supreme Court's ruling declaring illegal then-'elected' president Gen. Zia's May 1988 dissolution of the National

Assembly did not come until several months after his death. In response to this, Zia's son was quoted as saying: 'I would have seen [*sic*] how the court dared to give that judgment had my father been alive' (Hussain 1993: 32). An anonymous analyst agreed with Zia's son: '[judgments of the superior court are] the real measure of the country's political situation. When a government becomes weaker, the courts become bolder (Hussain 1993: 32).[17]

It will never be known how the Nawaz Sharif government might have handled the 1999 SAB ruling, or how the never-implemented Ministry of Law's 'Anti-*Riba* Ordinance' would have affected Pakistani life. The banks might have come up with new terms, other than 'markup', to describe their lending operations. It is also possible that the banks would have been forced to actually take an equity stake in every enterprise they wished to do business with; or that the entire Pakistani financial system and economy might have collapsed as formal sector credit availability contracted. Of course, *informal-sector* credit[18] processes are not affected by *riba* considerations and could have been expected to expand, but their ability to take up the resulting slack would have been severely limited, and the rates charged by this sector are several times higher than the formal sector.[19]

In November 2002 the State Bank of Pakistan, the central bank, allowed a 'parallel' Islamic banking system to initiate operations and designated the existing system as 'conventional' banking. The resulting Islamic banking subsystem is functionally virtually indistinguishable from the conventional one but this practical convergence is in light of the 2002 SAB ruling and directly contradicts the 1999 ruling that mandated direct 'equity participation' as the sole permissible Islamic financing mode. It cannot be determined, without the 2002 SAB ruling, what the effect of implementing the 1999 SAB ruling would have been by looking at the current Pakistani Islamic banking model. It is clear that what constitutes contemporary Islamic banking in Pakistan (as is the case of Islamic banking in the rest of the world) would not have passed muster with the 1991 FSC or the 1999 SAB.

What is also clear is that, under the Constitutionally-mandated structure of the SAB and the FSC, the *ulema* will have a disproportionate say in all decisions taken by these bodies. As amply demonstrated by the 1991 and 1999 rulings, the likelihood of regular judges consistently opposing *ulema* judges is minimal; the 2002 SAB review ruling was possible only after the most blatant court-packing. Therefore, until the Constitution is amended and the FSC and the SAB are dissolved, the risk to the Pakistani financial system will remain. But how likely is it that the FSC or the SAB will stand by their earlier rulings? The answer is 'very.' Despite the fact that genuine grassroots agitation against *riba*/interest/usury, or for the radical restructuring of the banking system, or the conversion of the country into a true stakeholder society, is virtually non-existent, all of the Islamist parties remain firmly committed to abolishing an interest-based banking system in Pakistan and no non-Islamist party has the courage or conviction to stand up to their demands.

The reasons for this hard-line stance are quite straightforward. Firstly, as discussed in more detail in Chapter Three, in its original genesis, as argued by Kuran, the actual economic/financial efficiency/practicality aspects of Islamic economic thought are irrelevant; it exists to fulfil the overall aim of 'identity creation and protection' and inoculate against 'Westoxication.' This aspect of Islamization is exemplified by Imam Khomeini's pithy comment that 'This revolution is not about the price of watermelons' when pressed about his regime's plans to stabilize the Iranian economy after the 1979 Islamic Revolution (Looney 2006: 29) and Maududi's concerns about 'partial Muslims' becoming the norm in Pakistan. Secondly, the Islamist parties see the anti-*riba* campaign as a potent weapon to use against Pakistani governments and have not hesitated to deploy it even against such ostensible allies as the Nawaz Sharif administration. The Islamist parties view the Pakistani establishment as being irredeemably pro-Western and so by definition insufficiently Islamic. The anti-*riba* campaign is a valuable lever against the establishment since it cannot be denied that Pakistan's economy is built upon an interest-based financial system.

As long as no Pakistani government is prepared to amend the 1973 Constitution to remove the more overtly Islamist clauses, the Islamist parties will continue to have a potent and constitutionally mandated threat to use against the Pakistani state. The self-described 'moderate Islamic' government of General Pervez Musharraf was perhaps the last hope of a reversion to the 1960s tradition of a more progressive interpretation of Islam in Pakistan. Despite his professed personal admiration for Mustafa Kemal of Turkey, Musharraf displayed a marked unwillingness to make fundamental changes to the Pakistani constitutional and legal structure as far as the official role of Islam and *Shariah* was concerned. If a *de facto* military dictatorship, one not dependent upon smaller political parties for support or answerable to a relatively conservative electorate, is unable or unwilling to make such changes, it is extremely unlikely that any future civilian government will have the power to do so – even if it has the inclination.

The 2002 reboot of Islamic banking in Pakistan

In 2015 Pakistan will have completed three decades since its then military ruler Gen. Zia ul Haq first ordered all banks to switch over to 'Islamic banking' by 1985. And it will have been well over a decade since the State Bank of Pakistan (SBP) in 2002 ordered a 'reboot' of Islamic banking in Pakistan.

The purpose of this reboot was extremely straightforward. Pakistan's central bank, the State Bank of Pakistan, could not have been any blunter: it was to 'make Islamic banking the banking of first choice for the providers and users of financial services' and accordingly it would act to 'promote and develop Islamic banking industry in line with best international practices, ensuring Shariah compliance and transparency' (SBP 2008a: iii). The major changes implemented by the SBP were the creation of a formal '*Shariah*

Compliance Framework' along the lines specified by the Bahrain-based Accounting and Auditing Organization for Islamic Financial Institutions (AAOIFI), and capital adequacy, risk management, corporate governance, and other criteria for Islamic financial institutions laid down by the Malaysia-based Islamic Financial Services Board (IFSB), of which Pakistan is a member and where it has some input in the standards-setting process.

The non-*Shariah* components of the AAOIFI and IFSB are very closely aligned with the norms and standards for banks set by the Swiss-based Bank for International Settlements (BIS – the central banks' bank) such as bank capital adequacy, regulation, and supervisory standards set by the various Basel rounds of negotiations. Thus the most important regulatory aspects of Pakistan's newly renovated Islamic banking framework would be very closely aligned with the global financial system and designed to ensure that Pakistan's Islamic banking framework would be compatible with them. It would not use capital adequacy, regulation, and/or supervisory standards that were derived from any principles organic to Islamic economics or finance or even to Islam itself.

The major differences between the post- and pre-2002 forms of Islamic banking in Pakistan had to do with the requirement that all Islamic banks have a State Bank-approved *Shariah* advisor although they may choose to appoint a panel of three advisors rather than just one. The individual banks' *Shariah* advisor has to follow the rulings/guidelines set by the SBP's *Shariah* Board and the bank has to use a broadly standardized set of forms ('duly vetted by their *Shariah* Adviser') for its Islamic financing transactions. The Islamic and non-Islamic modes of financing have to be kept in separate accounts and the Islamic bank has to carry out an annual *Shariah* audit of its Islamic financings.[20]

The SBP concluded that the earlier attempt at Islamic banking failed for three main reasons: 'it did not adequately address issues such as putting in place an effective Shariah compliance mechanism, [not] giving emphasis to capacity building, and [not] opting for a flexible and evolutionary approach' (SBP 2008a: vii). Thus by creating a layer of *Shariah* scholars/advisors whose function it is to scrutinize all Islamic banking transactions that the Islamic commercial bank carries out and to train the bank's personnel in the financial principles of *Shariah*, the SBP's aim was to remove the perception that there was no difference between Islamic and conventional banking. To enhance 'capacity building' in Islamic finance and to alleviate the chronic shortage of bank employees trained in the principles of *Shariah*-compliant banking, the SBP's National Institute of Banking and Finance (its in-house training center) started intensive training programs in Islamic banking methods that were open to personnel from commercial banks; it also coordinated with the Institute of Bankers – Pakistan (the body that administers various professional banking certification exams for Pakistani bankers) to include formal training in Islamic banking methods in its course and certification offerings, and it also coordinated with various academic institutions in the country to ensure that Islamic banking theory, methodology, and practice figured prominently in their accounting and finance curricula (SBP 2008a: 51). Finally, by allowing both conventional and Islamic banking, it would allow an organic growth path to emerge: Islamic banking would grow at the rate at which the people wanted it to, not at the rate mandated by the government – an overnight transition.

Accordingly, the SBP issued guidelines, including officially approved transaction forms, for the following fourteen types of approved Islamic banking transaction (see SBP 2008b for more details).

Participatory (profit- or loss-sharing, PLS) modes

- *Mudaraba* – partnership, with one partner contributing capital and the other expertise.
- *Musharaka* – taking a direct equity stake in a firm.
- Diminishing *musharaka* – financing a tangible asset in partnership, with one partner buying the other out over time.[21]
- Equity participation – direct purchase of shares in a corporate entity.

Trading (non-PLS) modes

- *Ijara* or *Ijara wa Iqtina*: a lease.
- *Murabaha* – sale of goods to a client on a deferred payment basis with the client knowing the bank's cost; see Chapter Six for more details.
- *Musawamah* – same as a *murabaha* but the client does not know the bank's cost of purchase.
- *Salam* – advance payment in full for future delivery of completely specified goods; repurchase agreements (repos) specifically excluded.
- *Istisna* – essentially the same as above but for goods that will be manufactured to order.
- *Tawarruq* – purchase of a commodity on a deferred payment basis, which item is then turned around and sold on the spot market (perhaps to the original seller) for a lower price; requires prior approval from the SBP; see Chapter Six for more details.

Debt-based modes

- *Qard* – a non-interest-bearing loan.

Other modes

- *Wakalah* – agency agreement for a set service fee.
- Assignment of debt – from one party to another; must be done at the debt's face value; no discounting of commercial paper or accounts receivable.

- *Kafalah* – third-party guarantee for the payment of a debt between two parties.

So what is the state of Islamic banking in Pakistan now? Has Islamic banking in Pakistan reached a stage where it is truly a different form of finance? How does the Pakistani version of Islamic banking differ from the version discussed in Chapter Six?

Size and scope of Islamic banking in Pakistan

In late 2002, Meezan Bank was the first new Islamic bank to get a banking license under the reboot, the 'new and improved' version if you will, of Islamic banking that was to be implemented in the light of the scathing criticism of the 'old' version of Islamic banking enunciated in the 1991 FSC and 1999 SAB rulings. Since then Islamic banking has grown quite rapidly from officially 'nil' in 2002 to, by end-March 2014, 9.4 per cent of Pakistan's total banking system assets and 10.7 per cent of total banking system deposits, with both assets and deposits often growing at 20–30 per cent plus annually (SBP 2014b).

The State Bank divides Pakistani Islamic banking into two categories, although no one type is preferred officially as such.[22]

- **Islamic banks** (i.e., all of the banks' operations are Islamic and fully '*Shariah*-compliant').

  Five banks: Al Baraka Bank, BankIslami Pakistan, Burj Bank, Dubai Islamic Bank (Pakistan), and Meezan Bank.

- **Islamic branches of conventional banks** (i.e., only the 'Islamic branch' is fully '*Shariah*-compliant').

  Fifteen banks: Askari Bank, Bank Al Habib, Bank Al Falah, Faysal Bank, Habib Bank, Habib Metropolitan Bank, MCB Bank, National Bank of Pakistan, Silkbank, Soneri Bank, Standard Chartered Bank (Pakistan), Summit Bank, Bank of Khyber, Bank of Punjab, and United Bank.

The composition of banks in the system has changed slightly over the past two or so decades as smaller banks have entered, been taken over by others or left[23] but the major banks have stayed dominant with only relatively minor changes in their size and market position. The ten largest banks in Pakistan in 2012 were: National, Habib, United, MCB, Allied, Al Falah, Bank al Habib, Standard Chartered, Askari, and Habib Metropolitan (Asian Banker 2012); the largest wholly Islamic bank in Pakistan, Meezan Bank, has never made the list of the ten largest.

Again starting from officially none in 2002, there are now 1,218 branches and 96 sub-branches[24] of Islamic banks or Islamic branches of conventional banks in the country, with the largest branch network belonging to Meezan Bank (349 branches), followed by Bank Al Falah (140 branches), and Dubai Islamic (124 branches). However, even Pakistan's largest Islamic bank's branch network, Meezan's, is small compared with the largest conventional branch network – Habib Bank with 1,540 branches and a presence in 25 countries worldwide.

Meezan Bank's asset and deposit base is similarly relatively small. In 2013 Meezan had total assets of Pakistani rupees (PKR) 329.74 billion (then approximately US$3.3 billion) and total deposits of PKR289.8 billion (then approximately US$2.9 billion) (Meezan Bank 2014). While small compared with, say, Habib Bank's 2012 assets of PKR1,610 billion and deposits of PKR1,215 billion (Habib Bank 2013), Meezan is the undisputed leader in both Islamic finance and Islamic financial product innovation in Pakistan. It has a large and creative 'Product Development and Shariah Compliance' department which has pioneered several Islamic financial products (e.g., *Takaful* insurance and *Musharaka*-based running finance – line of credit) and sponsored many conferences and training seminars for Islamic bankers. Meezan Bank is the main intellectual force behind Islamic banking in Pakistan.

So, while certainly growing faster than the conventional banking sector, Pakistan's Islamic banking sector is barely a tenth of the conventional system and poses no immediate threat of displacing the latter, glowing official tributes to the Islamic banking sector notwithstanding. Furthermore, despite the 'reboot' of Islamic banking in 2002, nothing has actually changed in the form and function of Islamic banking in Pakistan. In both cases it works exactly the same as the system of Islamic banking described in Chapter Six (other than the Malaysian case). In other words, Pakistani Islamic banking is still overwhelmingly 'markup'-based and *ipso facto* indistinguishable from conventional interest-based banking. Baele et al (2014: 2) calculate, after analyzing all credit extended by the Pakistani banking system in the period April 2006 to December 2008, that 'pure profit and loss sharing contracts' comprised no more than 3 per cent of all Pakistani banking sector credit advanced.

Analyzing data from 'Table 17: Advances by mode of financing' of the State Bank of Pakistan's *Statistics on Scheduled Banks in Pakistan* (SBP 2014c) for the six months ending December 2013 confirms Baele *et al.*'s (2014) analysis. The 'Table 17' data present a picture of Pakistani banking as shown in Table 7.1.[25]

Table 7.1 Credit extended by Pakistani banks in 2013 by type

Type of financing	*Credit (billion PKR)*
Total 'advances' (i.e., credit extended) by all banks in Pakistan	3,915.9
Of this, explicitly characterized as 'interest-based'	325.2
Characterized as 'Islamic modes'	3,590.6

Upon further examination, of the Islamic modes of financing, PKR3061.6 billion was immediately identifiable as *de facto* interest-based. This includes lending categories such as 'markup in price on deferred payment basis,' 'leasing,' 'hire purchase,' and so on. These all use, as mandated by the State Bank of Pakistan, the Karachi Interbank Offer Rate (Kibor) for their pricing basis and these are all different names for the same sorts of categories as discussed in Chapter Six. For example, 'markup in price on deferred payment basis' is of course the definition of *murabaha*-type transactions and at PKR2,774.8 billion, these *alone* totaled 77.28 per cent of all Islamic-mode credit advanced by all (conventional and Islamic) Pakistani banks.

So, in total, 85.27 per cent of all 'Islamic modes' of credit extended was immediately identifiable as *murabaha* or *ijara* or similar types of financing and only PKR38.1 billion (1.06 per cent) was explicitly identified as '*musharaka* or profit-and-loss' sharing. It is possible that other forms of 'strongly Islamic' types of financing were being carried out by the banking system as PKR471.9 billion (13.14 per cent of the total 'Islamic modes' of credit extended) fell in the category of 'other Islamic modes' and no further breakdown on this was available. However, given that 'other Islamic modes' would include items such as *Bai Salam* (deferred delivery of paid-for items), *Bai Muajjal* (deferred payment, i.e., credit, sales), and similar modes which also use 'markup'-type pricing, the overwhelming majority of all credit extended by Pakistani banks (including that extended under 'Islamic modes') was on a *de facto* interest-rate basis.

In fact, the State Bank of Pakistan is sometimes very forthright and forgets to disguise what it sees as the crucial role of interest rates in the Pakistani financial system. Although the State Bank usually pays at least lip-service to Islamic terminology and sensibilities, it does occasionally make a slip. This is clearly the case regarding the following definition from the section titled 'II. Explanatory Notes' of its *Statistics on Scheduled Banks in Pakistan* (SBP 2014c: xi):

> **Rate of Interest/Return.** This is the cost of using borrowed money expressed as a rate, or a percentage of the principal amount for a period of time usually a year. In case of Islamic modes of financing it is referred as rate of mark-up.

Ironically, given the massive interest rate cuts implemented by Western central banks since the start of the great recession in 2008, the 'markup rate' for Pakistani advances under 'Islamic modes of financing' has been consistently far higher than the rate charged on explicitly interest rate-based advances (SBP 2014c: xviii). In all fairness, however, it should also be said that the rate paid to depositors under 'Islamic modes' has also been far higher than the 'interest rate' paid on non-Islamic mode deposits (SBP 2014c: xvi).

Excluding conventional Pakistani banks from the analysis does not materially affect the picture. As of December 2013, the explicitly markup-based financing modes comprised 88.7 per cent of all credit extended by Pakistani Islamic banks, with *murabaha* (40.6 per cent), diminishing *musharaka* (30.8 per cent), and *ijara* (7.7 per cent) the three largest financing modes. This is, however, still an improvement over 2007 when *murabaha, ijara*, and diminishing *musharaka* totaled 94.14 per cent of all credit extended by the Pakistani Islamic banks (SBP 2008a: 36).

Explicitly 'PLS' modes comprised only 6.9 per cent (*musharaka* 6.7 per cent and *mudaraba* 0.2 per cent) of the total financing of Pakistani Islamic banks. Finally, 4.4 per cent of total credit extended was categorized as 'others;' again, these are likely to also be 'markup'-based.[26] Thus while Pakistani Islamic banks are substantially more likely to have 'PLS' partnerships with their clients, the actual value of these types of partnership is a very, very small, if not totally insignificant, component of Pakistani Islamic banking.

There is, however, one seeming anomaly in the data on Pakistani Islamic banks. 'Table 10: Earnings and profitability' of the SBP's *Islamic Banking Bulletin – December 2013* (SBP 2014a: 12) gives the ratio of 'non-mark up income to gross income' as 21.5 per cent. That is, just over a fifth of total income earned by Pakistani Islamic banks did not come from 'markup' (interest rate)-based earnings. It would appear that the 6.9 per cent of total credit extended by Pakistani Islamic banks that went to explicitly 'PLS' modes of financing contributed a vastly disproportionate portion of Islamic banks' income. How is this possible?

It is not. 'Non-mark up' income covers all of the banks' non-interest-based income. This includes items such as account maintenance charges, returned/cancelled check charges, check collection fees, account verification charges, travelers checks commissions, electronic fund transfer charges, charges for issuing letters of credit, performance bonds/bank guarantees, and the dozens of other fees and commissions all banks charge their customers for the myriad of services they provide. The most lucrative and desirable, from the banks' perspective, are the fees they earn for issuing letters of credit and performance bonds/bank guarantees.[27] For example, Standard Chartered Bank – Pakistan's Islamic banking arm, Saadiq, charges a standard rate of PKR2 million per calendar quarter for issuing an import letter of credit for PKR200 million (i.e., a 90-day PKR200,000,000 import sight L/C).[28] So it earned a straight 1 per cent of the transaction amount per quarter for handling the paperwork involved and guaranteeing payment for imported goods worth PKR200 million; if for some reason the transaction is not completed within one quarter, it would charge its client another PKR2 million. Obviously major clients will have negotiated a much more favorable rate for themselves than the standard one. This is a contingent liability for the bank as it is only on the hook for the payment if and when its client defaults – and all banks, conventional and Islamic, take steps to minimize this risk.

Thus even after the 2002 reboot, Islamic banking in Pakistan did not change in any significant way from the *de facto* conventional banking norms detailed in Chapter Six. The Kuran thesis – that banking form will follow function in this regard – is still applicable here and accurately describes why post-reboot Pakistani banks are still virtually indistinguishable from conventional ones. Indeed, since Pakistani Islamic banks have to adhere to AAOIFI and IFSB standards, which in turn are tightly coordinated with the Basel-based BIS standards for banks (i.e., the various Basel rounds of international banking standards), it can be logically concluded that Pakistani Islamic banks are *ipso facto* the functional equivalent of conventional banks. As Chapter Eight will show, extensive interviews, discussions, and meetings in Pakistan confirm the picture of Islamic banking in Pakistan depicted above. The major exception to this are the views of bankers from Meezan Bank who adhere strongly to the Islamic Shariah-compliant party line.

Notes

1 For a while some Pakistani analysts referred to the results of Gen. Zia's extensive amendments to the 1973 Constitution as the 1985 Constitution but this never really caught on despite the fact that none of his Islamic amendments were removed (as opposed to those granting the President substantial executive powers in a Westminster-style parliamentary system).

2 The FSC actually exercises original (including *suo moto*), revisional, appellate, and review jurisdiction, depending upon the exact circumstances involved. See the Court's website for more details on its functions and powers: www.federalshariatcourt.gov.pk/index.html.

3 The current Constitution and its various amendments are available online at www.pakistani.org/pakistan/constitution.

4 See successive amendments to Clause 203(b) of the Pakistani Constitution for details.

5 I can personally attest, as a corporate banker in Pakistan in 1988–90, to seeing pre-1985 forms being used where the word 'interest' had been erased and replaced with 'markup.'

6 Rumor has it that the new Benazir Bhutto government (her first term as Prime Minister was December 1988 to August 1990) simply forgot to renew the exemption for a fourth time. Pakistani governments have rarely been known for their administrative competence.

7 Nomani (2003: 49) holds that there were 119 cases challenging 22 separate laws. However, Hassan and Azfar's numbers (115 law suits challenging 20 laws) are probably more accurate as they are lawyers based in Pakistan whereas Nomani is a French academic.

8 The original ruling was issued by the FSC during Nawaz Sharif's first term as prime minister (November 1990 – April 1992) and the appeal was finally heard by the *Shariat* Appellate Bench of the Supreme Court during his second term as prime minister (February 1997 to October 1999).

9 The exact differences between the Prime Minister and the Chief Justice involved several issues, including which courts would have jurisdiction over terrorism/violent crime cases, who could nominate judges to existing vacancies on various benches, and so on. Matters came to a head when the Chief Justice instituted contempt of court proceedings against the Prime Minister, which would have removed him from office if convicted. The Prime Minister ordered several busloads of his party workers, led by cabinet members and MPs, to literally storm the Supreme Court building on November 28, 1997, roughing up several Court officials and forcing the justices to flee through the rear entrance. Following the refusal of the Army's

leadership to provide military protection for the justices, and the refusal of several justices to accept his authority and their continually staying whatever orders he issued, the Chief Justice resigned on December 2, 1997. See Khan (2001: 820–30) for a detailed discussion of the dispute.

10 Portions of the judgment are available online at http://albalagh.net/Islamic_economics/riba_judgement.shtml. Jafar (2000) gives the length as 1,100 pages, Kennedy (2004: 110–111) describes the full text as running to 534 pages while Hassan and Azfar (2001: 24) give it as only 400 pages but still lengthy 'even by Pakistani standards.' The differences in length have to do with whether or not one counts the various appendices and other ancilliary material solicited by the Bench. In addition to those, the SAB itself solicited numerous expert opinions from several scholars, both Pakistani and foreign, on the issues involved. It should be clear that the Bench did not rule hastily although it was careful to only solicit opinions from traditional/orthodox *ulema*.

11 In an interesting twist, the SAB also cited Western economists as being extremely critical of interest-based finance and concluding that even many Western economists were in favor of an interest-free financial system and economy. Pal (2006) is extremely critical of the Western sources used by the SAB, concluding that most of them were, at best, on the fringes of mainstream Western economic thought and not at all representative of the mainstream view of the role of interest rates in the modern economy.

12 That doctrine in English Common Law which holds that exigent circumstances that preclude any other conduct might mean that some laws will have to be violated; i.e., necessity makes legal what otherwise would be illegal. It is often cited by Pakistani courts to justify/excuse successful military coups. The Islamic concept of *dharura* (necessity) is similar.

13 Presumably in the form of a Presidential decree dismissing the existing judges and appointing new ones in their stead. In short, the Pakistani version of President Franklin Delano Roosevelt's threat to 'stack' the United States Supreme Court in order to ensure the survival of his New Deal legislation in the 1930s.

14 This extension was later rescinded after much protest by the Pakistan Bar Association and other organizations.

15 Taqi Usmani might be distantly related to Maulana Shabbir Ahmad Usmani; I have not been able to confirm this.

16 As the November 2007 declaration of a State of Emergency by President Gen. Pervez Musharraf and the wholesale sacking of Supreme Court justices, including the recalcitrant chief justice, showed, independent benches have a short lifespan in Pakistan. The reconstituted Supreme Court endorsed all of President Musharraf's actions. The subsequent restoration of the chief justice and the more activist tinge taken on by the Court are anomalies in Pakistani judicial history. Since the retirement of the activist chief justice in 2013, the Pakistani courts have been relatively quiet.

17 From the quotation's context, it appears likely that the source was a former or sitting High Court judge.

18 This is not loan sharking but credit made available to businesses which, for whatever reason (usually lack of tax records, audited accounts, clear title to property, inadequate credit history, etc.), are not able to meet the formal sector's documentation requirements for loans. For example, in the 1990s the State Bank of Pakistan mandated a minimum and maximum bank lending rate of between 10 and 20 per cent per annum. Informal-sector loans to fairly large firms which, for whatever reason, were not willing or able to get formal sector credit were usually about 5 per cent a month – about 80 per cent on an annualized basis.

19 Given the way in which the world's credit markets froze in fall 2008 and recovered only after heroic and hitherto utterly unprecedented policy action by the US

Federal Reserve and other Western central banks, it is unlikely that the Pakistani economy would have survived its credit freeze since the State Bank of Pakistan would not have been allowed to deal in debt.

20 See SBP (2008a) for more details.

21 The most common form of Islamic home mortgage; but as discussed in Chapter Six, this is as much a PLS financing mode as are home mortgages in the USA.

22 Branch data from SBP 2014a.

23 For example, the Royal Bank of Scotland sold its Pakistani operations and those branches became Faysal Bank; Dawood Islamic Bank was taken over by Burj Bank.

24 Sub-branches have limited services (e.g., only accepting deposits and cashing checks), as opposed to a full-service bank branch which may deal in foreign currency, pay orders and drafts, issue personal and business loans, and so on.

25 Explicitly interest-based transactions are mainly those dealing in foreign currency transactions or dollar-denominated, domestically held accounts. Even conventional banks adhere to Islamic lending norms for the most part, at least as far as eschewing explicit mention of 'interest rates' and often using the correct Islamic terminology to describe their accounts and practices.

26 Data calculated from 'Table 5: Financing mix' of SBP's *Islamic Banking Bulletin – December 2013* (SBP 2014a: 9).

27 Letters of credit (universally referred to as 'elcees') are invaluable for financing both domestic and especially international trade as the party responsible for making the payment to the seller/exporter is not the buyer/importer but the bank issuing the buyer's/importer's letter of credit; it is up to the bank to pursue its client if the buyer/importer defaults on his contractual obligation. This makes eminent sense as the counter-party risk perception is automatically greatly reduced if the counter-party for a British exporter is, say, Standard Chartered Bank, Pakistan (i.e., the Pakistani subsidiary of one of Britain's largest banks) rather than the Karachi Industrial Chemical Imports Ltd. which may well be an unknown quantity to the British firm. Performance bonds/bank guarantees are widely used in Pakistan and elsewhere as a way of reassuring the principal/client/contractee that the winning bidder on a contract will live up to the terms of the contract. In case of, say, default or the contractor being unable to complete the project on time or as per specifications, and the principal/client/conractee calling it in, the bank that has issued the performance bond will automatically make a pre-determined payment to the principal/client/contractee. It is up to the bank to seek reimbursement from its client.

28 Information from Standard Chartered Saadiq's 2014 *Schedule of Charges*.

8 Three decades of the Pakistani experiment

The purpose of this chapter is to see, in the opinion of Pakistani bankers and some of their corporate clients, how, if at all, the post-2002 reboot of Pakistani Islamic banking differs from its earlier incarnation. By interviewing those most intimately involved in the actual practice of Islamic banking in Pakistan, I hope to determine whether or not those who practice it see it differently from my analysis of it in Chapter Six. My aim is to provide the reader with both a 'big picture' overview as well as what I feel are some crucial 'in the weeds' details of the Pakistani Islamic banking sector. Accordingly, the chapter includes the views of a fairly broad sample of Pakistani Islamic and conventional bankers and others involved in the Pakistani financial sector; and an examination of the behavior of the Pakistani retail and corporate clientele of both Islamic and conventional Pakistani banks with an emphasis on highlighting the differences between those that use Islamic versus those that use conventional banks. The main focus of this chapter therefore is on the actual practice of Islamic banking in Pakistan and secondarily on the strength of Islamist feelings in the population. However, further compelling evidence does emerge that supports my overall argument about the importance of Islam for the average Pakistani.

The bankers', Islamic and others', view of Islamic banking

In 2008 and 2010 I conducted extensive interviews with Pakistani bankers (both conventional and Islamic), *Shariah* advisors to Islamic banks, some businessmen, and a prominent management consultant specializing in financial matters. I am keeping the identity of almost all of my interviewees confidential as they were assured that their identities and/or their professional affiliations would not be revealed. Where the interview was on the record and no assurance given of maintaining confidentiality, I will identify the interviewee and/or give their affiliation. In some cases, for reasons that will become obvious, I assured the person being interviewed that neither they nor their employer or, where relevant, their professional affiliation, would be given.

The persons that I interviewed, in some cases more than once, had current or prior affiliations with the following banks in Pakistan: Allied Bank, Citibank, Dubai Islamic Bank, Faysal Bank, Grindlays Bank, Habib Bank, HSBC Pakistan, Meezan Bank, National Bank, Silkbank, and Standard Chartered Bank. Their positions ranged from account managers/executives to the head of their bank's respective Islamic, corporate, retail, or product development divisions. The businessmen, in one case a former banker himself, were in textiles, commodity export, and sub-contractors/suppliers for multi-national firms operating in Pakistan.[1] The interviews were carried out in August 2008, January 2010, and June 2010. In some cases the interviewees were known to me beforehand[2] while others were generous enough to extend their time and knowledge to a complete stranger, albeit one who had been introduced to them by someone they knew well.

Interview 1 at a large conventional bank with Islamic banking branches

The most succinct, indeed pithy, summing up of the differences between Islamic and conventional banking in Pakistan was by a very senior (i.e., at the policy-making level) Islamic banking executive, *A*, who stated outright that '*Asal mein, yeh to sub marketing gimmick heh; hum apnay brochures par masjid ki tasweer lagga kar logon ko baewakoof banatay hein*' ('In reality this is all a marketing gimmick; we put pictures of mosques on our brochures and make fools of people'). *A*'s *Shariah* advisor, who was present at the meeting, looked troubled by this blunt statement and attempted to temper it by acknowledging that, as in Malaysia, what the *Shariah* board approved is often not what is actually marketed and implemented, and that is where the troubling aspects of Islamic banking practice come from. The *Shariah* advisor went on to make a direct analogy with the US mortgage market: what was specified by the regulators can be, and often was, very different from what was carried out by the actual practitioners; so the regulations laid down were good but the implementation was bad. *A* hastened to agree with this interpretation/clarification. Both he and the *Shariah* advisor estimated that approximately 10 per cent of total Pakistani banking sector clients were strictly conventional banking clients (mainly large Pakistani firms and multinationals), 20 per cent were strictly *Shariah*-compliant banking, and 70 per cent would probably prefer *Shariah*-compliant banking if all else were equal but would use conventional banking if there was a significant pricing difference. Their bank had plans to expand profit- and loss-sharing (PLS) transactions in principle but were not sure how effective modalities to safeguard the bank's interests could be worked out. They both stated categorically that there was no pressure from the SBP for favoring Islamic banking over conventional.

Interview 2 at a mid-sized conventional bank with Islamic banking branches

This interview was with an upper-middle management-level executive, *B*, who had worked for two different banks, currently a mid-sized conventional bank with separate Islamic branches and earlier a mid-sized Islamic bank. *B* had been hired away from the Islamic bank as his current employer wanted to expand its Islamic banking operations. *B* was quite cynical about Islamic banking and, in effect, confirmed the point made by *A*'s *Shariah* advisor about the difference between the ostensible Islamic banking rules in place and actual Islamic banking practices. Since I had been vouched for by a close friend of his, *B* was quite open and indeed quite outspoken. He described several instances where all of the documents relating to the various stages of a fairly complex *murabaha* transaction were signed in one meeting and the entire amount disbursed at the same time: 'When the client tells you he is too busy to waste time on three different meetings and needs all of his money today, what else can you do? Are you going to send him away to our competitors?' *B* was quite critical of his bank's *Shariah* advisors who, according to him, lived in a fool's paradise if they thought that actual banking could be done the way they taught it in Islamic banking classes: '*Client ki majboorian hein; hamari bhi majboorian hein; to aur kya kar saktay hein*?' ('The client has his exigencies; we have our exigencies; what else can we do?').

This issue might require some explanation for the non-expert in Islamic finance. Suppose a firm (the Islamic bank's client) needs to finance raw materials, and intermediate goods, and to purchase some finished parts to manufacture its widgets. As a *murabaha* is supposed to be financing 'real' items and not a line of credit, in theory each of these steps should be a separate transaction with separate sets of documentation and each transaction should be carried out at the appropriate point of the actual widget-making process. So it may take days or even weeks to disburse the funds in three separate installments whereas a line of credit is available for the customer to draw upon as and when needed at its discretion.

Similarly, since a *murabaha* finances a discrete 'real' transaction, it cannot be automatically rolled over upon expiry as is the norm for lines of credit for clients in good standing. Unless a client has several different *murabaha* transactions with different expiry dates ongoing simultaneously and can transfer funds from one to the other easily, it is entirely possible that the client may have to settle the whole *murabaha*, wait two or three days and then initiate another one. The *murabaha* settlement or the gap between the two *murabaha* has to be met from other resources, i.e., the client has to arrange very short-term and so usually quite expensive bridge financing. *B* had gone to the extent of helping clients arrange such bridge financing (usually through informal sector credit sources) till the second *murabaha* transaction could be disbursed.

Overall, *B* expressed considerable unhappiness with how Islamic banking was actually practiced and stated that he had started his banking career very favorably disposed to the entire concept of Islamic banking and had not wished to work for a conventional bank but now he would actually prefer working for a conventional bank as 'They are straightforward; they don't try to hide what they are doing and try to fool people into believing they are somehow different.' *B*'s estimate was that for the typical Small and Medium

Enterprise (SME)[3] client (the prime target for most Islamic banking corporate divisions and his particular area of specialization although he handled some larger clients also), Islamic banking was at least one percentage point annually more expensive for the standard *murabaha* working-capital transaction than conventional banks.

Interview 3 at a mid-sized conventional bank considering opening Islamic branches

I had two interviews with senior executive *C*, the head of his mid-sized conventional bank's Small and Medium Enterprise (SME) division. I knew *C* quite well from my earlier time in Pakistan and he was instrumental in arranging some interviews for me. *C* was extremely luke-warm about his bank's expansion into Islamic banking, considering it to be probably more trouble than it was worth in terms of the increased documentation and other transactions costs associated with Islamic banking; perhaps a trial branch was OK but no investment more substantial than that.

I said to *C* that, anecdotally, I had heard that the owners of many SME firms were very religiously conservative and would not use conventional banks; why not then open up a separate Islamic branch to handle them? *C* responded that yes, that was absolutely correct and he gave the example of firms in the leather industry and firms owned by members of the Chinioti[4] community. *C* went on that both of these SME sectors would not ordinarily touch conventional banking 'with a ten-foot pole' but simply opening up an Islamic branch would not convince them that what was previously *haram* was now *halal*; perhaps if the entire bank was Islamic, then they might bank with us but not otherwise. *C* said one Chinioti *seth* (tycoon) put it to him quite bluntly: the Bank's funds were kept all in one place and so the Islamic and the conventional branch drew the money out of the same polluted pool – in any case, *C* laughed, the *seth's* cash flow was such that he probably didn't really need a bank! Perhaps when and if some of the better educated, younger generation took over they might use the Islamic branch but not now.

I asked *C* about competition from Meezan Bank, which I had heard was very aggressively going after the SME market. He agreed that Meezan had made initial inroads: when Meezan Bank expanded its operations it lured a few fairly large clients away from him with a lower interest rate for working capital needs but, six months later, he had most of them back. I asked *C* if he had had to cut his own rates? *C* laughed and said not at all, they came back at exactly the old rate! He gave the example of a fairly large manufacturing firm, near the limit of the SME category, run by its founder, a self-made man with relatively little formal education, who had come to him expecting *C* to match (or at least lower the rate) on the firm's working capital facility after the *seth* had been approached by Meezan Bank. *C* said he told the *seth* that Meezan might appear cheaper but it was actually more expensive. *C* went on to explain to the *seth* that a *murabaha* was charged at the full rate on the entire amount financed from day one while a 'real' working capital facility worked on a daily product basis. So although the working capital line of credit might be at a higher interest rate, the firm was only charged for the actual amount drawn on that day and, *C* went on:

> I said to the *seth* you always deposit all of your proceeds at the end of the day and always try to minimize the balance at Saturday's closing. We only charge you for what you actually use for as long as you actually use it, but Meezan will charge you for the full amount for the full time. Even if you have cash sitting idle in the bank, Meezan will be charging you markup on the *murabaha*. If you aren't convinced, try Meezan for three months and I guarantee that you won't have saved any money by switching. And the *seth* was back with us three months later.[5]

C's view was that Islamic banking was fine for those who had a strong religious motivation for not using conventional banking but it made no financial sense for anyone who was concerned with minimizing time, documentation, and financial costs. *C* considered Meezan Bank to be a fairly second-rate operation and one he did not view as being his competition, which were other large and mid-sized conventional banks, e.g., Allied Bank or Askari Bank. In his view Meezan was leeching off the religious sensibilities of the pious, and a bank that hired mainly those MBA graduates who could not get jobs at the top banks – as he put it, 'I wouldn't hire their people, [well-established bank] wouldn't hire their people; no good bank would. Look around my floor and compare them to the Meezan people you'll meet' (I had informed him that I would be visiting Meezan Bank as well).

Interview 4 at a mid-sized conventional bank with established Islamic branches

This interview was with senior executive *D*, the head of the bank's Islamic banking division, and someone who had written extensively on issues relating to Islamic finance. I had been personally introduced to *D* by another former banking colleague of mine who asked *D* to help me out in any way possible. *D* had begun his career in a very large, conventional Pakistani bank well before Islamic banking was initiated in Pakistan; he had also worked in the Middle East for some time and was only a few years short of retirement.

Surprisingly, or unsurprisingly perhaps, as someone who had written extensively on Islamic finance, *D* was quite critical of many Islamic banking/finance practices. For example, *D* dismissed commodity *murahaba* (discussed extensively in Chapter Six) as an outright 'sham transaction' and said that it had been invented by Dubai Islamic Bank[6] to handle its excess liquidity problems. *D* had insisted that his bank could not take part in it even though many other Islamic banks in Pakistan did, and he intimated that his attitude had not gone over well with his top management: 'not everyone agreed with me' (with a roll of his eyes upwards).

D's view of Islamic banking practices was that banks' *Shariah* boards had no choice but to strive for the 'maximum level of compromise with practical necessity' and that there were very few *Shariah* scholars who had the necessary ability to judge adequately how a transaction was actually carried out, and when misused (which was very often) the *Shariah* board had no way of stopping abuses even if they were aware of them. *D* again intimated that he had tried to curtail some of the worst abuses but had not been very successful: 'I did try for a while ....'

D was very forthright that Islamic banking was not for everyone. If clients wanted maximum tax deductibility, effortless transactions, to minimize paperwork/documentation, standalone transactions, immediate rolling over of facilities, etc., then Islamic banking would not work for them. The Islamic banks, *D* stated quite forcefully, must 'look for clients who are willing to work with the bank; the typical client is not for us; we tell him to go to the conventional side.' This was obviously a sore topic with *D* and a point he had made more than once.

Finally, *D* opined that it was 'impossible for any Islamic bank to move away from *murabaha* [and similar transactions such as *ijara* and diminishing *musharaka*]; maybe for individual transactions with trusted clients' but not for routine business. True PLS, *D* went on, was not possible on a large scale as no client [and again the Islamic banking target market was mainly SME firms] would show the bank their real set of books. According to *D*, 'some customers have said that we'll share the real profits but we can't show it officially' so the payment will have to be made under the table. *D* was of the opinion that this might have happened with some Islamic banks[7] but that he had not agreed to any such deals. *D* refused to say which Islamic banks he suspected of doing this; he would only say 'some of the bigger ones.'

Interview 5 at Meezan Bank – the largest Islamic bank in Pakistan

I carried out two sets of interviews with six different people at Meezan Bank, among them senior executives at the policy-making level, in Meezan's 'Product Development and Shariah Compliance' department. People I knew at other banks introduced me to a Meezan bank executive who very kindly arranged the first interview. The Meezan Bank officers were extremely informative and unfailingly courteous and patient with my questions, except at the very end of one interview when my questions apparently struck a nerve in a senior bank executive. I was given a rundown of the bank's operations, the modalities of Islamic banking (i.e., the discussion in Chapter Six but without the critique), and the steps taken by Meezan Bank to provide new *Shariah*-compliant products.

The assessment of the Meezan bankers was that Islamic banking (in both Pakistan and the world) was merely in its first stage which was to, in effect, replicate the conventional banking model along *Shariah*-compliant lines.

They stressed, however, that this was not a *hila* (a legal ruse to avoid a prohibition) but a legitimate attempt to provide needed services to their clientele. Their argument was that it is the providers' intent that makes the difference between a *Shariah*-compliant product and one that is religiously suspect, not whether or not the products happen to have a functional similarity. They made the specific analogy that there is no discernible difference between *halal* meat (that from an animal slaughtered according to Muslim rites) and *jhatka* meat (that of an animal slaughtered according to Hindu or Sikh rites) but only the former is permissible for Muslims to eat. As I was told more than once during my Meezan meetings: 'You must start with the right intentions! [Our] intention is not to circumvent *Shariah*'s *riba* ban but to meet genuine customer needs.'

They then gave the example of automobile financing (under diminishing *musharaka*) and leasing (*ijara*) as a way Meezan met the actual needs of its clients through *Shariah*-compliant products. Meezan then had approximately 100,000 cars financed by these Islamic products and a minimum of 50 per cent of these clients were 'fully Islamic,' i.e., they maintained only current (checking) accounts with Meezan and would not have been able to finance their automobiles any other way. An upper-mid-level Meezan executive estimated that about 90 per cent of their current SME clients would have remained unbanked if Islamic financial products from an Islamic bank had not been available and he reiterated *C*'s point in Interview 3 that most of these clients would shy away from the Islamic branch of a conventional bank. As he joked: '*Nimbu-soda peanay ki ijazat heh muggar thoRa sa sharaab Daalenin us mein to sara glass haram ho ja ta heh!*' ('Lemon with club-soda [a common drink in Pakistan] we are allowed to drink but put a little alcohol in it and the whole glass is forbidden!')

Meezan also helped pioneer *takaful* insurance (i.e., mutual or cooperative insurance)[8] in Pakistan and for a while, before this type of insurance product was approved by the Pakistani Government, Meezan carried on its books some PKR2–3 billion of Meezan-financed uninsured home purchases as *Shariah*-compliant insurance was not available. They also informed me that Meezan was in the process of trying to develop *Shariah*-compliant forms of repurchase (a sale and buyback agreement at pre-set prices, universally known as a repo) and reverse-repo arrangements as a tool to handle the excess liquidity problem all Islamic banks faced as the standard overnight loan market was not available to them; this was very much in the discussion stage as yet and no product roll-out date was envisaged.

The second stage of Islamic banking, according to Meezan's product development executives, was when the Islamic bank ceases to act as a source of credit and moves towards something more akin to a trading house cum financier cum business consultant. For example, in some cases Meezan had itself purchased and then sold an SME's finished inventory after the firm had run into difficulties. Presumably the third (final?) stage would be when the

Islamic bank acts as a direct equity partner in most enterprises but we never reached discussion of this stage in the interviews.

The only discordant note occurred near the end of the second set of interviews when I pressed a senior executive about *murabaha* being more expensive than standard running finance (working capital) agreements and the need for clients to use expensive bridge financing between *murabaha*. His answer was that 'improper modes of financing gave rise to higher costs of Islamic banks' but that this was in the past and was not the case now. Was it true, I asked him, that Islamic banks were still more expensive than conventional ones due to bridge financing needs and that Meezan, so I had been told, was rolling-over *murabaha* automatically for clients? He somewhat testily denied that there had been any *murabaha* rolling-over and asked '*agar aek do fe sad ziyadah*' (if 1 or 2 per cent more) wasn't a small price to pay for being *Shariah*-compliant? And if such a small price was too high for the client, they were better off with a conventional bank – and he then excused himself as he had another meeting to go to. I continued talking with a somewhat embarrassed mid-level executive about some questions I had regarding Meezan's corporate clientele. As per his estimate, perhaps a third of the total SME firms were 'exclusively rate-conscious' and would always attempt to minimize their financing costs and, he admitted, they would continually try to play Meezan off against conventional banks. The impression I got was that he would have admitted that Meezan's account managers might have cut a few corners every now and then but, given his superior's statement, would not admit it now. While Meezan had tried to go after these firms very aggressively at first, they had now concluded that these weren't worth the trouble as, he stated, there were continual complaints about the amount of documentation required, fund disbursement schedules, *Shariah* compliance issues, and so on. Thus the Meezan interviews confirmed *D*'s observation in Interview 4 that Islamic banking was not for everyone, or at least not for the 'exclusively rate-conscious.' It required a clientele that was particularly cooperative with the bank and one that saw *Shariah* compliance as the most important aspect of the transaction.

Interview 6 at the Islamic finance partner of a major Pakistani consulting firm

This interview was with a partner, *F*, who handled issues relating to Islamic finance for a major Pakistani business consultancy that had affiliations with a large international consulting firm. *F* had also written extensively on Islamic financial topics including a guide on how to handle personal financial issues in a *Shariah*-compliant manner. I was introduced to *F* by an old friend.

F had been involved in a peripheral way in the 2002 decision by the State Bank to relaunch Islamic banking in Pakistan and, *F* stated, it was the result of a complex set of interactions between three distinct groups within the State Bank and 'there was no demand for it from the business side.' These three groups within the State Bank were the:

- 'secularists' who were happy with conventional banking;
- 'opportunists' who saw Islamic banking as a rapidly growing field and 'did not want us [Pakistan] to miss the bus';
- 'true believers'.

F was critical of current Islamic banking practices in ways already discussed above (e.g., 'Commodity *murabahas* are designed to finance conventional banks,' he stated categorically), which for reasons of space I will not go into again. *F* also highlighted some other issues with contemporary Islamic banking in Pakistan. For example, *F* pointed out that there were absolutely no requirements for external *Shariah*-compliance audits of any Islamic bank in Pakistan and that a 2009 State Bank of Pakistan draft proposal on this had gone nowhere after Islamic banks had voiced their strenuous opposition to it.[9] *F*'s own experience, when he had conducted a rare *Shariah*-compliance external audit of Islamic banks, was that he was not allowed to challenge 'the design and structure of [financial] transactions' but only allowed to 'check and challenge [their] implementation.' That is, he could not challenge the actual transaction being carried out but only whether or not the procedures for that transaction had been followed correctly. And that, as he said, 'is not a proper *Shariah*-audit.'

Interview 7 with G, *senior Government of Pakistan official*

G had held a very senior position in the Pakistani Government where he had major input into the policy-making process during the period when the State Bank was restructuring the Pakistani version of Islamic banking. *G* had also served, originally on secondment from the Pakistani Government, in a multilateral donor agency for several years and had advanced degrees from Western universities. Despite his extremely busy schedule, I was able to meet with *G* briefly twice.

G's views on Islamic banking and its position in Pakistan were extremely straightforward. He saw it 'as an integral part of international finance' and that it was nothing other than conventional finance. Or, as he put it, 'Islamic banking *is* lending' and accordingly Islamic finance would perforce 'emulate and mimic major features' of conventional finance. This is of course the Kuran thesis, discussed at length in Chapter Six. In *G*'s view, Islamic banking and finance was not anything more exotic than, say, ethical investment funds that eschewed buying shares in tobacco companies or arms manufacturers. His view was that, just like green or ethical funds, Islamic banking and finance would also occupy a niche bracket in the world of investment and finance.[10] As far as direct equity participation was concerned, *G* was of the opinion that true PLS would never be a significant component of Islamic banking and finance due to severe 'risk management' issues.

According to G, who had been a key participant in the State Bank's and the Pakistani Government's policy-making meetings discussing the relaunch of Islamic banking, the State Bank's reason for ordering the relaunch in 2002 was nothing other than to create a parallel banking system in Pakistan. This would give a 'free choice for consumers' to opt for whichever banking system they preferred and 'draw in devout Muslims who are hitherto unbanked.'[11] It seems probable that *G* would fall in the intersection of the 'secularists' and 'opportunist' camp (identified by *F* earlier of those in the Pakistani Government who had no personal commitment to Islamic banking but rather saw it as an opportunity for Pakistani banking to avail.

Interview 8 with the general manager of a family-owned, mid-sized Pakistani manufacturing firm

Businessman *H* was an old friend of mine from my school days in Pakistan and, prior to taking over the day-to-day running of his family firm, had spent several years as a corporate banker in Pakistan with a large foreign bank. *H* had also served in fairly senior positions in the Karachi Chamber of Commerce and Industry (KCCI) and various other industry advocacy groups. Extensive discussions with *H* confirmed (or led me to ask questions which then later confirmed many of *H*'s comments) the view of Pakistani Islamic banking and finance presented here. For example, *H* readily agreed that many in the SME sector were extremely religiously conservative and personally very devout and were extremely unlikely ever to use conventional banks. When, for example, an associate of his – the finance manager of a fairly large Pakistani firm – had stated that he had changed to Meezan Bank from a conventional one, *H* had explained to him that as there was no functional difference between conventional and Islamic banking, nothing had really changed as such other than his costs. *H*'s associate agreed that that may well be the case but now '*gunnah to unkay sar par heh; mairay peh nahin! Jo mein kar sakta hoon, woh mehneh kiya*' ('The sin is on their head now, not on mine! What I could do, I've done'). *H* had been approached by representatives from Meezan and other Islamic banks but had stated to them that he wasn't interested in increasing his transaction costs unless the rate differential was over 2 per cent on *murabaha* working capital (his personal estimation of the cost differential between conventional and Islamic banking for his firm)[12] and unless they gave him better terms on his letters of credit and bank guarantees. As *H* put it:

> Their pitches to me are never on cost or what they can do for [my firm] but always on how by doing business with them, I can avoid *riba* and so save my soul. I'll look after my own soul, thank you very much! Their whole sales pitch is how their transactions are structured to avoid *riba* and who is on their *Shariah*-board that has certified that their transactions are *riba*-free. If you push them on cost and convenience, they get very defensive and imply that you're not being a good Muslim. They've finally stopped bothering me now.

Interview 9 with the chief executive officer of a family-owned, mid-sized Pakistani manufacturing firm

Businessman *I* was also an old friend of mine from my schooldays in Pakistan; he had gone to work in the family business right out of college. *I*'s early experience with Islamic bankers was very similar to *H*'s except that *I* had used some Islamic banking facilities but had gone back to his conventional bank. In *I*'s estimation, it wasn't worth the added inconvenience of increased documentation and other costs although he readily admitted that according to some of his professional colleagues 'Islamic banking apparently is a lot simpler now [2010] than when I tried it.' *I* was also of the opinion that after 9/11 many of the Western firms doing business in Pakistan had shied away from anything labelled 'Islamic' and that gave conventional banks an advantage in soliciting their business. For example, given *I*'s business field (his firm was a subcontractor/supplier to Western firms in Pakistan), his clients preferred to avoid anything to do with Islamic banking and his customers were happier dealing with a 'foreign' conventional bank – although, as he laughed, 'there are no foreigners working in it any more!'[13]

The above interviews, with the possible exception of the Meezan Bank ones, seem to indicate that there are minimal, if any, differences between Islamic and conventional banks, at least in the view of their practitioners. However, this would be somewhat overstating the case. It turns out that Islamic and conventional banks do differ in some significant ways.

So what makes Islamic banking different from conventional banking?

As a matter of fact, there are some substantive differences between conventional and Islamic banking, not on their product side but in their clientele. Ayesha Khalid Khan, during the course of research for her dissertation, carried out an extensive analysis of the clientele of two banks, one Islamic (Meezan Bank) and the other conventional (Habib Bank) (Khan 2010a: 95). Her research team contacted 5,133 bank customers (3,628 Islamic and 1,504 conventional) spread out across 30 (15 'matched pairs' of Islamic and conventional) branches in different areas of Karachi (Pakistan's largest city and industrial center) and 1,480 (853 Islamic and 627 conventional) of them agreed to be interviewed (Khan 2010a: 105–107). Care was taken to ensure that the 30 'matched pairs' of Islamic and conventional branches were geographically very close together (usually within a mile of each other, and in two cases in the same building) (Khan 2010a: 97).

Khan's research produced some interesting results. Across the board, Islamic bank customers had higher savings account balances than conventional bank customers (Khan 2010a: 105) (see Table 8.1).

The Islamic bank customers were on average older, better educated, travelled more overseas ('to countries other than those visited for religious purposes'), and had switched to the Islamic bank from a conventional one (Khan

Table 8.1 Islamic versus conventional bank customers

Average savings account balances	*Islamic bank (PKR)*	*Conventional bank (PKR)*
For all 9,078 customers in sample	162,924	82,761
For all 5,133 customers contacted	127,498	72,184
For all 1,480 customers surveyed	102,045	83,338

2010a: 106). The customers surveyed also had a slightly higher level of trust in the conventional bank than in the Islamic one and, most surprising, the Islamic bank's customers tended to have a second account at a conventional bank as well (Khan 2010a: 108).

Khan (2010a: 110) gives, as the four most important reasons cited by Islamic banking customers for having an account there, (i) the bank offering *Shariah*-compliant products (62 per cent); (ii) their employer having a salary deposit agreement with the bank (13 per cent); (iii) convenient location (10 per cent); and (iv) friend's/family member's recommendation (8 per cent). For the conventional bank the reasons were: (i) the branch's location (44 per cent); (ii) salary accounts (16 per cent); (iii) better service (12 per cent); and (iv) family member already had an account there (12 per cent).

Unsurprisingly, Islamic bank customers, even in a country that is very religious and conservative across the board, were much more religiously observant than conventional bank customers. They were more likely to have performed *Haj*, have a beard if male, pray five times daily, and regularly attend religious classes, and the differences on these scores between Islamic and conventional bank customers were significant at the 5 per cent level or better. Khan (2010a: 113–114, 116–118) also tested several different LOGIT (logistic regression) models and found that, across various model specifications and robustness tests, the best predictor for selecting an Islamic bank was whether or not the customer had performed the *Haj* (Khan 2010a: 115). Khan terms this the 'faith premium' and concludes that:

> For the managers of existing Islamic banks, it is important to note that the most significant source of demand for their products comes from the faith premium that is generated by the individual belief that Islamic banking products are religiously appropriate and necessary. As such, as Islamic banks continue to grow, they should take extreme care to remain within the boundaries of strict *Shariah* interpretations. In fact, Islamic banks should actively signal their religious commitments to their customers by employing the most credible religious scholars on their boards

> and adopting the most stringent, voluntarily transparent product structuring and operating processes.
>
> (Khan 2010a: 119)

Khan's 'faith premium' manifests itself in a different way as well. Baele *et al.* (2014) analyzed all business loans outstanding in Pakistan from April 2004 to December 2008 using official data reported to the State Bank of Pakistan's Credit Information Bureau database. It seems as if the default rate (defined as loans that are 90 or, in some versions of their econometric models, 180 days late on their payments) on Islamic banking loans is far lower than that for conventional loans, even after adjusting for loan and borrower types.

After excluding all loans smaller than PKR500,000 (then approximately US$7,700, for which running a beneficiary credit check or reporting all loan details to the Consumer Information Bureau is not required), inter-bank loans, loans to sundry government bodies and official government agencies or development projects, microfinance loans (below PKR50,000 or about US$770), and loans over PKR419,000,000 (approximately US$6.5 million), Baele *et al.* were left with 152,370 new loans issued in this period to 22,723 borrowers by 40 different banks; approximately 5 per cent of these were Islamic loans (Baele *et al.* 2014: 12). For any given month, the default rate on Islamic bank loans (0.5 per cent) was lower than that for conventional bank loans (0.9 per cent) and this difference was statistically significant; however, while the default rate for loans by Islamic branches of conventional banks (0.2 per cent) was lower than the default rate for loans by these banks' conventional branches (0.7 per cent), this difference was not statistically significant (Baele *et al.* 2014: 14). Baele *et al.* (2014: 20) also found that the default rate after one year (the median duration of all loans) on conventional loans (5.2 per cent; 'not uncommon for loans in a developing economy') was substantially higher than that on Islamic loans (3.1 per cent; 'more equal to the default rate on loans … in developed countries').

Baele *et al.* carry out several 'robustness checks' to determine whether their findings stand up to changing the parameters of their regression models. So, for example, they account for where the loan was made (different regions of Pakistan), in what industry category, whether the loan was collateralized or unsecured, long term or short, for capital improvements or working capital, large or small, and so on. Baele *et al.* (2014: 22) find that except for longer-term Islamic loans (which had a higher default rate than other Islamic loans) 'none of the estimated coefficients on the other interactions is statistically significant' and Islamic loan default rates are still lower than conventional ones.

Baele *et al.*'s most interesting findings came from analyzing the 44,335 loans (out of their sample of 152,730) where the same borrower had taken out essentially identical Islamic and conventional, short-term (under one year), fully collateralized loans. They found that 'the [default] hazard on the Murabaha loans is about half the hazard (= $e^{-0.587}$) than on the very similar conventional loan' (Baele *et al.* 2014: 23).

Baele *et al.* conclude that:

> [T]he more pious ones among them may choose (and are legally and observably able) to default on their conventional rather than on their Islamic loans. Our finding that the hazard rate on Islamic loans of the same borrower taking both conventional and Islamic loans from the same bank is only one fifth the hazard rate on conventional loans confirms ... that *the same borrower is less likely to default on an Islamic than on a conventional loan*.
>
> (Baele *et al.* 2014: 4, emphasis added)

What could explain this counterintuitive result since, for any given borrower, the *ex ante* assumption would have been that the two (identical) loans should have the same default risk for the same borrower? One possible reason for this could be that, in an overtly religiously observant community, the borrower may not want to be known as someone who would harm other pious Muslims (the Islamic bankers) but reneging on debts owed to the impious (the conventional bankers) would carry much less opprobrium. If this is the correct reason, it shows both the depth of religious conservatism in Pakistan and how important it is for many persons to be seen to be doing the right thing religiously.

Baele *et al.* also try to test specifically for Islamic piety as a determining factor in loan defaults. Accordingly they test to see if default on Islamic loans declines during the month of Ramadan[14] and is lower in those areas where Islamist political parties (ostensibly committed to enforcing the *Shariah*) receive a larger share of the vote. They find that 'during Ramadan months defaults on Islamic loans drop by more than half' and that 'Islamic loans are relatively less likely to default' when the share of the vote in the 2002 general elections received by Islamist parties increased (Baele *et al.* 2014: 30–31).[15] Thus it seems very likely that the reasons for the differing default rates have to do with both the personal piety of the borrowers and the religious conservatism of their community.

Supplying a non-existent demand?

By adhering very closely to the AAOIFI and IFSB standards for Islamic financial institutions, it is clear that the State Bank of Pakistan was not motivated by any attempt to truly Islamize Pakistani banking as it is these same AAOIFI and IFSB standards that all of the Islamic banks discussed in Chapter Six adhere to. As an analysis of the breakdown of 'advances' by Pakistani banks shows, Pakistani Islamic banking follows the same lending patterns as discussed in Chapter Six: minimally Islamic and maximally conventional, down to using standard market interest rates as benchmarks for Islamic lending practices. Unsurprisingly then, Pakistani Islamic banking looks very similar to its conventional competitor in terms of its lending patterns and preferences.

Detailed interviews with banking professionals (both Islamic and conventional), management consultants, businessmen, and a former senior government servant confirms this impression: there is minimal difference between Islamic and conventional financial products but those customers that opt for the one over the other may well exhibit very different characteristics. Ayesha Khan's and Baele *et al.*'s empirical findings support some of the qualitative findings from my interviews in Pakistan: the characteristics of most of those who opt for Islamic over conventional finance are substantially different. Unsurprisingly, as some of my interviewees noted, individual religious piety and not cost differences may prompt the decision to choose the Islamic product over the similar conventional one, and borrowers for whom religious compliance is of paramount importance are much better credit risks than 'regular' borrowers, at least for Islamic banks. Again, as some of my interviewees noted, directly or indirectly: if saving 2 per cent on your rate is more important than your soul, go to the conventional bank.

Thus Islamic banking is clearly tapping into an as yet relatively small but rapidly growing pool of 'Islamist bourgeoisie,' if you will, of SME owners who value personal piety and orthopraxic form – conducting Islamic financial transactions with an Islamic bank – over financial efficiency and cost reduction. And there is a dedicated group of Islamic bankers in Pakistan who appear to gravitate to Meezan Bank, which has taken the lead in developing new Islamic financial products to cater to this 'Islamist bourgeoisie.' It is far too soon to say whether or not this phenomenon will result in the creation of a Pakistani version of Turkey's Justice and Development Party (AKP)[16] but the rapid growth of Islamic banking in Pakistan, and the fact that many of those who favor Islamic over conventional banks appear to be better educated and more prosperous than the average conventional bank customer, is bothersome to those concerned about the growing strength of political Islam in Pakistan.

None of this changes the fact that in Pakistan Islamic banking was and continues to remain a supply-driven and not a demand-driven phenomenon. The Pakistani central bank, the State Bank of Pakistan, mandated the revamp and transformation Islamic banking underwent in 2002. The earlier (1985) incarnation was also mandated from above by the then military ruler of Pakistan. This is despite the fact that there has been absolutely no popular movement for Islamizing Pakistani finance. However, every Pakistani constitution and Council of Islamic Ideology report on the subject has required that *riba* be banned and banking and finance be appropriately Islamized. The Federal *Shariat* Court and the *Shariat* Appellate Bench of the Supreme Court have also sided with the 1973 Constitution in this regard and so we have the existence of a 'separate but equal' dual banking system in Pakistan. The state then continues to implement the continuing Islamization of the country despite the fact that, in this particular case at least, there is minimal popular demand for it.

Notes

1 A management consultant, with extensive experience in both management consulting, chartered accountancy and banking, requested that no identifying information be given about him as he would be easily identifiable to people with knowledge of the Pakistani management consulting field.

2 From 1988 to 1990 I was in the Corporate Banking Division of ANZ Grindlays Bank in Karachi, then the largest foreign bank in Pakistan. Grindlays, operating in South Asia since 1854, was bought by Australia's ANZ group in 1984 and then sold to Standard Chartered Bank in 2000 and merged with Standard Chartered's existing Pakistani operations.

3 Small and Medium Enterprise (SME) is an official government designation in Pakistan but different federal and provincial government agencies employ different definitions of what constitutes a 'small' versus a 'medium' enterprise. For the State Bank of Pakistan (SBP), Small enterprises are defined as those having up to 20 employees and sales/turnover up to PKR 75 million (approximately US $750,000 in 2014) (SBP 2013: 6). Medium ones have two separate categories: 21 to 250 employees for manufacturing and service sector firms, and 21 to 50 for trading firms; annual turnover for both categories had to be PKR75–400 million (approximately US$0.75–4 million) (SBP 2013: 9). Keeping in mind the realities of business life in Pakistan and the near impossibility of finding 'proper' accounts for many smaller firms, the SBP does not require banks to obtain audited accounts for small firms before lending to them although maximum bank exposure is capped at PKR15 million (approximately US$150,000); audited accounts are required before loans can be made to Medium enterprises (SBP 2013: 6, 9).

4 Chiniot is a district (administrative division) of Pakistan's Punjab province. Before independence in 1947, contrary to the general view that Sunni Muslims in South Asia were not interested in or capable of doing well in business or trading ventures, individuals from Chiniot acquired a reputation for being shrewd businessmen with a strong entrepreneurial streak.

5 *C* has highlighted a major weakness in the cost structure of *murabaha* transactions. This is probably why Meezan Bank has rolled out, on a trial basis, the revised Islamic Running Finance Facility discussed in Chapter Six to deal with precisely this problem.

6 Incorporated in Dubai in 1975, it is one of the world's oldest Islamic banks and also has a significant presence in Pakistan.

7 From my experience in the Pakistani corporate banking sector, the modalities for an under-the-table payment could be easily worked out in a *prima facie* legal way in many instances. For example, it is common for banks to charge their smaller (or sadly, their more vulnerable) clients an 'annual account review fee' that is often half or three-quarters of a per cent of their entire financing arrangement. So if XYZ Co. has various *musharaka*, *murabaha*, etc. arrangements with ABC Islamic Bank totaling PKR500,000,000, then ABC Islamic Bank could charge PKR3.75 million or more for its annual review fee to get its under-the-table payment without the client having to officially disclose its real profits. Or XYZ Co. could agree to let ABC Islamic Bank charge a higher rate on, say, its letters of credit to ensure that ABC Islamic Bank received its 'fair' share of the actual profits from the PLS transaction.

8 A mutual insurance structure is where the company is owned by its policyholders and thus it has connotations of a 'mutual assistance' society where each will help

the others out in time of need; this is what makes it '*Shariah*-compliant.' Standard insurance is not considered *Shariah*-compliant as it is considered to be akin to gambling where the premiums are considered a *de facto ante* or purchase of a lottery ticket.

9 The State Bank (SBP 2008b) mandates an internal *Shariah*-compliance audit of an Islamic bank's procedures by the bank's own *Shariah*-board. News reports indicate that the State Bank's revised guidelines for Islamic banks, expected to be issued in October 2014, will mandate an annual external *Shariah*-compliance audit (APP 2014). See also the discussion on this topic in Chapter Six.

10 This is also the view of Dr. Shamshad Akhtar, Governor of the State Bank of Pakistan from 2006 to 2009, who stated that 'the development of IF [Islamic Finance] in tandem with conventional finance will help broaden and deepen [global] financial markets' (Akhtar 2010: 122).

11 During a conversation I had with a semi-retired Pakistani businessman, formerly the chief operating officer of one of Pakistan's largest business groups, he dismissed the idea that Islamic banking had anything to do with increasing the banking sector's penetration into the population of hitherto unbanked Pakistanis. He pointed out that the State Bank in this time period had allowed banks to close both unprofitable and outlying branches, especially those in smaller and more remote towns and poorer parts of large cities, and open up more branches in already heavily served areas. So while this may have increased competition in some parts of the banking system, it actually had the effect of reducing overall banking system accessibility to the poorer parts of the population. He was of the opinion that the relaunch was nothing other than Islamic window dressing to allow the government to live up to its assurances to the multilateral donor agencies that no radical change would be carried out in the Pakistani financial system; any other considerations were purely secondary. I am not entirely convinced of this but it certainly was a major factor in the decision-making process.

12 This was confirmed by Baele *et al.*'s study (2014: 14) which also showed that Islamic *murabaha* type transactions were about 2 per cent (on an annualized basis) more expensive than the similar conventional product.

13 This aspect of Pakistani finance was also relayed to me in an earlier meeting with a former supervisor of mine from ANZ Grindlays days. Muslim Commercial Bank (one of the largest banks in Pakistan and universally referred to there as MCB) had officially changed its name to MCB Bank as it had been denied a banking license to establish new branches in Western Europe because it had 'Muslim' in its name. I cannot vouch for the accuracy of this, but MCB has officially changed its name.

14 Pronounced 'Ramzaan' in Urdu; Ramadan, the month of fasting, is one of the holiest months of the Muslim calendar as keeping the fast is a central tenet (one of the Five Pillars) of Islam. The end of Ramadan is immediately followed by *Eid ul Fitr*, the second biggest holiday/festival in Islam.

15 There were also some unsurprising findings about Islamic bank loans in Baele *et al.* (2014): that longer-term Islamic loans had higher default rates than shorter-term ones, that Islamic loans in urban areas had higher default rates than Islamic loans in rural areas, and so on.

16 See Taspinar (2012) for more on the AKP and Turkey's Islamist bourgeoisie.

9 *Quo vadis* Islamic banking?

The purpose of this chapter is to conclude this examination of the Islamization of Pakistan's banking system by summarizing my main arguments and findings and to indulge in some mild speculation about the future Islamization of the banking sector in particular and Pakistan in general.

An Islamic banking system for an Islamic Republic

As I hope I have shown by this point, it is not possible to understand why the Pakistani banking system became 'Islamic' in 1985 without understanding Pakistan's tortured relationship with political Islam. For committed Islamists, Islamic banking and finance is just one facet of an entirely Islamic social, economic, and political system. For its Pakistani advocates such as Shabbir Ahmad Usmani, Syed Abul Ala Maududi, and those who followed the path set by them, the former without the latter is meaningless. Even before Pakistan came into existence, there were very strong forces determined to push it along the path of Islamic Maximalism in order to create a fully Islamic state. Indeed, it was to be the first truly Islamic state since the time of the Prophet and his four immediate successors[1] and thus to serve as the natural leader of the Muslim world.[2] Rather than being an end in itself, the effort to Islamize banking in Pakistan is simply one front of an overall campaign for the full Islamization of the country. What appear to be defeats for the Islamists (e.g., the 2002 *Shariat* Appellate Bench (SAB) ruling that reversed the 1999 and 1991 judicial rulings), I argue, are not actually defeats but merely successful holding actions fought by the relatively few Islamic Minimalists and the even fewer secularists left in Pakistan. Actions such as the rulings are not permanent victories since the underlying system – General Zia's amendments to the 1973 Constitution – that produced the 1991 and 1999 court rulings has not changed. The odd 'victory' won by the rearguard of a defeated and retreating army does not change the final outcome; it merely delays the inevitable by offering a temporary respite but it possibly might allow for a better terms to be negotiated.

An Islamic state without *riba*?

The development of Islamic economics in South Asia was the result of the desire of Islamic revivalists to develop and strengthen an Islamic identity among South Asian Muslims. For people such as Maududi, the founder of Pakistan's most important Islamist political party, the great fear was that the centrality of Islam in the lives of Muslims would be reduced to the point where religion was relegated by them to the private sphere. That is, religion might become as relevant to their lives as Christianity was to the lives of most Westerners: something that the majority of the population trotted out only on Sundays and at weddings, christenings, and funerals. The result would then be that the essential and most fundamental questions of public and private life, key matters of state and legislation, would no longer have an Islamic answer; just as in the West they no longer had a Christian answer. They would have a secular, areligious answer. The consequence of this would be, in Maududi's term, a nation of 'partial Muslims' who would soon lose their way entirely.

This was the essence of Maududi's opposition to Sir Syed Ahmad Khan's Islamic Modernism and Jinnah's espousal of Sir Syed's 'Two Nation Theory,' and the Muslim League's (Jinnah's political party) resulting call for Pakistan. Maududi, backed by his amazingly prolific pen – which wrote exegesis on the Koran, volumes on Islamic political and constitutional thought, and reams on Islam's views of economics, interest, land reform, and whatever else came within the purview of his inexhaustible writing ability – was a major force in demanding that Jinnah's Dominion of Pakistan become not merely a national home for Muslims but an explicitly and avowedly Islamic Republic with an overtly confessional cast to it.

Jinnah's death in September 1948, just over a year after independence in August 1947, left the Muslim League no-one who could counter the Maududi-led demand for an Islamic state. In the all-important 1946 All-India general elections, the last held in the unified British Indian Empire, the Muslim League had used blatant appeals to Islam and stoked anti-Hindu Muslim religious sentiments. This was done to counter the opposing Hindu-dominated Congress Party's use of conservative Islamic scholars from the Deoband *Madrassa* and their affiliated *Majlis e Ahrar e Islam* (Association of Free Muslims[3]) who, opposed to anything that smacked of Western-style modernity or education, denounced the Muslim League's demand for Pakistan. In the *Ahrar*'s view the demand for Pakistan was the work of a Godless secularist like Jinnah, who was so far removed from Islam that he had not only married a non-Muslim but had allowed his daughter to marry one as well: no true Muslim could follow such a *kafir* (infidel) as his leader unless he wanted to condemn his soul to hell.

The resonance of the call for an Islamic politico-constitutional structure for the new state among a large portion of the populace and many in the political classes, including not a few in Jinnah's Muslim League, caused Jinnah's chief lieutenant and successor Prime Minister Liaquat Ali Khan to pass the

Objectives Resolution in the Constituent Assembly in 1949. The apparent overtly Islamic nature of the Resolution, which begins 'Sovereignty belongs to Allah alone …' and goes on from there, was not the capitulation to the Islamists that it may appear at first glance to be. Liaquat's real aim was to give the Islamists the *form* but not the *substance* of their demands and by so doing remove from their arsenal the potent charge that his Muslim League government was un-Islamic. Thus, by conceding Islamic Minimalism, Liaquat was trying to avoid Islamic Maximalism. Liaquat never meant it to be the first step in achieving Islamic Maximalism. While on the face of it the Objectives Resolution seems to lay out a clearly Islamic *grundnorm* for the new state's future constitution, it really does nothing of the sort.

The Objectives Resolution makes only general and somewhat vague references to the Quran and *Sunnah* and none at all to *Shariah, fiqh, dhimmis*, and the role of the *ulema* in vetting (if not actually formulating) legislation for conformity to the strictures of any Muslim *madhab*. Without all this no state can actually be considered 'Islamic.' At one level then the Objectives Resolution was not all that much more of a statement of actual Islamist political thought than the US Pledge of Allegiance, with its reference to 'One nation, under God,' or US coinage with 'In God we trust' stamped on it, are statements of 'Christianist' political thought. Liaquat undoubtedly intended a certain level of 'ceremonial deism' to be the norm for Pakistan, but the actual level he intended, and whether he could really have held the Islamists at bay when he did not deliver on his apparent promise to Islamize Pakistan, will never be known. Prime Minister Liaquat Ali Khan was assassinated in October 1951.

Liaquat's successors as leaders of the Muslim League were much weaker than he was *vis à vis* both the Islamists' demands for an 'Islamic state' and attempts by some within the League's myriad factions to use the Islamists for their own political ambitions (most notably in the anti-Ahmadiyya pogroms of 1953). Drafts of the proposed constitution were strongly criticized for being insufficiently Islamic, with one of the most potent charges being that if a secular constitution was desirable, then why leave India? Accordingly, the Constitution that was eventually approved by the Constituent Assembly in 1956 had a decidedly Islamist ring to it: the country was renamed from the Dominion of Pakistan to the Islamic Republic of Pakistan, the president of the republic had to be a Muslim, instruction in the Koran was compulsory for all Muslims, *riba* was to eliminated and formal institutions were to be established to scrutinize all laws and practices to ensure their conformity to established Islamic norms. In short, the question of whether Pakistan was to be a republic of Muslims or a Muslim Republic had been affirmatively answered in favor of the latter. However, on the spectrum range from 'Islamic Minimalism' (*pro forma* invocation of Islam in an appropriately ceremonial deist fashion) to 'Islamic Maximalism' (where all formal and informal institutions, public and private actions, and all rules and laws have to adhere to specific *Shariah/fiqh* interpretations), the 1956 Constitution was probably equidistant between the two. But the principle of the Islamic state, so important to Maududi and the Islamist political parties, had been conceded. And, as the proverb has it, once the camel's nose is in the tent, it is merely a matter of time before the rest of the camel follows. Clause 29f of the 1956 Constitution that banned *riba* ensured that Islamizing the Pakistani economy and financial system was a constitutional requirement. But since *riba* was not defined in the constitution, it was left to the courts and/or the *ulema* to interpret what exactly was being prohibited if it should come to the test. Since the 1956 Constitution took longer to craft than it existed as the supreme law of the land, this push never came to shove.

The 1958 military coup that brought in General Ayub Khan's Islamic Modernist and somewhat reforming government to power replaced the 1956 Constitution with the 1962 one. The 1962 Constitution attempted to move closer to the Minimalist end of the spectrum by, among other things, removing the 'Islamic' qualifier from the name of the country: it was now simply 'The Republic of Pakistan.' However, the strength of Islamism in Pakistan can be gauged by the fact that the first amendment to the Constitution reinstated the 'Islamic' modifier in the country's official name. The Islamists had triumphed once more. The same amendment also required the government to ensure that all existing laws were in conformity to Islam. Clearly the strength of Islamist feelings in Pakistan were too much for even a military dictatorship to disregard: Ayub Khan's Islamic Modernism clearly had its limits and he was no Mustafa Kemal Ataturk.

The 1962 Constitution kept the formal review bodies such as the Central Institute of Islamic Research (CIIR) and the Council of Islamic Ideology (CII), created earlier. However, Ayub Khan, who had attended Sir Syed Ahmad Khan's Aligarh Muslim University before leaving for the Royal Military Academy at Sandhurst, and clearly admired Sir Syed Ahmad Khan, the father of Islamic Modernism in South Asia, made sure to appoint fellow Modernists such as Fazlur Rahman to head these bodies. Ayub's Islamic Minimalism and acute Modernist tendencies, especially where finance was concerned, are fully displayed in the details of his Constitution. While Article 8(18) of the 1962 Constitution also called for eradicating *riba*, it is the only one of Pakistan's three constitutions to actually define it and by so doing explicitly safeguard conventional banking. Article 8(18) reads clearly: 'Riba (Usury) should be eliminated.'

This is crucial in the story of Pakistan's financial sector Islamization since scholars such as Fazlur Rahman drew a clear distinction between *riba* and interest, and argued that *riba* was best translated as usury and not interest (*sood*). From a contextual reading of the scriptures, Rahman argued, it was clear that the Koranic prohibitions applied to usury (i.e., to exploitation, injustice, and the unjust taking of property) rather than bank interest charged on a conventional loan. Conventional banking continued undisturbed in Pakistan as the first CII report recommending the imposition of an 'Islamic' banking system there was not issued until late 1969 – after the departure from the scene of both Ayub Khan and Fazlur Rahman (the former under house arrest and the latter in self-imposed exile in the USA). Ayub Khan resigned after mass street protests convinced him that he had lost the populace's confidence; the protests (which included leftists, workers, students, and many Islamists) did not have as one of their demands the elimination of *riba* from the economy. No Pakistani government was interested in moving Pakistan closer to the Maximalist end of the spectrum, at least not on financial matters, and the 1969 CII Report gathered dust for a decade.

The 1973 Constitution, Pakistan's most Islamic one and adopted by a democratically elected parliament following the disastrous 1971 civil war that saw the loss of East Pakistan and the creation of Bangladesh, reiterated all of the Islamist clauses of the earlier ones and added new ones to it. The civilian government of Prime Minister Zulfikar Ali Bhutto decided to frame a new Constitution for the country following the Second Partition but chose to ignore the negation of the Two Nation Theory implied by the secession of East Pakistan. Bhutto chose, as it were, to 'double down' on Islam as both Pakistan's *raison d'être* and its guiding light, and his supposedly Socialist government even went so far as to call itself 'Islamic Socialist.' Bhutto thereby avoided the unforgivable Muslim sin of *shirk* (idolatry) by replacing the questionable 'God of Socialism' (Karl Marx) and his prophet (Vladimir Ilyich Lenin) with the one and only true God and his Prophet. Among the 1973 constitution's many Islamic clauses was the old standby which required that the State 'eliminate *riba* as early as possible' (Clause 38f) but, unlike in 1962, care was taken not to define *riba*. Bhutto's government, though quick to amend the Constitution to declare certain sects (the Ahmadiyya) as non-Muslim, chose neither to define *riba* nor to act to eliminate it – although this last was again a constitutional requirement. It was left to the new military government of General M. Zia ul Haq who seized power after tainted elections in 1977 (and ruled till his death in 1988) led to massive street protests and bloody riots.

The Zia regime was to Islamic Maximalism what Ayub Khan's was to Islamic Minimalism. Zia asked the CII to review and update its 1969 report that had equated *riba* to commercial interest and the Council came back with a stronger report than before. This one did not gather dust on the shelves of some government ministry but was implemented forthwith. The 1980 CII report formed the basis on which Zia ordered all Pakistani banks to cease conventional banking operations by 1985. There was minimal protest on the part of the banks to this because, as detailed in Chapter Six, the difference between what they were doing and what they were now told to do was only semantic. So they willingly charged 'markup' instead of 'interest.'

But Zia also created the Federal *Shariat* Court (FSC) and the *Shariat* Appellate Bench (SAB) of the Pakistani Supreme Court by amending the 1973 Constitution, and transformed the Objectives Resolution from being the end point of Islamization in Pakistan to being the beginning. While scrutinizing Pakistani laws for *Shariah*-compliance had been required by the 1956, 1962 (in its first amendment), and 1973 constitutions, no government or court had actually bothered to do so until now. The FSC could and did take up cases filed by people who claimed that certain financial laws were un-Islamic.

Since the Chief Justice of the FSC in 1991, Tanzil ur Rahman, was the chief author of the 1980 CII report that recommended a fully Islamic financial system, he was more than willing to take on cases challenging the then distinction-without-a-difference Pakistani banking system. The 1991 FSC ruling and the much broader, indeed sweeping, 1999 SAB one (issued after Pakistani banks appealed to it against the FSC ruling) scrapped the existing system in favor of an actual profit- and loss-sharing (PLS) system. The SAB gave the Pakistani Government a relatively brief time period (later extended to July 2002) to implement its ruling.

While the government of Gen. Pervez Musharraf, who had seized power in a military coup in 1999, appeared at first to go along with the 1999 ruling, Musharraf changed the composition of the SAB hearing the appeal petition against the 1999 ruling in mid-2002. Citing multiple errors in the 1999 ruling, the reconstituted ('packed') SAB duly sent the case back to the FSC to be reheard afresh. The SAB did not overturn the decision. It has languished there unheard since 2002 and there seems to be no pressure on the FSC to take it up any time soon.

However, rather than reverting to the 1985 form of 'interest-free' (Islamic) banking that had been the norm till then, the State Bank of Pakistan (SBP) decided to reboot Islamic banking in Pakistan using global *Shariah*-compliance standards. General Pervez Musharraf's government, despite his self-professed admiration for Mustafa Kemal Ataturk of Turkey and his oft-repeated call for 'enlightened moderation' in religion, did not feel strong enough to dispense with any of General Zia's Islamic innovations or amendments to the Constitution since he needed civilian political support to make his regime more palatable to the USA – Pakistan's largest foreign assistance giver. However, Pervez Musharraf was willing to move Pakistan back incrementally and stealthily towards the Minimalism end of the Islamic spectrum. Accordingly, the form of Islamic banking that was implemented in 2002 was not what the 1991 FSC and 1999 SAB rulings envisaged Islamic banking as being. It was the exact form described in detail in Chapter Six and so clearly the form proscribed by the 1999 and 1991 court rulings. Like Liaquat Ali Khan before him, Pervez Musharraf was probably hoping that if the Islamists were given the form publicly, they could be denied the substance of their demands privately. And there Pakistani Islamic banking sits: functionally indistinguishable from conventional banking right down to substantive conformity with the Basel Accords on bank regulation.[4]

Pakistani Islamic banking: the hidden victory of Islamic Minimalism?

It seems clear from the various directives issued by the State Bank of Pakistan (e.g., SBP 2008b) that Islamic banking in Pakistan will keep to the norms and regulations for financial transactions issued by the Bahrain-based Accounting and Auditing Organization for Islamic Financial Institutions (AAOIFI) and the Kuala Lumpur (Malaysia)-based Islamic Financial Services Board. These two organizations coordinate with the Bank for International Settlements in Basel, Switzerland, which houses the Basel Accords secretariat, to ensure that Islamic banks and other financial institutions adhere very closely to the regulatory norms set for the world's financial institutions. That is, Islamic banking *is* conventional banking.

Governors of the SBP have made no bones about their commitment to ensuring that Pakistani banking, including Islamic banking, strictly follows global banking regulatory norms. Dr. Ishrat Husain, SBP Governor from 1999 to 2005, instituted the requirement that Islamic banking in Pakistan follows AAOIFI and IFSB standards. Dr. Shamshad Akhtar, SBP Governor from 2006 to 2009, also made that absolutely clear when she said in unequivocal terms that 'The development of Islamic prudential regulatory and supervisory frameworks, which subscribe to Basel standards of conventional banking, will pave the way for the development of IF [Islamic Finance] while tweaking the regulations to accommodate the special risk characteristics of IF' (Akhtar 2010: 123). Since it makes sense to 'subscribe to the Basel standards' only if Islamic banking is now functionally equivalent to conventional banking and is expected to remain so in the future, it is extremely unlikely that Islamic banking in Pakistan will move beyond the 'first stage,' where they replicate conventional finance in a '*Shariah*-compliant' manner, described to me by Meezan Bank's 'Shariah Compliance and Product Development' staff.

Thus Islamic banking and finance in Pakistan and elsewhere will in all likelihood continue to remain functionally indistinguishable from its conventional counterpart. In fact, as the AAOIFI and IFSB actions have shown, it will coordinate very closely with its conventional counterparts to ensure that it moves strictly in tandem with conventional finance. This is of course at least a partial victory for Islamic Minimalists in Pakistan, who have kept the substance of Islamic Modernism (the practice of conventional banking and finance) even if they have had to concede the form (the nomenclature it uses).

The importance of this victory cannot be overstated even if it is one that cannot really be celebrated. A truly Islamic PLS financial system of the sort envisaged by the 1999 SAB ruling might (probably would) have been absolutely disastrous for Pakistan. It could have been the final push that the Pakistani economy needed to push it over the edge. While Pakistan seems particularly adroit at dancing on the edge of the precipice, in the short run at least the absolute collapse of formal sector credit that would have been the inevitable result of a serious attempt to implement the 1999 ruling could well have been the final misstep that pushed Pakistan over the edge.

That this is not just scaremongering or ridiculous hyperbole is shown by the credit implosion in the USA and Western Europe caused by the 2007–08 financial crisis that led directly to the Great Recession worldwide. As banks became less and less sure of the creditworthiness of their financial sector counterparties, they essentially stopped lending to each other and the large corporations: the commercial paper market dried up completely. Very few outside the financial and economic worlds realize just how close the West and probably the world came to complete disaster because the West's central bankers, led by the US Federal Reserve's Ben Bernanke, literally flooded the world with liquidity. The US Federal Reserve's balance sheet expanded from about US$0.5 trillion in domestic open market assets (i.e., bonds and other items purchased by the US central bank) in December 2008 to about US$2.1 trillion by December 2009 and finally to US$3.8 trillion by early 2014.[5] That is, the US central bank alone had injected about 3.3 *trillion* dollars into the US and other countries' economies during this time. In the case of Pakistan, if the country's banks contracted credit as they would have had to do to take a direct equity stake in every enterprise, the ability of the State Bank to take up the slack would have been virtually non-existent.

A different 'Islamic' alternative?

The form that contemporary Islamic banking and finance has taken is what the prominent Islamic economist Professor M. Amin El-Gamal has scathingly criticized as '*Shariah* arbitrage:' where the correct Islamic name is applied to a Western financial product. For advocates of Islamic finance like him, the path not taken for Islamic banking was the 'mutual banking' route. Here, instead of the bank taking a PLS stake in the venture, the venture's principals take an ownership stake in the bank. That is, the bank's depositors are its owners (e.g., as is the case of credit unions in the USA) and the bank lends only to those who have an ownership stake in it. This is actually a very old Western financial concept but one that El-Gamal argues fits extremely well into the ethical concepts behind Islamic banking and finance as:

> [M]utuality in Islamic banking can in fact bring to the industry large numbers of depositor/investors as well as managers who are committed to Islamic ideals of social and economic development, as opposed to profit- and fee-oriented Shari'a arbitrageurs. … Hence, the best Islamic alternative for conventional commercial banking may in fact be adopting mutual banking structures that have been in existence in the west for well over a century …
>
> (El-Gamal 2006: 166, 171)

El-Gamal is of course arguing for a small-scale banking solution that, in effect, provides the fabled 'home town bank' of yore.[6] The mutuality approach would also, El-Gamal (2006: 171) argues, allow these institutions to charge low rates of interest that would not violate the spirit of the Koran's ban on *riba*. This utopian view of what Islamic banking and finance could achieve if only it was unshackled (decolonized) from gigantic Western banking corporations is one that is shared by other Islamic bankers who despise the current form of 'distinction without a difference' Islamic finance.[7] The opposition of this type of Islamic banker is not to charging interest on financial transactions but to the complete disappearance of what in a bygone age used to be referred to as the 'prudent man standard'[8] for people with fiduciary responsibilities (e.g., trustees and guardians) for funds not their own. This standard prohibited speculating in non-investment grade bonds, short sales, margin accounts, questionable business ventures, and the like. In short, would 'prudent investors' who very carefully weigh the risks and benefits of any venture in order to minimize losses commit their funds to any given undertaking? These Islamic bankers would opt for an 'extremely prudent investor' standard even at the expense of sacrificing most of an economy's economic growth. For them the emphasis is always on loss-avoidance rather than profit-maximization.

The Federal Shariat Court, again?

As I believe I have shown in Chapter Seven, the 2002 SAB ruling that sent the case back to the Federal *Shariat* Court for a re-hearing was the result of a very careful 'stacking' of the judicial bench to ensure that the 'correct' ruling was given. The case has sat there unheard for the past thirteen years and no-one seems concerned about re-opening hearings. Is it likely to stay like this?

The Federal *Shariat* Court itself took up the original case in 1991 only because there was a new and highly activist Chief Justice there determined to enforce 'real' Islamic banking. Therefore, if a more overtly Islamic Maximalist Chief Justice is again appointed to the Federal *Shariat* Court, it is entirely possible that he will re-open hearings and issue another ruling similar to the 1991 one – after carefully considering all the points raised in the 2002 SAB ruling that sent the original case back to his court. In this case then we are back again to the earlier situation where all Pakistani banks have to turn themselves into direct equity investment houses. In short, venture capitalists and not lenders against excellent collateral.

As I have also argued in Chapter Seven, the Pakistani judiciary is usually discreet to a fault and has come up with extremely creative ways to show its discretion and hide its valor. However, on several occasions, there have been judges who have thrown caution to the winds and issued bold rulings that have infuriated the executive branch of the Pakistani government. The latest such case was former Chief Justice of the Supreme Court of Pakistan Iftikhar Muhammad Chaudhury (chief justice 2005–07; 2009–13) who refused to kow tow to General Pervez Musharraf and discreetly resign after several rulings issued by him infuriated General Musharraf. The furor over his arrest and dismissal eventually brought down the Musharraf military regime and forced his successor, President Asif Ali Zardari, to restore Chaudhury to the bench. Thus it cannot be simply assumed that no Pakistani court will rule against the current form of Pakistani Islamic banking simply because the executive branch and the financial sector is against it and there is no popular agitation in favor of any radical change.

This last presumes that there is not a more overtly, even radically, Islamist regime in power in Pakistan. While this of course cannot be ruled out, it is an extremely unlikely scenario and possible only if the Pakistan Army itself has gone Islamist. If the true Islamists ever actually take power in Islamabad, the Islamization of the Pakistani financial system will be the least of anyone's worries.

The Islamization of Pakistan is a foregone conclusion. All that is left is to argue about is how far towards Islamic Maximalism the country will go and how much substance will have to be conceded to go along with the form. At the moment, for the banking and financial sector at least, it is so much more form than substance that Islamic banking is *de facto* conventional banking. And we all hope it shall remain that way.

Notes

1 The rule of the first four caliphs of Islam from 632–661 CE is known as the *Khilafat e Rashidun* (Rightly Guided Deputies) and is held by devout Sunni Muslims to be the Golden Age of Islam despite the fact that three of the four were murdered.

2 It was attitudes such as this that led King Farouk of Egypt, who saw his Egypt as the natural leader of the Arab/Muslim world, to remark caustically that if one believed the Pakistanis, Islam was born on August 14, 1947 (Pakistan's independence day).

3 The *Ahrar* initiated the 1953 pogrom against the Ahmadiyya and took the lead in the killings; see Chapter Three for more details.

4 The Basel I, II, and III Accords are the effort made by the Basel Committee on Banking Supervision to improve global banking system regulations with regard to risk management, capital adequacy requirements, reporting, transparency in reporting, and so on.

5 Calculated from 'Chart 1: Size and composition of SOMA Domestic Securities Holdings,' FRBNY (2014: 2).

6 As exemplified in the perennial American Christmas classic film, 1946's *It's a Wonderful Life*. It stars Jimmy Stewart as a despondent small-town banker contemplating suicide on Christmas Eve, who is shown by an angel what life would have been like for his small town had he never been born; unsurprisingly the townsfolk would have suffered greatly without the compassionate Stewart sacrificing his happiness for that of his fellow men and women.

7 For example, Tarek El-Diwany (2010), a principal of Kreatoc Zest investments and Usman Hayat, Director Islamic Finance and Environmental, Social and Governance Investing at the CFA Institute (http://blogs.cfainstitute.org/investor/author/usmanhayat) have in their own ways argued for the importance of tying bank lending absolutely to the real economy and of massively curbing financial speculation and *de facto* financial gambling.

8 Now referred to as the 'prudent investor' standard, when it is referred to at all.

Glossary of key terms and abbreviations

AS *Alleh us Salam*, peace be upon him. A common invocation uttered as a sign of respect whenever the name of the Prophet Muhammad or any other prophet of God is mentioned; often written 'pbuh' in Pakistan.

Ahmadi See *Jamaat e Ahmadiyya.*

Akhil Bharat Hindu Mahasabha All India Hindu Assembly. Relatively mainstream Hindu chauvinist movement founded in 1914 as the Hindu counter to both the (secular) Indian National Congress and the (eventually separatist) Muslim League.

Alim Muslim religious scholar, plural *ulema.*

CA Constituent Assembly.

CII Council of Islamic Ideology. Constitutionally mandated body that advises the Pakistani government on the compatibility of Pakistani laws with *Shariah* (i.e., *fiqh*).

Constituent Assembly Legislature cum Constitution-writing assembly of Pakistan from 1947 to 1958. The first of three official Pakistani constitutions was the product of years of deliberation by the Assembly and was officially adopted in March 1956.

Deobandi Adhering to the teachings of, or affiliated with, the *Madrassa Dar ul Uloom Deoband*, India, founded in 1866 and offering a conservative and traditionalist interpretation of classical *fiqh* of the *Hanafi* Sunni madhab. Its Pakistani daughter madrassas have become considerably more conservative and Saudi-influenced than the mother *madrassa* in India.

Dhimmi A protected person in an Islamic state, pronounced '*zimmi*' in Pakistan. Used to refer to non-Muslim citizens of an Islamic state who are accorded specific but limited citizenship rights upon payment of the *jizya* (poll tax) by adult, able-bodied males, and who are then exempt from compulsory military service.

Fatwa Muslim religious ruling/opinion issued by a *mufti* (an *alim* judged competent to issue a fatwa) regarding whether or not something is consonant with Islamic *fiqh*. It is binding only on those who accept the *mufti*'s competence to issue such rulings.

Federal *Shariat* Court Penultimate Islamic appellate court in Pakistan established in 1980 by the then military ruler Gen. Zia ul Haq to determine whether Pakistan's laws are *Shariah*-compliant; three of its eight members have to be established ulema. It enjoys original (including *suo moto*), revisional, appellate, and review jurisdiction.

Fiqh Muslim jurisprudence; what is erroneously often termed *Shariah*, *fiqh* is the attempt by fallible humans to interpret *Shariah*.

FSC Federal *Shariat* Court.

GoP Government of Pakistan.

Hadith Accounts by third persons of the words and actions of the Prophet Muhammad AS; sometimes termed the 'Prophetic traditions.' Pronounced '*hadees*' in Pakistan, these form a major component of Islamic fiqh and have undergone a vetting process by collectors such as the Sunni Imam Malik (eighth century CE) and Imams Bukhari and Muslim (ninth century CE) as to their *isnad* (chain of transmission) and there is a graduated scale as to their reliability with the most reliable being termed *sahih* (authentic/correct).

Halal That which is permissible for Muslims to do or consume.

Haram That which is forbidden for Muslims to do or consume.

Hiyal Ruse or legal stratagem designed to circumvent Islamic prohibitions.

IBF Islamic banking and finance.

Ijara Finance lease.

Ijtihad Independent reasoning. One of the four (along with the Koran, Sunnah, and *qiyas*) sources of Islamic *fiqh*.

Indian National Congress Political party founded in 1884 that led India to its independence from the British Empire in 1947. Jawaharlal Nehru as its President became India's first prime minister.

Islamiat Study of Islam. A course of study prescribed for Pakistani Muslim schoolchildren.

Jamaat e Ahmadiyya Party of Ahmad. A heterodox Sunni Muslim sect founded in 1889. Its founder Mirza Ghulam Ahmad claimed to be a prophet, albeit a minor one, sent by God as a reformer. Since 1974 its adherents have been officially designated as non-Muslims in Pakistan.

Jamaat e Islami Party of Islam. Political party founded by Maulana Syed Abul Ala Maududi in 1941 to propagate his views on Islamic political and social thought. Since the 1950s it has been the leading proponent for an Islamic state in Pakistan.

Jamiat e Ulema e Hind Party of the Scholars of India. Political party of *ulema* from the *Deoband Madrassa*, allied with the Indian National Congress and opposed to M. A. Jinnah and the Muslim League.

Jamiat e Ulema e Islam The Party of the Scholars of Islam. Breakaway faction of *Jamiat e Ulema e Hind* led by Maulana Shabbir Ahmad Usmani that allied with M. A. Jinnah and the Muslim League.

JI *Jamaat e Islami.*

JUH *Jamiat e Ulema e Hind.*

JUI *Jamiat e Ulema e Islam.*

***Khilafat* Movement** Indian political movement 1919–24 aimed at restoring the Ottoman Sultan to his position as Caliph (khalifa) of Sunni Islam. While it had Mahatma Gandhi as its ostensible 'leader,' it was an overwhelmingly Muslim political movement with minimal direct non-Muslim involvement.

Khudai Khidmatgar Servants of God. Muslim political party in the former North-West Frontier Province (now renamed Khyber Pakhtunkhwa in Pakistan) of India. It was allied with Mahatma Gandhi and the Indian Congress and opposed to M. A. Jinnah and the Muslim League.

Madhab School of Muslim *fiqh*; pronounced *mazhab* in Pakistan. There are currently four main Sunni and one main Shia school extant in the world today.

Madrassa An Islamic school/seminary associated with a particular *madhab* (or a particular interpretation of a *madhab*).

Madrassatul Uloom Musalmanan e Hind Institution of Learning for the Muslims of India. The original name for what became Aligarh Muslim University in 1920, the major seat of Islamic Modernism in pre-Independence India.

Majlis e Ahrar Association of Free Muslims. A radical Deobandi offshoot from the Khilafat Movement; also allied with the Indian National Congress and opposed to M. A. Jinnah and the Muslim League. It led the agitation to declare the *Jamaat e Ahmadiyya* as non-Muslims in the 1950s.

Maulana 'Learned' or 'scholar;' used to denote an accomplished *alim* or *fuqaha* (jurist).

ML Muslim League. Muslim political party founded in 1906 and later led by M. A. Jinnah. Achieved independence of Pakistan from the British in 1947.

Murabaha A cost-plus, deferred-payment sale where the Islamic financier purchases an item on behalf of its client and sells it to the client on a 'marked up' basis.

Musharaka Direct equity participation by the Islamic financier. A declining musharaka, i.e., 'rent-to-own,' is a common way of financing home purchase in an Islamic financial system.

Nizam e Mustafa System of the Chosen One, one of the epithets of the Prophet Muhammad AS. A fairly common way of referring to the establishment of an Islamic State along classical *fiqh* lines; this was how, e.g., General Zia (r. 1977–88) referred to it in the Pakistani context.

pbuh See AS.

Qiyas Deduction by analogy. One of the four (along with the Koran, Sunnah, and *ijtihad*) sources of Islamic *fiqh*.

Rashtriya Swayamsevak Sangh National Patriotic Organization. Extreme right-wing Hindu party founded in 1925. It was opposed to British rule and to M. A. Jinnah and the Muslim League as well as to Mahatma

Gandhi's moderate Hinduism and the Indian National Congress's secularism.

Riba Literally meaning 'increase.' Its usage in the financial sense is held to equate to 'usury' by Islamic Modernists but to 'interest' by Islamic Maximalists.

Riba al-nasiah The *riba* of deferment; i.e., lending at interest, also known as *riba al-jahiliyah*: *riba* of the age of ignorance.

SAB *Shariat* Appellate Bench.

Sadaqah Charity.

Satyagraha Insistence on truth. The name given by Mahatma Gandhi to his 1920 political movement against British rule in India.

SBP State Bank of Pakistan.

Shaikh ul Islam Chief of the Muslim *ulema*. The title usually refers to the senior most Muslim *alim* in a region/country.

Shariah Literally 'path,' but here the Divine Path or Law laid down by Allah that all observant Muslims must follow. *Shariah* is immutable, but in this context see also *fiqh*.

***Shariat* Appellate Bench** The Bench of the Supreme Court of Pakistan designated to hear appeals for rulings issued by the Federal Shariat Court. Two of its five members must be ulema.

State Bank of Pakistan The country's central bank.

Sukuk Islamic bonds, singular *sukk*. The most common type of issue is a *sukuk al ijara*, a lease-revenue bond.

Sunnah The teachings and practices of the Prophet Muhammad AS that form binding examples for subsequent generations of Muslims. It is one of the major sources of Islamic *fiqh*.

Tanzil ur Rahman Report 1980 report issued by the CII committee, chaired by Mr. Justice Tanzil ur Rahman, that formed the basis of the 1985 institution of Islamic banking in Pakistan. Rahman later served as the Chief Justice of the FSC and in that capacity issued the 1991 ruling that led eventually to the rebooting of IBF in 2002.

Ulema Muslim religious scholars, singular *alim*.

Zakat Poor tax; usually assessed at the rate of 2.5 per cent annually of one's movable assets by Sunnis.

Bibliography

Ahmad, A. (1993) *Contemporary Practices of Islamic Financing Techniques*, Research Paper #20, Jeddah: Islamic Research and Training Institute, Islamic Development Bank. Online. Available at: www.irti.org/English/Research/Documents/IES/154.pdf (accessed 16 August, 2006).

Ahmad, A. U. F. and M. K. Hassan (2006) 'The time value of money concept in Islamic finance,' *American Journal of Islamic Social Sciences*, 23: 66–89. Online. Available at: www.iefpedia.com/english/wp-content/uploads/2009/11/The-Time-Value-of-Money-Concept-in-Islamic-Finance.pdf (accessed 14 September, 2013).

Ahmed, A. S. (1997) *Jinnah, Pakistan and Islamic Identity: The Search for Saladin*, London: Routledge.

Ahmed, H. (2002) *A Microeconomic Model of an Islamic Bank*, Research Paper #59, Jeddah: Islamic Research and Training Institute, Islamic Development Bank. Online. Available at: www.irti.org/English/Pages/Publications.aspx?pid=968 (accessed 15 April, 2008).

Ahmed, O. B. (2001) *Islamic Financial Instruments to Manage Short-Term Excess Liquidity*, Research Paper #41, Jeddah: Islamic Research and Training Institute, Islamic Development Bank. Online. Available at: www.irtipms.org/PubDetE.asp?pub=43 (accessed 2 February, 2008).

Akbar, M. J. (2011) *Tinderbox: The Past and Future of Pakistan*, New York: HarperCollins.

Akhtar, S. (2010) 'Islamic finance: authenticity and innovation – a regulator's perspective,' in S. N. Ali (ed.) *Islamic Finance: Innovation and Authenticity*, Harvard, MA: Harvard University Islamic Legal Studies Project, pp. 111–123.

Al Baraka Islamic Bank (2007) *Annual Report 2006*, Karachi: Al Baraka Islamic Bank.

Al Nasser, L. (2008) 'Islamic banking and external auditing,' *Ashraq Alawast*, English edn, February 16.

Alavi, H. (1989) 'Nationhood and the nationalities in Pakistan,' *Economic and Political Weekly*, July 8, 24: 1527–1534.

Algaoud, L. M. and M. K. Lewis (2007) 'Islamic critique of conventional financing,' in M. K. Hassan and M. K. Lewis (eds) *Handbook of Islamic Banking*, Cheltenham and Northampton, MA: Edward Elgar, pp. 38–48.

Ali, R. (2001) 'Riba deadline frozen by a year: SC refuses extension till 2005,' *Dawn Wire Service*, 16 June. Online. Available at: www.lib.virginia.edu/area-studies/SouthAsia/SAserials/Dawn/2001/jun1601.html (accessed 15 July, 2006).

Ali, R. (2002) 'Usmani's monetary interest led to his removal,' *Dawn Wire Service*, 12 June. Online. Available at: www.dawn.com/news/42482/usmani (accessed 16 July, 2006).

AMEinfo (2006) *Corporate Sukuk Market Growing in the Middle East*. Online. Available at: www.ameinfo.com/96842.html (accessed 11 January, 2008).

Amin, M. (2009) 'The tax treatment of Islamic finance in Western countries and Muslim majority countries,' in A. Khorshid (ed.) *Euromoney Encyclopedia of Islamic Finance*, 2nd edn, London: Euromoney Institutional Investor, pp. 367–376.

Anderson, P. (2012) *The Indian Ideology*, Gurgaon, India: Three Essays Collective.

Ansari, A. S. B. (1963) 'Review of J. M. S. Baljon Modern Muslim Koran Interpretation (1880–1960) (Leiden: E. J. Brill 1961),' *Islamic Studies*, 2: 290–293.

Anwar, H. (2012) 'Moody's cuts Pakistan credit rating deeper into junk,' *Bloomberg*-July 13. Online. Available at: www.bloomberg.com/news/2012-07-13/moody-s-cuts-pakistan-credit-rating-deeper-into-junk.html (accessed 9 December, 2013).

APP (2014) 'State Bank issues Shariah governance framework of IBIs,' *Associated Press of Pakistan*. Online. Available at: www.brecorder.com/pakistan/banking-a-finance/165917-state-bank-issues-shariah-governance-framework-of-ibis.html (accessed 16 July, 2014).

Arab Law Quarterly (1985–1986) 'Noel J. Coulson,' *Arab Law Quarterly*, 1: 473.

Asad, M. (1980) *Message of the Qu'ran: Translated and Explained*, Gibraltar: Dar Al-Andalus.

Asiamoney (2006) 'Islamic finance: the inner circle,' *Asiamoney*, September. Online. Available at: http://business.highbeam.com/435599/article-1G1-159405425/islamic-finance-inner-circle (accessed 27 August, 2015).

Asian Banker (2012) *Asia Pacific Largest Banks: Pakistan*. Online. Available at: www.theasianbanker.com/ab700/2012-2013/asia-pacific-largest-banks-extended (accessed 3 July, 2014).

Axelrod, R. (1984) *The Evolution of Cooperation*, New York: Basic Books.

Axelrod, R. and W. D. Hamilton (1981) 'The evolution of cooperation,' *Science*, 211: 1390–1396.

Ayub, M. (2002) *Islamic Banking and Finance: Theory and Practice*, Karachi: State Bank of Pakistan.

Ayub, M. (2007) *Understanding Islamic Finance*, Chichester: John Wiley and Sons.

Baele, L., M. Farooq and S. Ongena (2014) *Of Religion and Redemption: Evidence from Default on Islamic Loans*, Center Discussion Paper Series No. 2012–2014; forthcoming, *Journal of Banking and Finance*.

Bahrain Monetary Agency (2006) 'Banking Statistics.' Online. Available at: www.bma.gov.bh/cmsrule/media/pdf/statistics/bulletin/July2006small.pdf (accessed 6 October, 2009).

Baljon, J. M. S. (1964) *The Reforms and Religious Ideas of Sir Sayyid Ahmad Khan*, 3rd edn, Lahore: S. M. Ashraf.

Balraj, K. (2008) *India's Bismarck: Sardar Vallabhai Patel*, New Delhi: Indus Source Books.

Bank Islam (n.d.) *Property Financing-i (Tawarruq) – Baiti Home Financing*. Online. Available at: www.bankislam.com.my/en/pages/BaitiHomeFinancing.aspx?tabs=3&mlink=HomeFinancing (accessed 5 December, 2013).

Baring, E. (1908) *Modern Egypt*, Vol. II, London: Macmillan.

BBC (2009) *Abu Dhabi Gives Dubai $10bn to Help Pay Debts*. Online. Available at: http://news.bbc.co.uk/2/hi/8411215.stm (accessed 12 December, 2013).

Binder, L. (1961) *Religion and Politics in Pakistan*, Berkeley and Los Angeles, CA and New York: University of California Press.

Bloomberg (2013) *Malaysia exposes Shariah scholars to jail for breaches.* Online. Available at: www.gulf-times.com/business/191/details/363694/malaysia-exposes-shariah-scholars-to-jail-forbreaches (accessed 16 December, 2013).

Callard, K. (1957) *Pakistan: A Political Study*, New York: Macmillan.

Central Bank of Bahrain (2014) *Statistical Bulletin*, April. Online. Available at: www.cbb.gov.bh/page.php?p=statistical_bulletin (accessed 1 June, 2014).

Chandavarkar, R. (2003) *The Origins of Industrial Capitalism in India: Business Strategies and the Working Classes in Bombay, 1900–1940*, Cambridge: Cambridge University Press.

Chapra, M. U. (2004) 'Mawlana Mawdudi's contribution to Islamic economics,' *Muslim World*, 94: 163–180.

Chapra, M. U. (2008) 'Islamic economics: what it is and how it developed,' in R. Whaples (ed.) *EH.Net Encyclopedia.* Online. Available at: http://eh.net/encyclopedia/islamic-economics-what-it-is-and-how-it-developed (accessed 11 May, 2011).

Chaudhuri, N. C. (2001/1951) *The Autobiography of an Unknown Indian*, New York: New York Review of Books Classics.

Chin, V., K. Storholm, S.-O. Vathje, N. A. Razali and M. Badi (2008) *Islamic Banking: Can You Afford to Ignore It?* Boston, MA: Boston Consulting Group. Online. Available at: www.bcg.se/documents/file15221.pdf (accessed 14 September, 2009).

Chong, B. S. and M. H. Liu (2009) 'Islamic banking: interest-free or interest-based?' *Pacific-Basin Finance Journal* , 17: 125–144.

Cizakca, M. (1996) *A Comparative Evolution of Business Partnerships: The Islamic World and Europe, with Specific Reference to Ottoman Archives*, The Ottoman Empire and its Heritage Series, Vol. 8. Leiden, Netherlands: E. J. Brill.

Coulson, N. J. (2007/1964) *An Introduction to Islamic Law*, reprint edn, Edinburgh: Edinburgh University Press.

Council of Islamic Ideology (2006) *Elimination of Riba From the Economy & Islamic Modes of Financing*, web version of 2nd edn (2002), Islamabad, Pakistan: Council of Islamic Ideology. Online. Available at: www.cii.gov.pk (accessed 2 April, 2013).

Dawn (2001) 'AG hints at invocation of doctrine of necessity: Riba issue,' *Dawn Wire Service*, 16 June. Online. Available at: www.lib.virginia.edu/area-studies/SouthAsia/SAserials/Dawn/2001/jun1601.html (accessed 15 July, 2006).

Dawn (2002a) 'Two ulema made SAB ad hoc judges,' *Dawn Wire Service*, 25 May. Online. Available at: www.dawn.com/2002/05/25/nat16.htm (accessed 16 July, 2006).

Dawn (2002b) '6 SC judges validating army coup get retired,' *Dawn Wire Service*, 6 December. Online. Available at: www.dawn.com/2002/12/06/nat9.htm (accessed 16 July, 2006).

Desai, M., S. H. Rudolph and A. Rudra (eds) (1984) *Agrarian Power and Agricultural Productivity in South Asia*, Berkeley and Los Angeles, CA and New York: University of California Press.

Devji, F. (2013) *Muslim Zion: Pakistan as a Political Idea*, Boston, MA: Harvard University Press.

Dhulipala, V. (2008) 'Rallying the Qaum: The Muslims of the United Provinces and the Movement for Pakistan, 1935–1947,' PhD thesis, University of Minnesota.

Dhulipala, V. (2011) 'A nation state insufficiently imagined? Debating Pakistan in Late Colonial North India,' *Indian Economic & Social History Review*, 48: 377–405.

Dow Jones Sukuk Index (2013) *Fact Sheet*. Online. Available at: www.djindexes.com/mdsidx/downloads/fact_info/Dow_Jones_Sukuk_Index_Fact_Sheet.pdf (accessed 9 December, 2013).

Economist (2012) 'Islamic finance,' *The Economist*, April 10. Online. Available at: www.economist.com/blogs/graphicdetail/2012/04/focus-2 (accessed 3 December, 2013).

El-Diwany, T. (2006) 'How the banks are subverting Islam's ban on usury,' *Financial Times*, July 14: 15.

El-Diwany, T. (2010) *The Problem With Interest*, 3rd edn, London: Kreatoc.

El-Gamal, M. A. (2000) *A Basic Guide to Contemporary Islamic Banking and Finance*, Plainfield, IL: Islamic Society of North America.

El-Gamal, M. A. (2003) '"Interest" and the paradox of contemporary Islamic law and finance,' *Fordham International Law Journal*, 27(1): 108–149.

El-Gamal, M. A. (2006) *Islamic Finance: Law, Economics and Practice*, New York: Cambridge University Press.

El-Hawary, D., W. Grais and Z. Iqbal (2004) *Regulating Islamic Financial Institutions: The Nature of the Regulated*, World Bank Policy Research Working Paper #3227, Washington, DC: World Bank.

Embree, A. T. (2011) 'Pakistan: the burden of Islam,' in R. Kalia (ed.) *Pakistan: From the Rhetoric of Democracy to the Rise of Militancy*, London and New York: Routledge, pp. 217–242.

Epstein, S. B. (1996) 'Rethinking the constitutionality of ceremonial deism,' *Columbia Law Review*, 96: 2083–2174.

Esposito, J. L. (1998) *Islam and Politics*, 4th edn, Syracuse, NY: Syracuse University Press.

Euromonitor International (2005) *Investment Banking and Venture Capital in the USA*, London and Chicago, IL: Euromonitor International.

Farooq, M. O. (2009) 'The riba–interest equation and Islam: reexamination of the traditional arguments,' *Global Journal of Finance and Economics*, 6: 99–111. Online. Available at: http://ssrn.com/abstract=1579324 (accessed 10 May, 2013).

Farooq, M. O. (2011) 'Self-interest, Homo Islamicus and some behavioral assumptions in Islamic economics and finance,' *International Journal of Excellence in Islamic Banking and Finance*, 1: 52–79. Online. Available at: http://ssrn.com/abstract=1740729 (accessed 5 October, 2013).

Faroqhi, S. (1997) 'Crisis and change: 1590–1699,' in H. Inalcik and D. Quataert (eds) *An Economic and Social History of the Ottoman Empire*, Vol. II, Cambridge: Cambridge University Press, pp. 411–635.

Feldman, H. (2001) *The Herbert Feldman Omnibus*, Karachi: Oxford University Press. Comprising '*Revolution in Pakistan: A Study of the Martial Law Administration*,' '*From Crisis to Crisis: Pakistan 1962–1969*,' and '*The End and the Beginning: Pakistan 1969–1971*.'

Firoozye, N. (2009) 'Wa'd and the completeness of Islamic markets,' *Opalesque*, August 23. Online. Available at: www.opalesque.com/OIFI116/Featured_and_the_completeness_of_Islamic16.html (accessed 1 July, 2014).

Fitch Ratings (2007) 'Fitch's approach to rating sukuk,' *Fitch Ratings Criteria Report*, March 7.

FRBNY (2014) *Domestic Open Market Operations During 2013*, New York: Federal Reserve Bank of New York. Online. Available at: www.newyorkfed.org/markets/omo/omo2013.pdf (accessed 19 June, 2014).

Fremont, R. (2000) 'Islamic democracy and Islamic governance,' seminar at The Middle East Institute, Washington, DC, May 5. Online. Available at: www.drsoroush.com/English/By_DrSoroush/E-CMB-20001121-Islamic_Democracy_and_Islamic_Governance.html (accessed 25 December, 2006).

Gaborieau, M. (2002) 'Islam and politics,' in C. Jaffrelot (ed.) and G. Beaumont (trans.) *A History of Pakistan and its Origins*, London: Wimbledon Publishing Co., pp. 235–249.

Gassner, M. S. (2005) 'Reasons to issue sukuk and the structures behind them,' *Banker Middle East*, 56.

Gaudefroy-Demombynes, M. and J. P. Macgregor (trans.) (1968/1950) *Muslim Institutions*, 4th edn, London: Allen & Unwin.

Ghazanfar, S. M. (ed.) (2003) *Medieval Islamic Economic Thought: Filling the 'Great Gap' in European Economics*, London and New York: RoutledgeCurzon.

Gibb, H. A. R. (1975/1947) *Modern Trends in Islam*, reprint edn, New York: Octagon Books.

Gibb, H. A. R. and H. Bowen (1960/1950) *Islamic Society and the West: A Study of the Impact of Western Civilization on Moslem Culture in the Near East, Vol. 1: Islamic Society in the Eighteenth Century*, reprint edn, London: Oxford University Press.

Gilmartin, D. (1988) *Empire and Islam: Punjab and the Making of Pakistan*, Berkeley and Los Angeles, CA and New York: University of California Press.

Glaeser, E. I. and J. A. Scheinkman (1998) 'Neither a borrower nor a lender be: an economic analysis of interest restrictions and usury laws,' *Journal of Law and Economics*, 41: 1–36.

Habib Bank (2013) *Annual Report – 2012*, Karachi: Habib Bank Ltd. Online. Available at: http://hbl.com/downloads/pdf/annual/HBL_AnnualReport_2012.pdf (accessed 2 July, 2014).

Haque, Z. and A. A. Kazmi (1993) 'The nature and significance of the medieval and modern interpretations of "riba",' *Pakistan Development Review*, 32: 933–946.

Haron, S. and N. Ahmad (2000) 'The Islamic banking system in Malaysia: some issues,' in N. Ali (ed.) *Islamic Finance: The Task Ahead*, Proceedings of the Fourth Harvard University Forum on Islamic Finance, Cambridge, MA: Harvard University Press, pp. 155–163.

Hasan, M. (1980) 'Communal and revival trends in Congress,' *Social Scientist*, 8: 52–66.

Hassan, P. and A. Azfar (2001) *Moving Toward an Islamic Financial Regime in Pakistan*, Harvard Law School Islamic Legal Studies Program Occasional Publication No. 2, Cambridge, MA: Harvard Law School.

Hathaway, R. H. and W. Lee (eds) (2004) *Islamization and the Pakistani Economy*, Washington, DC: Woodrow Wilson International Center for Scholars.

Healy, P. O. (2005) 'For Muslims, loans for the conscience,' *New York Times*, 7 August. Online. Available at: www.nytimes.com/2005/08/07/realestate/for-muslims-loans-for-the-conscience.html (accessed 21 February, 2008).

Henderson, A. (2009) 'The regulation of Shari'a-compliant financial services and products: approaches and challenges,' in A. Khorshid (ed.) *Euromoney Encyclopedia of Islamic Finance*, 2nd edn, London: Euromoney Institutional Investor, pp. 377–385.

Henry, C. M. and R. Wilson (2004) 'Introduction,' in C. M. Henry and R. Wilson (eds) *The Politics of Islamic Finance*, Edinburgh: Edinburgh University Press, pp. 1–14.

Hoffman, L. (1948) 'India: main population concentrations,' *Geographical Journal*, 111: 89–100.

Hoodbhoy, P. (2007) 'Jinnah and the Islamic State: setting the record straight,' *Economic and Political Weekly*, 42: 3300–3303.

Howladar, K. (2009) *The Future of Sukuk: Substance Over Form?* 31 May. Online. Available at: www.cpifinancial.net (accessed 15 October, 2009).

Hussain, Z. (1993) 'The judiciary on trial,' *Newsline*, February: 32–33.

Ibrahim, B. el D. A. (2006) 'The "missing link" between Islamic development objectives and the current practice of Islamic banking – the experience of Sudanese Islamic banks (SIBs),' *Humanomics*, 22: 55–66.

Inalcik, H. (1995) 'The Ottoman state: economy and society 1300–1600,' in H. Inalcik and D. Quataert (eds) *An Economic and Social History of the Ottoman Empire*, Vol. I, Cambridge: Cambridge University Press, pp. 9–387.

Iqbal, Sir A. M. (1930) 'Sir Muhammad Iqbal's 1930 Presidential Address,' speech delivered at the 25th Session of the All-India Muslim League, Allahabad, India, 29 December 1930. Online. Available at: www.columbia.edu/itc/mealac/pritchett/00islam links/txt_iqbal_1930.html (accessed 3 July, 2014).

Iqbal, Sir A. M. (2004/1934) *The Reconstruction of Religious Thought in Islam*, reprint edn, Lahore: Sang-e-Meel Publications.

Iqbal, M., A. Ahmad and T. Khan (1998) *Challenges Facing Islamic Banking*, Occasional Paper #1, Jeddah: Islamic Research and Training Institute, Islamic Development Bank.

Iqbal, M. and P. Molyneux (2005) *Thirty Years of Islamic Banking: History, Performance and Prospects*, Basingstoke and New York: Palgrave Macmillan.

Islamic Bank of Britain (2007) *Home Finance: Key Features Guide*, Birmingham and London: Islamic Bank of Britain.

Islamic Development Bank (2004) *29th IDB Annual Report 1424H (2003–2004)*, Jeddah: Islamic Development Bank. Online. Available at: www.isdb.org/irj/portal/a nonymous?NavigationTarget=navurl://fc89183034cf9829cd053376f798af07 (accessed 16 August, 2006).

Islamic Development Bank (2007) *32nd IDB Annual Report 1427H (2006–2007)*, Jeddah: Islamic Development Bank. Online. Available at: www.isdb.org/irj/portal/a nonymous?NavigationTarget=navurl://fc89183034cf9829cd053376f798af07 (accessed 8 December, 2008).

Islamic Research Institute (2009) 'The Objectives Resolution,' *Islamic Studies*, 48: 89–118.

Jafar, I. (2000) 'Judgment on riba: an analysis,' *Dawn Wire Service*, 17 March. Online. Available at: www.lib.virginia.edu/area-studies/SouthAsia/SAserials/Dawn/2000/ma r17.html (accessed 10 June, 2006).

Jalal, A. (1994/1985) *The Sole Spokesman: Jinnah, the Muslim League and the Demand for Pakistan*, reprint edn, Cambridge: Cambridge University Press.

Jalal, A. (2000) *Self and Sovereignty: Individual and Community in South Asian Islam Since 1850*, London and New York: Routledge.

Jalal, A. and A. Seal (1981) 'Alternatives to Partition: Muslim politics between the wars,' *Modern Asian Studies*, 15: 415–454.

Jalali-Naini, A. R. (2000) 'The structure and volatility of fiscal revenue in MENA countries,' paper presented at the Mediterranean Development Forum, Cairo, Egypt. Online. Available at: www.ibrarian.net/navon/paper/The_Structure_and_Vola tility_of_Fiscal_Revenue_in.pdf?paperid=3518460 (accessed 15 February, 2008).

Jawed, A. (2009) *Secular and Nationalist Jinnah*, Karachi: Oxford University Press.

Jennings, R. C. (1973) 'Loans and credit in early 17th century Ottoman judicial records: the sharia court of Anatolian Kayseri,' *Journal of the Economic and Social History of the Orient*, 16: 168–121.

Kamali, M. H. (1999) 'Law and society: the interplay of revelation and reason in the Shari'ah,' in J. L. Esposito (ed.) *The Oxford History of Islam*, Oxford and New York: Oxford University Press, pp. 107–153.

Kamali, M. H. (2005) *Principles of Islamic Jurisprudence*, 3rd edn, London: Islamic Texts Society.

Kemal, M. A. (2007) *A Fresh Assessment of the Underground Economy and Tax Evasion in Pakistan: Causes, Consequences, and Linkages with the Formal Economy*, Pakistan Institute of Development Economics Working Paper 2007:13. Online. Available at: http://mpra.ub.uni-muenchen.de/2226/01/MPRA_paper_2226.pdf (accessed 15 February, 2008).

Kennedy, C. H. (2004) 'Pakistan's Superior Courts and the prohibition of riba,' in R. Hathaway and W. Lee (eds) *Islamization and the Pakistani Economy*, Washington, DC: Woodrow Wilson International Center for Scholars.

Khairi, S. (1995) *Jinnah Reinterpreted: The Journey from Indian Nationalism to Muslim Statehood*, Karachi: Oxford University Press.

Khan, A. K. (2010a) 'Essays on faith and finance,' PhD thesis, Cambridge, MA: Harvard Business School.

Khan, F. (2008a) 'Islamic banking by judiciary: the "backdoor" for Islamism in Pakistan?' *South Asia: Journal of South Asian Studies*, 31: 535–555.

Khan, F. (2010b) 'How "Islamic" is Islamic Banking?' *Journal of Economic Behavior & Organization*, 76: 805–820.

Khan, H. (2001) *Constitutional and Political History of Pakistan*, London and Karachi: Oxford University Press.

Khan, M. A. (1967) *Friends Not Masters: A Political Autobiography*, New York, London and Karachi: Oxford University Press.

Khan, M. F. (1991) 'Time value of money and discounting in Islamic perspective,' *Review of Islamic Economics*, 1: 35–45.

Khan, M. N. and M. I. Bhatti (2008) *Developments in Islamic Banking: The Case of Pakistan*, Basingstoke and New York: Palgrave Macmillan.

Khan, M. S. A. (1929) 'The Mohammedan laws against usury and how they are evaded,' *Journal of Comparative Legislation and International Law*, 11: 233–244.

Khan, S. (2008b) 'Working capital,' in H. Anwar (ed.) *Islamic Finance: A Guide for International Business and Investment*, London: GMBH Publishing, pp. 65–74. Online. Available at: www.kantakji.com/fiqh/Files/Finance/N248.pdf (accessed 9 December, 2013).

Khnifer, M. (2011) 'Shocking: 21 defaulted sukuk cases in the last 20 months!' *Business Islamica Magazine*, 24–26.

Knight, J. (2010) 'Big banks go cold on Islamic products,' *The Independent*, 18 July. Online. Available at: www.independent.co.uk/money/spend-save/big-banks-go-cold-on-islamic-products-2029081.html (accessed 9 December, 2013).

Krasicka, O. and S. Nowak (2012) *What's in It for Me? A Primer on Differences Between Islamic and Conventional Finance in Malaysia*, IMF Working Paper 12/51, Washington, DC: International Monetary Fund. Online. Available at: www.imf.org/external/pubs/ft/wp/2012/wp12151.pdf (accessed 11 December, 2013).

Kumar, R. (2007) *Sardar Vallabhai Patel: The Maker of United India*, New Delhi: Gyan Publishing House.
Kumar, V. (1999) 'Place Vande Mataram in correct context,' *The Times of India*, 1 July.
Kuran, T. (1993) 'The economic impact on Islamic fundamentalism,' in M. Marty and S. Appleby (eds) *Funamentalisms and the State: Remaking Polities, Economies, and Militance*, Chicago, IL: Chicago University Press, pp. 302–341.
Kuran, T. (2004) *Islam and Mammon: The Economic Predicaments of Islamism*. Princeton, NJ: Princeton University Press.
Looney, R. (2006) 'The Iranian economy: crony capitalism in Islamic garb,' *Milken Institute Review* (First Quarter). Online. Available at: http://faculty.nps.edu/relooney/Milken-Iran.pdf (accessed 5 August, 2006).
Lothian, Marquess of (1932) 'India and the franchise problem,' *International Affairs*, 11: 593–617.
Ludden, D. (1984) 'Productive power in agriculture: a survey of work on the local history of British India,' in M. Desai, S. H. Rudolph and A. Rudra (eds) *Agrarian Power and Agricultural Productivity in South Asia*, Berkeley and Los Angeles, CA and New York: University of California Press, pp. 51–99.
Mahmudabad, Raja M. A. A. K. (1997/1993) 'Some memories,' in M. Hasan (ed.) *India's Partition: Process, Strategy, and Mobilization*, New Delhi: Oxford University Press, reprint edn, pp. 408–430.
Malaysian International Islamic Financial Centre (2013) *Global Sukuk Report 2Q*, July. Online. Available at: www.mifc.com/index.php?ch=28&pg=72&ac=44&bb=uploadpdf (accessed 9 December, 2013).
Malik, H. (2006) *Political Profile of Sir Sayyid Ahmad Khan*, New Delhi: Adam Publishers and Distributors.
Maududi, S. A. A. and K. Ahmad (ed. and trans.) (1960) *The Islamic Law and Constitution*, Lahore: Islamic Publications.
Maududi, S. A. A. with K. Ahmad (ed.) and R. Husain (trans.) (1997) *Economic System of Islam*, 4th edn, Lahore: Islamic Publications.
Mawdudi, S. A. A. with K. Ahmad (ed.) and A. I. S. Hashemi (trans.) (2011) *First Principles of Islamic Economics*, Leicestershire: Islamic Foundation.
McGrath, A. (1996) *The Destruction of Pakistan's Democracy*, Karachi and Oxford: Oxford University Press.
Meenai, A. A. (1996) *Riba and Common Interest: A Rejoinder*, Karachi: Shafiq Press.
Meenai, S. A. (2004) *Money and Banking in Pakistan*, 5th edn, Karachi: Oxford University Press.
Meezan Bank (2014) *The Art of Values: Annual Report 2013*. Online. Available at: www.meezanbank.com/docs/AnnualReport2013.pdf (accessed 3 July, 2014).
Meezan Bank (n.d.) *Easy Home: Islamic Home Financing*. Online. Available at: www.meezanbank.com/easyhome.aspx (accessed 14 December, 2013).
Metcalf, B. (2004) *Islamic Contestations: Essays on Muslims in India and Pakistan*, New Delhi and Oxford: Oxford University Press, reprints of papers first published 1978–2002.
Metcalf, B. and T. Metcalf (2006) *A Concise History of Modern India*, 2nd edn, London and New York: Cambridge University Press.
Mills, P. S., and J. R. Presley (1999) *Islamic Finance: Theory and Practice*, New York: St Martins Press.

Minault, G. (1982) *The Khilafat Movement: Religious Symbolism and Political Mobilization in India*, New York: Columbia University Press.

Mishkin, F. S. (2013) *The Economics of Money, Banking and Financial Markets*, 10th edn, New York: Addison-Wesley.

Mittal, S. C. (1977) *Freedom Movement in Punjab 1905–1929*, New Delhi: Concept Publishing.

Moody's Investor Services (2008) *Credit Opinion: Al Rajhi Bank*, November. Online. Available at: www.alrajhibank.com.sa/en/media-centre/reports/documents/moodys_investors_report.pdf (accessed 19 December, 2008).

Moore, E. (2013) 'Should you buy into Islamic finance?' *Financial Times*, November 1. Online. Available at: www.ft.com (accessed 8 December, 2013).

Morais, R. C. (2007) 'Don't call it interest,' *Forbes*, 23 July, 122–132 (not inclusive).

Mortimer, E. (1982) *Faith and Power: The Politics of Islam*, London: Vintage.

Munir, M. and R. Kayani (1954) *The Report of the Court of Inquiry Constituted Under the Punjab Act II of 1954 to Enquire into the Punjab Disturbances of 1953*, Lahore: Government of Punjab. Online. Available at: https://ia601709.us.archive.org/31/items/The1954JusticeMunirCommissionReportOnTheAntiAhmadiRiotsOfPunjabIn1953/The-1954-Justice-Munir-Commission-Report-on-the-anti-Ahmadi-Riots-of-Punjab-in-1953.pdf (accessed 4 April, 2010).

Nanda, B. R. (2010) *Road to Pakistan: The Life and Times of Mohammad Ali Jinnah*, New Delhi: Routledge India.

Nasr, S. V. R. (1994) *The Vanguard of the Islamic Revolution: The Jama'at-i Islamic of Pakistan*, Berkeley and Los Angeles, CA and New York: University of California Press.

Nasr, S. V. R. (1996) *Mawdudi and the Making of Islamic Revivalism*, New York and Oxford: Oxford University Press.

National Venture Capital Association (n.d.) *Total Venture Capital Investment by Year 2009–Q3 2013*. Online. Available at: www.nvca.org/index.php?option=com_content&view=article&id=344&Itemid=103 (accessed 6 December, 2013).

Nehru, J. (1941) *Toward Freedom: The Autobiography of Jawaharlal Nehru*, New York: John Day.

Nomani, F. (2003) 'The problem of interest and Islamic banking in a comparative perspective: the case of Egypt, Iran and Pakistan,' *Review of Middle East Economics and Finance*, 1: 36–69.

Nomani, F. (2006) 'The dilemma of riba-free banking in Islamic public policy,' in S. Behdad and F. Nomani (eds) *Islam and the Everyday World: Public Policy Dilemmas*, London: Routledge, pp. 193–223.

Oakley, D. (2007) 'Market for Islamic "mortgages" to soar,' *Financial Times*, March 31.

Oakley, D. (2008) 'Sukuk market: clarification of rules does market a favour,' *Financial Times*, June 19.

OED Online (2014) 'usury, n.,' in *Oxford English Dictionary*, Oxford: Oxford University Press. Online. Available at: www.oed.com/view/Entry/220740?rskey=Fnm7TW&result=1 (accessed 2 January, 2015).

Oldenburg, P. (2010) *India, Pakistan and Democracy: Solving the Puzzle of Divergent Paths*, London and New York: Routledge.

Pal, I. (2006) *Islam and the Economy of Pakistan: A Critical Analysis of Traditional Interpretation*, Karachi: Oxford University Press.

Pandey, D. (1978) 'Congress–Muslim League relations 1937–1939: "the parting of the ways",' *Modern Asian Studies*, 12: 629–654.

Parker, M. (2006) 'Dow Jones Citigroup Sukuk Index launched,' *Arab News*, 22 May. Online. Available at: www.arabnews.com/node/285064 (accessed 26 February, 2008).

Presley, J. R., and J. G. Sessions (1994) 'Islamic economics: the emergence of a new paradigm,' *Economic Journal*, 104: 584–596.

Qureshi, A. I. (1991/1967) *Islam and the Theory of Interest*, 2nd edn, Lahore: Sh. Muhammad Ashraf.

Qureshi, M. N. (1999) *Pan-Islam in British Indian Politics: A Study of the Khilafat Movement, 1918–1924*, Leiden: Brill Academic Publishers.

Rahman, F. (1964) 'Riba and interest,' *Islamic Studies*, 3: 1–43; M. Siddiqi trans. (1963) '*Tahaqiq-i-Riba*,' *Fikr-o-Nazar*.

Raja, S. A. (2003) 'Islamisation of laws in Pakistan,' *South Asian Journal*, 1: 94–109.

Rammal, H. G. (2004) 'Financing through Musharaka: principles and application,' *Business Quest: Journal of Applied Topics in Business and Economics*. Online. Available at: www.westga.edu/~bquest/2004/musharaka.htm (accessed 3 February, 2008).

Riedel, B. (2012) *Deadly Embrace: Pakistan, America, and the Future of the Global Jihad*, revised edn with new preface, Washington, DC: Brookings Institution Press.

Rubin, J. (2009) 'Social insurance, commitment, and the origin of law: interest bans in early Christianity,' *Journal of Law & Economics*, 52: 761–777.

Rudolph, L. and S. H. Rudolph (2006) *Post Modern Gandhi and Other Essays: Gandhi in the World and at Home*, Chicago, IL: University of Chicago Press.

Saeed, A. (1996) *Islamic Banking and Interest: A Study of the Prohibition of Riba and Its Contemporary Interpretation*, Studies in Islamic Law and Society Vol. 2, Leiden, New York and Koln: E. J. Brill.

Sarkar, T. (2006) 'Birth of a Goddess: "Vande Mataram", "Anandamath", and Hindu Nationhood,' *Economic and Political Weekly*, 41 (Sep. 16–22): 3959–3969.

Saudi British Bank (n.d.) *Terms & Conditions of SABB Amanah Credit Cards*, Saudi British Online. Available at: www.sabb.com/1/PA_1_083Q9FJ08A002FBP5S00000000/content/SABB/en/personal/attachments/Amanah-Tawarruq-CreditChipCard.pdf (accessed 1 December, 2013).

SBP (2005) *Rate of Returns under Export Finance Scheme*, Karachi: State Bank of Pakistan. Online. Available at: www.sbp.org.pk/incentives/efs/efs-rates.htm (accessed 3 February, 2008).

SBP (2008a) *Pakistan's Islamic Banking Sector Review 2003 to 2007*, Karachi: State Bank of Pakistan. Online. Available at: www.sbp.org.pk/ibd/Islamic-Bkg-Review-03-07.pdf (accessed 3 July. 2014).

SBP (2008b) *Annexure 1 of IBD Circular No: 02 of 2008: Instructions for Shariah Compliance in Islamic Banking Institutions*. Online. Available at:www.sbp.org.pk/ibd/2008/Annex-c2-1.pdf (accessed 14 July, 2014).

SBP (2013) *Prudential Regulations for Small & Medium Enterprise Financing*, Karachi: State Bank of Pakistan. Online. Available at:www.sbp.org.pk/publications/prudential/PRs-SMEs.pdf (accessed 14 July, 2014).

SBP (2014a) *Islamic Banking Bulletin – December 2013*, Karachi: State Bank of Pakistan. Online. Available at: www.sbp.org.pk/ibd/bulletin/2013/IBB-dec-2013.pdf (accessed 3 July, 2014).

SBP (2014b) *Islamic Banking Bulletin – March 2014*, Karachi: State Bank of Pakistan. Online. Available at: www.sbp.org.pk/ibd/bulletin/2014/IBB-Mar-2014.pdf (accessed 3 July, 2014).

SBP (2014c) *Statistics on Scheduled Banks in Pakistan – December 2013*, Karachi: State Bank of Pakistan. Online. Available at: www.sbp.org.pk/publications/schedule_banks/Dec-2013.htm (accessed 14 July, 2014).

SBP (n.d.) *Islamic Export Refinance Scheme*, Karachi: State Bank of Pakistan. Online. Available at: www.sbp.org.pk/incentives/iers/Scheme.pdf (accessed 3 February, 2008).

Schneider, F. (2006) *Shadow Economies and Corruption All Over the World: What Do We Really Know?* Institute for the Study of Labor, Discussion Paper #2315. Online. Available at: http://ftp.iza.org/dp2315.pdf (accessed 8 January, 2013).

Schumpeter, J. (1996/1954) *History of Economic Analysis: With a New Introduction*, Oxford: Oxford University Press.

Shakoor, A. (2005) *Congress–Muslim League Tussle 1937–1940: A Critical Analysis*, New Delhi: Aakar Books.

Sharif, M. A. (1994) *Searching for Solace: A Biography of Abdullah Yusuf Ali, Interpreter of the Qur'an*, Kuala Lumpur: Islamic Book Trust.

Siddiqui, M. N. (2002) *Dialogue in Islamic Economics*, Islamabad: Institute of Policy Studies.

Siddiqui, M. (2011) 'Muddassir Siddiqui comments' at the Panel on Islamic Finance: Bankruptcy, Financial Distress and Debt Restructuring, Harvard Law School, September 26. Online. Available at: http://ifpprogram.com/login/view_pdf/?file=Bankruptcy_Panel.pdf&type=lectures (accessed 8 December, 2013).

Sharma, J. N. (2008) *Encyclopaedia of Eminent Thinkers #13: The Political Thought of M. A. Jinnah*, New Delhi: Concept Publishing Company.

Sigmund K., E. Fehr and M. A. Nowak (2002) 'The economics of fair play,' *Scientific American*, January: 82–87.

Singh, A. I. (1991/1987) *The Origins of the Partition of India 1936–1947*, reprint edn, Delhi: Oxford University Press.

Singh, J. (2010) *Jinnah: India, Partition, Independence*, New York: Oxford University Press.

Smith, K. (2004) 'The Kuwait Finance House and the Islamization of public life in Kuwait,' in C. M. Henry and R. Wilson (eds) *The Politics of Islamic Finance*, Edinburgh: Edinburgh University Press, pp. 168–190.

Soliman, S. (2004) 'The Islamic banking model in Egypt,' in C. M. Henry and R. Wilson (eds) *The Politics of Islamic Finance*, Edinburgh: Edinburgh University Press, pp. 265–285.

Standard and Poor's (2004) *Islamic Development Bank*. Online. Available at: www.zawya.com/researchreports/zawyapr/IslamicDevelopmentBankrating.pdf (accessed 6 March, 2008; no longer available online).

Standard Chartered Saadiq (2014) *Schedule of Charges*, Karachi: Standard Chartered Bank Pakistan. Online. Available at: www.sc.com/pk/_documents/Saadiq-SOC-14.pdf (accessed 8 July, 2014).

Stiansen, E. (2004) 'Interest politics: Islamic finance in the Sudan, 1977–2001,' in C. M. Henry and R. Wilson (eds) *The Politics of Islamic Finance*, Edinburgh: Edinburgh University Press, pp. 155–167.

Stiglitz, J. E. and A. Weiss (1981) 'Credit rationing in markets with imperfect information,' *American Economic Review*, 71: 393–410.

Sundarajan, V. and L. Errico (2002) *Islamic Financial Institutions and Products in the Global Financial System: Key Issues in Risk Management and Challenges Ahead*, IMF Working Paper #192, Washington, DC: International Monetary Fund.

Supreme Court of Pakistan (2002) *Civil Shariat Review Petition No. 1 of 2000*, Islamabad: Supreme Court of Pakistan. Online. Available at: www.supremecourt.gov.pk/web/user_files/File/JR_Detailed_Judgment_in_Riba_Case.pdf (accessed 15 July, 2006).

Talbot, I. (1999) *Pakistan: A Modern History*, London: Palgrave Macmillan.

Taspinar, O. (2012) 'Turkey: the new model?' in R. Wright (ed.) *The Islamists are Coming: Who They Really Are*, Washington, DC: United States Institute of Peace, pp. 127–136. Online. Available at: www.brookings.edu/research/papers/2012/04/24-turkey-new-model-taspinar (accessed 23 July, 2014).

Tedds, L. M. (2010) 'Keeping it off the books: an empirical investigation of firms that engage in tax evasion,' *Applied Economics*, 42: 2459–2473.

Tett, G. (2006) 'Banks seek Islamic scholars versed in finance,' *Financial Times*, 19 May. Online. Available at: http://search.ft.com/ftArticle?queryText=sharia+scholar&aje=true&id=060519008895 (accessed 2 February, 2008).

Townsend, R. (1979) 'Optimal contracts and competitive markets with costly state verification,' *Journal of Economic Theory*, 21: 265–293.

Transparency International (2013) *Corruption Perceptions Index 2013*. Online. Available at: http://cpi.transparency.org/cpi2013/results (accessed 5 December, 2013).

Tripathi, D. (2004) *The Oxford History of Indian Business*, Oxford: Oxford University Press.

Udovitch, A. L. (1970) *Partnership and Profit in Medieval Islam*, Princeton, NJ: Princeton University Press.

UK Trade & Investment (2013) *Opportunities for Islamic finance in the UK*, 28 October. Online. Available at: www.gov.uk/government/news/opportunities-for-islamic-finance-in-the-uk (accessed 9 December, 2013).

UNCTAD (2006) *Islamic Finance and Structured Commodity Finance: Where the Twain Can Meet*, UNCTAD Study 2006/6, Geneva: United Nations Conference on Trade and Development. Online. Available at: http://unctad.org/en/Docs/ditccom20066_en.pdf (accessed 15 May, 2008).

Usmani, M. I. A. (2002a) *Meezan Bank's Guide to Islamic Banking*, Karachi: Darul Ishaat. Online. Available at: www.meezanbank.com/docs/GIBcomplete.pdf in a slightly different reprint edn.

Usmani, M. T. (2002b) *An Introduction to Islamic Finance*, Arab and Islamic Law Series, The Hague: Kluwer Law International.

Uysal, E. (2007) 'Kinalizade's views on the moral education of children,' *Journal of Moral Education*, 36: 333–341.

Venardos, A. M. (2005) *Islamic Banking and Finance in Southeast Asia: Its Development and Future*, Singapore: World Scientific.

Visser, W. A. M. and A. McIntosh (1998) 'A short review of the historical critique of usury,' *Accounting, Business and Financial History*, 8: 175–189.

Warde, I. (2000) *Islamic Finance in the Global Economy*, Edinburgh: Edinburgh University Press.

Warde, I. (2010) *Islamic Finance in the Global Economy*, 2nd edn, Edinburgh: Edinburgh University Press.

Warde, I. (2011) 'Ibrahim Warde presentation,' Panel on Islamic Finance: Bankruptcy, Financial Distress and Debt Restructuring, Islamic Finance Workshop, Harvard

Law School, September 26. Online. Available at: http://ifpprogram.com/login/view_pdf/?file=Bankruptcy_Panel.pdf&type=lectures (accessed 8 December, 2013).

Wasti, T. (2009) *The Application of Islamic Criminal Law in Pakistan: Sharia in Practice*, Leiden: Brill Academic Publishers.

Weiss, A. (1985) 'Women's position in Pakistan: sociocultural effects of Islamization,' *Asian Survey*, 25: 863–880.

Wigglesworth, R. (2009) 'Credit crunch May test industry beliefs,' *Financial Times*, May 5.

Williamson, S. D. (1987) 'Costly monitoring, loan contracts, and equilibrium credit rationing,' *Quarterly Journal of Economics*, 102: 135–146.

Wilson, J. Q. (1993) *The Moral Sense*, New York: Basic Books.

Wolpert, S. A. (1984) *Jinnah of Pakistan*, Oxford: Oxford University Press.

Wouters, P. (2012) 'Goldman Sachs: genuine or ribawi sukuk in the making?' *Business Islamica*, February 16. Online. Available at: www.cimaglobal.com/Documents/Islamic%20finance/2011/GS%20-%20Genuine%20or%20Ribawi%20Sukuk-%20ISLAMICA%20JAN-FEB%202012.pdf (accessed 10 December, 2013).

Yousef, T. M. (2004) 'The Murabaha Syndrome in Islamic Finance: laws, institutions and politics,' in C. M. Henry and R. Wilson (eds) *The Politics of Islamic Finance*, Edinburgh: Edinburgh University Press, pp. 63–80.

Zaheer, S. and S. van Wijnbergen (2013) *Sukuk Defaults: On Distress Resolution in Islamic Finance*, Discussion Paper TI 13-087/VI/DSF57, Amsterdam: Tinbergen Institute, Duisenberg School of Finance. Online. Available at: http://papers.tinbergen.nl/13087.pdf (accessed 10 December, 2013).

Zaher, T. S. and M. K. Hassan (2001) 'A comparative literature survey of Islamic banking and finance,' *Financial Markets, Institutions and Instruments*, 10: 155–199.

Zaidi, S. M. Z. (2010) 'The assassination of the Prime Minister Liaquat Ali Khan: the fateful journey,' *Pakistan Journal of History and Culture*, 30: 71–101.

Zaman, A. (2008) *Islamic Economics: A Survey of the Literature*, Working Paper 22, Birmingham: Religion and Development Working Programme, International Development Department, University of Birmingham. Online. Available at: http://epapers.bham.ac.uk/1538/1/Zaman_IslamicEconomics.pdf (accessed 15 February, 2011).

Zaman, A. (2013) 'Mawlana Mawdudi and the genesis of Islamic economics,' paper presented at the Ninth International Conference on Islamic Economics and Finance, Istanbul, September 2013.

Zaman, M. R. (2002) 'Interest free Islamic banking: ideals and reality,' *International Journal of Finance*, 14: 2428–2442.

Zaman, M. R. (2008) 'Usury (riba) and the place of bank interest in Islamic banking and finance,' *International Journal of Banking and Finance*, 6: 1–15.

Zebiri, K. (1993) *Mahmud Shaltut and Islamic Modernism*, Oxford: Clarendon Press.

Ziring, L. (1997) *Pakistan in the Twentieth Century: A Political History*, New York and Karachi: Oxford University Press.

Index

Page numbers with '*n*' indicates note.

For Product Safety Concerns and Information please contact our EU representative GPSR@taylorandfrancis.com
Taylor & Francis Verlag GmbH, Kaufingerstraße 24, 80331 München, Germany

www.ingramcontent.com/pod-product-compliance
Ingram Content Group UK Ltd.
Pitfield, Milton Keynes, MK11 3LW, UK
UKHW011013180926
475701UK00004B/714
9780367232023